Strategic Decision Making in the Arts

For entrepreneurs in the creative fields, decision making is both a necessity and an art. Applying creativity to strategic decisions requires skills developed over time. This textbook provides arts entrepreneurship students a series of case studies centering on decision-making models applicable to launching and sustaining arts businesses.

Each case set in the book focuses on a particular arts entrepreneur within the context of a range of creative businesses, from performance to videography. To facilitate classroom adoption, the authors provide expert guidance on getting the most from case-study-based learning. Additional features include insights into the key decision-making models in each case, analysis by a leader in the arts entrepreneurship education field on the factors forcing a decision and a broad view on the arts ecologies surrounding each example.

Suitable for students in arts management programs as well, this book introduces readers to case-based learning via practical examples that give students insight into strategic decision-making in the creative industries.

Extensive teaching notes are available for instructors. To gain access, visit www.routledge.com/9781032539577.

Gary D. Beckman is Director of Entrepreneurial Studies in the Arts at North Carolina State University, USA.

Karl Androes is Co-founder of Whirlwind Performance Company, which became Reading In Motion, in Chicago.

Discovering the Creative Industries

Series Editor: Ruth Rentschler

The creative and cultural industries account for a significant share of the global economy. Gaining and maintaining employment and work in this sector is a challenge and chances of success are enhanced by ongoing professional development.

This series provides a range of relatively short, student-centred books which blend industry and educational expertise with cultural sector practice. Books in the series provide applied introductions to the core elements of the creative industries. In sum, the series provides essential reading for those studying to enter the creative industries as well as those seeking to enhance their career via executive education.

Understanding Cultural Policy
Government and the Arts and Culture in the United States
Carole Rosenstein

Legal Issues for Arts Organizations
A Practical Guide
Kristi W. Arth

The Creative Economy
Arts, Cultural Value and Society in Practice
Amanda J. Ashley, Carolyn G. Loh, Matilda Rose Bubb and Shoshanah B.D. Goldberg-Miller

Rural Arts Management
Elise Lael Kieffer and Jerome Socolof

Strategic Decision Making in the Arts
Case Studies in Arts and Cultural Entrepreneurship
Gary D. Beckman and Karl Androes

For more information about this series, please visit: www.routledge.com/Discovering-the-Creative-Industries/book-series/DCI

Strategic Decision Making in the Arts

Case Studies in Arts and Cultural Entrepreneurship

Gary D. Beckman and Karl Androes

Routledge
Taylor & Francis Group
LONDON AND NEW YORK

Designed cover image: olaser / iStock / Getty Images Plus

First published 2025
by Routledge
4 Park Square, Milton Park, Abingdon, Oxon OX14 4RN

and by Routledge
605 Third Avenue, New York, NY 10158

Routledge is an imprint of the Taylor & Francis Group, an informa business

British Library Cataloguing-in-Publication Data
A catalogue record for this book is available from the British Library

Library of Congress Cataloging-in-Publication Data
Names: Beckman, Gary D., 1961- author. | Androes, Karl, author.
Title: Strategic decision making in the arts : case studies in arts and cultural entrepreneurship / Gary D. Beckman and Karl Androes.
Description: Abingdon, Oxon ; New York, NY : Routledge, 2025. | Series: Discovering the creative industries | Includes bibliographical references and index.
Identifiers: LCCN 2024006890 (print) | LCCN 2024006891 (ebook) | ISBN 9781032539584 (hbk) | ISBN 9781032539577 (pbk) | ISBN 9781003414483 (ebk)
Subjects: LCSH: Entrepreneurship. | Arts--Economic aspects. | Decision making. | Creative ability.
Classification: LCC HB615 .B4157 2025 (print) | LCC HB615 (ebook) | DDC 706.8/4--dc23/eng/20240612
LC record available at https://lccn.loc.gov/2024006890
LC ebook record available at https://lccn.loc.gov/2024006891

ISBN: 978-1-032-53958-4 (hbk)
ISBN: 978-1-032-53957-7 (pbk)
ISBN: 978-1-003-41448-3 (ebk)

DOI: 10.4324/9781003414483

Typeset in Caslon
by SPi Technologies India Pvt Ltd (Straive)

Access the Support Material: www.routledge.com/9781032539577

For arts students who dare to dream…or just want to pay the rent….

CONTENTS

FIGURES

Tables

Acknowledgements

General thanks

We would like to thank the four individuals featured in these cases. They graciously shared their stories and trusted us to document and analyze those experiences. Obviously, this book would not be here without their collective courage. Additionally, we would like to thank Terry Clague at Routledge for his graciousness and belief in this effort.

Gary's thanks

My deepest thanks to Kate for her patience, encouragement and understanding. Thanks to all the members of the Quadrivium Project and Syn3 for their collective agreement to engage in something musical: it must be loud…the right key is also helpful. Lastly, a thanks to my past students for tolerating a passionate educator: a full refrigerator is important and it means more if you fill it yourself.

Karl's thanks:

My deepest thanks to the following individuals:

My wife Jean Clough, who cared as much as I did about the success of young children in under-resourced neighborhoods, and proved that every day with her time, listening skills, wise counsel and editing of just about every word I ever wrote.

My sons, Patrick and Joe, who inspire me every day to be better and do better.

My grandson, Ian, who reminds me why this work—the arts, building organizations to serve people, improving decision-making skills—is worth doing.

Gary Beckman, who suggested the first time we ever spoke that I write this book, then suggested WE write this book, then spent two very enjoyable years making it happen together.

Debra Snider for long ago believing I had a writer in me, then helping me become that writer.

Ed Crego for being an insightful and kind management consultant to me for 40 years, helping me build a business that (mostly) made good decisions.

Liz and Little, my best work colleagues for over 30 years each, who became my trusted friends.

Dale Rose, for teaching me how to measure things that matter and for being one of the most generous people I know.

Mihir Patel, for showing me the next generation has the curiosity and rigor to keep things running and improving.

Greg Pierce, who taught me how to ask people for what I needed, including a cab driver and the Mayor of Chicago.

Eric and Sally, for getting me started on my greatest adventure and feeding me until I could feed myself.

James Mattern, for teaching me trombone, life is not fair, take the gig then figure out how to do it, spend less than you make.

Lynn White, the best classroom teacher I ever met.

The dream team: Donna Bogosh, Amy Houston, Vivi Rogers, Cathy Meredith, Kristi Amendola, Avo Randruut, Sarah Surrain, Barbara Pawlikowski, Gaye Preston, Tiffany Lovell. We made something wonderful together.

Steve and Kathy McShane, Frank and Donna Marrese, Rick Andrew, Wally Burke, Jane Piggot, Jill Seltzer, Suzanne Kerbow, Nikki Stein, Mary Roney, Mark McKeown, Cindy Richards, Merle

Tresser and the many more who provided essential financial support, sage advice, encouragement and friendship.

Eileen Ryan and Hugh Spector, Rich Gage, Susie Buono-Diers, David Kornhauser and Shelley Gates, Ellen Hunt, Robert Blazek, John Maki and many more great friends who kept me going.

INTRODUCTION

1

THE IMPORTANCE OF DECISION MAKING

Welcome to the Madness

Decisions, decisions, decisions. They're everywhere. Everyday. Constantly. The problem with decisions is that they have consequences—sometimes good, sometimes bad and sometimes it doesn't matter. What makes decisions so maddening is that some only reveal their consequences in the future. To make it more frustrating, we are not provided a magic 8 ball to make the right decision, every time. No, there is no oracle. And no, phones are not oracles.

To illustrate the point, let's identify some of the decisions it takes to make a cup of coffee in the morning, just after waking up. Assuming you are fairly connected to your phone and use it to wake up, let's begin with the alarm going off and you hear it...

- Ignore alarm OR hit snooze OR turn off.
- Should you get out of bed OR go back to sleep?
- If you get out of bed, do you make coffee OR have a cup of something else OR check your phone. Which one comes first?
- If you want a cup of something else, what should it be?
- If you want coffee, do you only have one brand in the pantry OR multiple?

 DOI: 10.4324/9781003414483-2

- If you have multiple brands of coffee, which one should you choose?
- If you have cream and sugar in your coffee, how much of each should you put in?
- Should you use a spoon for your sugar?
- Should the spoon be clean?
- Should you measure the amount of cream OR just pour?
- How should you measure the cream?
- Where should you drink your coffee?
- Or do you want tea?

Obviously, we could get microscopic with the decisions in this example, but we're sure you see the point. We cannot live without decision making. It is an integral part of our lives and we can't get away from the (likely) thousands of miniscule decisions we make every day.

While the scenario and list above may fall under the heading of "decisions of little consequence," there are other life decisions that fall into the "decisions of significant consequence" category. These might include: choosing a college or university, choosing a major or a career, getting married, starting a family or a business, etc. Decisions like these typically require significant thought. Indeed, these decisions are made in various ways and we typically consider the goals and consequences of our decisions. When we are in the *process* of decision making, most of us are trying to achieve a goal of some kind: to create something, to eliminate a scenario or to avoid a consequence. It gets more complicated when one is trying to make a decision with multiple outcomes, goals, potential scenarios or consequences. Decision making, then, is a part of daily life and if we are making a decision about something of "significant consequence," we tend to put more effort into the process.

Who is This Book for, What are Case Studies Anyway and Why is this Collection Different?

To be clear, this book is written exclusively for undergraduate arts students interested in entrepreneuring their art. For most (unless you've taken a number of business classes) case studies will be a new experience.

They are certainly an experience far removed from arts history, music theory, improv or studio classes.

For business students, case study classes are a bit like recitals or performances. They provide an opportunity to apply material from previous classes in as realistic a manner as one can muster in a classroom. Basically, a case study is a *true* story of a business' opportunities or struggles. In the business school, the case study experience is student driven, which means that students do most—if not all—of the talking. The instructor is there to facilitate discussion, keep observations on topic and point out critical aspects of the case.

A typical business school class can focus on a case for one class period, or more, depending on its length or complexity. However, once the case is finished, one almost never knows what transpired after the case ends. This is where this collection of case studies differs. Specifically, this is a book of four case study *sets*. Each set focuses on the decisions a single entrepreneur made concerning their arts business or non-profit organization. What sets this collection apart is that each new case in a set builds on the decisions made from the previous case. This way, you see the *outcome* of the previous case's decision and encounter the additional decisions required to achieve the entrepreneur's goals. By the third or fourth case, it becomes clear how previous decisions helped reach, modify or attenuate these goals.

This collection gives you a more realistic glimpse of operating an arts business or organization. While business school students know quite a bit about commercial operations, an arts student's experience is different. If we follow the business school model, students are constantly offering opinions or suggestions about each case and their economics or management classes guide their thinking. For most arts students—since we're trained in the A(a)rts, not business—the traditional business school model is somewhat unfair since most have not taken fundamental economics classes. To help solve this problem, accompanying each case is an analysis addressing four areas: a **Summary** (an abstract of critical or interesting aspects of the case), **Factors Forcing the Decision** (identifying internal areas that may or may not be the entrepreneur's decision), the **Decision Model Used** (the models are introduced and discussed in the next chapter) and an **Ecology Discussion** (the ecologies are introduced below). The idea is to provide you with a way to engage the case *and* have some material you can talk about in the classroom. For example, the **Decision Model Used** section discusses both how to identify the decision model(s) used in the case and *why* you could consider different decisions, models, or contextual aspects impacting a decision.

An Introduction to the Concept of Patterns

As the brief example introducing this chapter demonstrates, there wouldn't be much time to get anything accomplished if we had to analyze all of the micro-decisions we encounter daily. In an effort to generate time for other things, we create patterns or routines to simplify these decisions—hence a morning wake up routine. Typically, it is the "decisions of little consequence" that are subject to these constructs (i.e.: patterns). When we create these constructs, we've made the required decisions in advance and are comfortable with the outcomes. For example, with a simple wake up routine where coffee is the desired outcome, the point is to engage in a series of actions resulting in a comfortable and predictable experience to achieve a certain goal. To do this, we create a shorthand set of decisions and execute them, which many call a "routine." However, when there are no coffee beans, the pattern is disrupted. Of course, this break in the pattern not only disrupts the wake up routine, it also disrupts the desired outcome.

The point about decision-making patterns is that they not only save time and mental energy, but they provide a sense of predictability, comfort and—importantly—an outcome. Not remarkably, this extends to "decisions of significant consequence" as well. As we learn to make decisions, we tend to rely on decision-making patterns. For example, some of us are quite analytical in our decision-making process, where we need to gather as much information as possible before making a decision. Some (as we'll see in the first Case Set) feel more comfortable speaking with friends, confidants and family before they make a decision. Others either make decisions impulsively or do everything they can to put off making a decision. When we learn that successful, *predictable* and *directed* outcomes are generated by these patterns, we become confident (i.e.: trust) in these patterns, which for most, creates comfort.

While we could go on and on about this aspect of decision making, the simple fact is that the way we develop a process of decision making is both unique to the individual and will inevitably use decision-making patterns of some kind. Yet the frustrating aspect of developing our decision-making patterns is that 1) experimentation is required, 2) our learned experiences will both color and guide this process and 3) we must frequently fail. This means our decisions, our models, our patterns, our desired outcomes—the entire process—is a uniquely developed pattern occurring throughout our lives. Whether we keep to one pattern of decision making, fluctuate between many or combine them, learning to make the best decisions possible is a life-long process. The purpose of this book is to provide the emerging A(a)rts entrepreneur some tools and practice when thinking about decisions, to speed this process along.

Patterns Part 2, the "If-then" Fundamental and a Caveat

Patterns and routines are about repetition. As artists, we understand both because we use them in our art in some way. Broadly speaking, we could say patterns tend to concern the art itself and routines tend to be the actions we engage in to create art. If we go outside of the arts, both are used somewhat interchangeably. The example introducing this chapter, for example, could be viewed as dissecting a routine where certain internal patterns are identified and interrogated.

For most, the decision-making process encompasses both patterns and routines. Once we have enough experiences in our adolescent lives, we find our own ways to make decisions. These "ways" tend to be based on routines where we broadly execute a series of patterns. For example, if one has a complex decision to make, they may want to be in a quiet location where they can think through a series of unique and personal decision-making patterns. Others may like to sit at a coffee shop because the multiple and varied sounds, smells or clientele act like white noise, which can silence internal banter. Routines, then, can create a platform for working with patterns.

If we put decision making into this equation, we could say that a decision-making routine can be quite varied: gathering people in a conference room, going to the pub with the rest of the band to plan a regional tour, gathering in an office to make decisions about a museum's next season, etc. In each case, the decision process begins with a routine of gathering at a specific location. In each location, patterns of decision making occur. Many of us simply find trusted ways to make a decision and stick with them our entire lives…or sometimes, they evolve. These patterns of decision making are "models."

We know decisions are meant to address a question or situation of some sort. It could be securing a startup loan, launching a new product, not closing a business, using a new marketing strategy for your next gallery show, etc. In this book, let's call the *desired* outcome of a decision a goal. Therefore, if there is a business decision you need to make, there is likely a goal you're trying to achieve. You'll begin a decision-making routine where you use various decision-making patterns (i.e.: models) in making a decision to achieve your goal.

If we look at the more meta aspect, ultimately, a decision comes down to a binary if/then statement to reach a goal of some kind: if I do *this*, then *that* happens. This, after all, tends to be the purpose of decisions—to make something occur (or not). For example: *if* I start this arts business, *then* I can make enough to not have a day job OR *if* I speak with the client about the cost for my A(a)rt, *then* I run the risk of losing the client OR *if* I hire this marketing consultant, *then* I can sell more tickets, etc.

However, we must add an important caveat: one decision-making model is not for everyone, *nor is there a "best" model.* While it is tempting to rely on easy-to-remember processes, there are frequently issues and contexts that demand one take a unique tact. Additionally, the way we make decisions evolves over time, through our experiences. For example, if the reader considers the process they used to make decisions five years ago versus the way they do now, most would likely admit at least a small evolution. Our suggestion is that you engage these models, consider how you typically make decisions and reflect on how the past outcomes of your decisions may have changed if you used an alternative model.

Authenticity

The cases in this book are real. It's one of the primary and critical characteristics of the case study method. Everything you read in the cases are true; they occurred and some are ongoing. Here's how we wrote them.

We informed each entrepreneur about our interest in writing a set of case studies on their businesses, organizations or careers. The authors interviewed them and formatted each interview into three to four case studies. Note, however, that the entrepreneurs, their company names and products are anonymized.[1] There are situations, however, where names of organizations, governmental agencies, venues or spaces *are* used when they cannot, thereby, reveal identities of our subjects.

A small word concerning trying to identify the subjects or companies in the cases. It is human nature to try and determine the "true" names of people, places and products. The temptation to solve the puzzle is great, we understand. However, one's time would be better spent engaging the cases and the decisions the entrepreneurs are wrestling with throughout. Simply put, if you think you know, does that make a difference? Does it help you understand the situation better? Our warning here is that cases are *not* entertainment. Those interviewed were kind enough to share their stories to help the reader and we ask you to engage these cases in the spirit the interviewees intended.

The New Arts Entrepreneur

Although these Case Sets are not intended to be a direct companion to *The New Arts Entrepreneur*, this is an ecology-based work.[2] *The New Arts Entrepreneur* is a textbook exploring the different "ecologies" an arts enterprise exists within and how to use this knowledge to foster venture success. In many respects, the ecologies are "the water an enterprise swims in," consisting of its larger supporting elements, broader economic systems, market issues, geographic impact and other contextual micro-elements.

There is an ecology discussion included in each case analysis.[3] Venture sustainability and sustainable decision making for most arts businesses centers on an understanding of a venture's ecological system—recognized as such or not. For example, it is valuable to increase the available if/thens when making a decision since it both generates options and provides a way to see the outcomes of these options. More "ifs" emerge when you understand a venture's ecological system and its elements. "Thens" increase as well because the more one can identify how elements in each ecology react when stressed or stimulated, the more possibilities (i.e.: "thens" or "outcomes") emerge. When combined, this increases the chance of making more informed decisions to achieve a venture's goal.

A venture's ecological system is better understood when an entrepreneur can historically predict the reaction of elements and their impact on similar ventures. One of the most frustrating aspects of venture sustainability is knowing you have a great idea, can prove it, yet can't get anyone else to buy in. Knowing a venture's ecological system helps the entrepreneur holistically determine *and communicate* their desired actions.

Defining "Entrepreneur"

In a book like this, one of the first things an A(a)rts student typically wants to know is the definition of an entrepreneur. Well, like A(a)rt, there is no easy definition.[4] To make this only slightly more frustrating, business school scholarship has not reached a *consensus* on a definition of entrepreneurship. While many definitions are available, however, they tend to center on a few *behaviors*.

To provide some guidance, we will use *The New Arts Entrepreneur*'s focus on three entrepreneurial *behaviors*. However, be aware that 1) behaviors occur uniquely to the individual, 2) all three do not necessarily have to be present for one to "be" an entrepreneur and 3) context of *all* kinds is crucial to determining if someone is behaving in an entrepreneurial manner. Additionally, we address two behaviors popular in some quadrants of the entrepreneurial space, to inform readers of *extensions* to the three behaviors listed above.[5]

Behaviors

The first is *risk*. On this point, most agree that entrepreneurs take risks. Yet these risks are not necessarily financial, as they could be risks to reputation, non-monetary investment, educational training, a myriad of family issues, etc. Literally, the list is both endless and unique to the individual. Most entrepreneurship textbooks suggest that one *mitigate* risk. (Mitigate simply means "reduce"). This is good advice; one should reduce the risk it will take to start an A(a)rts venture. For those wanting to strike out on their own immediately after college, rent, food and utilities require money. In order to do this, most take a "day job" having little to nothing to do with their future A(a)rts goals. Taking a "day job" is mitigating risk: you might not have enough money right now to start your business and the "day job" should pay enough to cover the basic expenditures of life, while you save money to start your business.

Next is *innovation*. Most textbooks will say that "successful" entrepreneurs develop an "innovative" product of some kind. (Elon Musk and his involvement in *PayPal* would fall into this category). The tricky part is that innovative A(a)rt is not always popular, money making nor accepted by all audiences. (Arnold Schoenberg, *Gentle Giant*, Jackson Pollock, Iris van Herpen are common examples). Perhaps the best way to think of this aspect is contextually, and demographics is an example. Let's say you're a rapper and two months after your latest drop, the median age of your live audiences increases to 45–50 years old. Obviously, your A(a)rt is appealing to this demographic and you may or may not understand why. However, the fact this is occurring could lead one to say you engaged in an effort to "innovate" your target market's demographics since this age group typically doesn't engage with the genre. (Of course, one may not want this to happen, but we're sure you get the point…). Read: A(a)rt can be innovative, but so can other aspects of an A(a)rts venture.

Last is *opportunity recognition*. This is perhaps the easiest to understand. Simply put, this is an entrepreneurial behavior where one is constantly alert for opportunities to advance one's A(a)rts business. This could include identifying new markets, ideas for new products, geographical opportunities, networking with those who could advance your venture, etc. For example, if you learn that a new art gallery just opened in a geographic area you have not targeted before, with a median household income higher than your present market, and secured a solo show at this new gallery, you both recognized and leveraged on an opportunity.

Extensions

The first and most popular *extension* is the creation of a legal business entity or platform of some kind (i.e.: a for-profit business, a non-profit organization or another type of legal platform). A second popular (if not vital) *extension* is related to the first: facilitate a value exchange.[6] Hopefully, the relationship is obvious: start a business or organization so one can *legally* create a value exchange to generate either a monetary return or financial support of some kind. The outcomes should also be obvious: a for-profit business wants to generate a profit and a non-profit would like to positively impact a community and it needs money to facilitate that impact.

To illustrate both of these extensions, let's examine the following. If you are a musician and secure a paying gig, you are typically paid by a venue, which is incorporated as either a for- or non-profit entity. When you are booked, you receive the intrinsic value of performing (i.e.: enjoyment) and a potential financial return (i.e.: money). These are values to you. When the venue secures your musical performance to host an audience, the audience will exchange money for a ticket to your performance. Here, the venue receives money (a value to the venue) and the audience will be entertained (a value to the audience).

It should be said that to act entrepreneurially does not necessarily *require* the first extension. One could make the case that acting entrepreneurially can occur internally. For example, if one is fearful of performing on stage and decides to overcome that fear, the decision/supporting actions are acts of self-growth and *perhaps* considered entrepreneurial to the individual. Since overcoming fear is typically valuable, we could say that an exchange of value occurs when an audience experiences performances that are efforts to address this fear. Therefore, when acting entrepreneurially through the A(a)rts, the authors assume that a value exchange *of some kind* is typically *embedded* in these actions—even if that value is non-monetary.

Notes

1 This is required due to Institutional Review Board (IRB) regulations on human subjects.
2 Gary D. Beckman, *The New Arts Entrepreneur: Navigating the Arts Ecologies* (London: Routledge, 2022).
3 Note that some words in the Discussion sections may be oddly capitalized. This is intended to help the reader identify various Ecological Elements under discussion.
4 We use the construction "A(a)rt" to indicate both fine and popular art.
5 Throughout each case analysis, we will use these five aspects (three behaviors and two extensions) to help determine if the entrepreneur is encompassing these aspects.
6 A value exchange is where two or more parties exchange anything of value.

Bibliography

Beckman, Gary D. *The New Arts Entrepreneur: Navigating the Arts Ecologies*. London: Routledge, 2022.

Bikart, Joseph. *The Art of Decision Making: How we Move from Indecision to Smart Choices*. London: Watkins Publishing, 2019.

Burns, Paul. *New Venture Creation: A Framework for Entrepreneurial Startups*. 2nd edition. London: Palgrave, 2018.

Meyer, Marc H. and Frederick G. Crane. *New Venture Creation: An Innovator's Guide to Entrepreneurship*. 2nd edition. Thousand Oaks, CA: SAGE Publications, 2014.

Spinelli, Stephen and Robert J. Adams. *New Venture Creation: Entrepreneurship for the 21st Century*. 10th edition. New York, NY: McGraw Hill Education, 2016.

2

Decision-Making Models and Groups

The Tyranny of One

Some readers of this text may be looking for a decision-making "rule" or model to facilitate quick or guaranteed entrepreneurial success. What must be said at the outset is critical: a single decision-making model *cannot* be relied on in all circumstances and a good decision-making model does not mean success is assured. It may appear that our mentors or those we look up to use the same model consistently—or at least advocate for its use. While it is true that some have success making decisions in the same manner they always have, others do not. Since the world is a complicated place with many unique and intertwined systems of operation and contexts, succeeding as an arts entrepreneur requires a facile engagement with these systems—perhaps a bit more than a non-arts entrepreneur.

Hopefully we would all agree that decisions about one's career and a restaurant order differ not simply as a matter of degree, but in contexts, expectations, risks, opportunities and results. While one could engage a single model for all decisions, this certainly isn't practical and not what we—as humans—are trained to do; Maslow's *Hierarchy of Needs* certainly proves this, as his lowest level is based more on primal needs while the ones at the top demand more intellectual finesse. This suggests

DOI: 10.4324/9781003414483-3

the decisions we confront naturally become more complex as we move towards self-actualization (i.e.: becoming an "adult" who reaches and realizes their full potential), and the decision-making models we use will become increasingly more complex and varied as well. More simply put, when one is moving towards self-actualization, models of decision making can—and likely should—be used fluidly. This implies that multiple models (or even borrowing aspects of different models) may be required to make the best decision possible in different circumstances.

As artists, we constantly use different decision-making models in the creation of art. For example, when balancing complexity and creativity, jazz musicians may use more Linear and Instinctive approaches. Watercolor artists, however, may rely on more Instinctive and Domain-based approaches due in part to their experience with the art form and knowledge of the medium's role. One could even make the case that some textile artists and fashion designers use all three groups as the complexities of a 2d medium (a textile) placed on a dynamic 3d object (a moving human being) requires technical, mechanical and creative decisions at almost every turn. As an artist moves into the world of entrepreneurship, it cannot be stressed enough that models for making rational, sustainable and entrepreneurial decisions are already a part of our art-making and creative life—again, perhaps more than non-artists. Artists, then, may be more naturally attuned to decision making, yet are never told that creating art is (at least in part) a complex array of decisions powered by creativity, intuition, technique, repetition, experience and a host of other skills.

Getting to the Models

In this text, we use six decision-making models arranged into three groups of two models each (Figure 2.1). Some of the models are well-known in leadership education and management circles, while others are hybrids of lesser-known models we've adapted for arts students. The authors have done their best to make sure the models used in the book reflect (as much as possible) some basic ways artists make decisions about and during their art-making. We've done this specifically to help the reader connect their art-making with this newer discussion of decision making.

The three groups are Linear, Domain and Instinctive. It is likely better to envision a continuum, where the Linear group is at one end, the Instinctive at the other and the Domain group somewhere in the middle. The **Linear** group contains the Rational and Analytical models. As their names suggest, these are models that are quite methodical and focused more on the gathering and analysis of data. The **Domain** group, consisting of the Intuitive and Expertise models, is more contextually based than the other two. Lastly, the **Instinctive** group contains the Creative and Heuristic models. While these may appear more suited for artists, they are better conceived as time-based models. The remainder of this chapter is an in-depth discussion of each model.

Identifying and analyzing these models is the primary concern of this chapter. As mentioned previously, there is a section in the analysis of each case explicitly discussing the decision model. Among other things, this is to help the reader connect the models with the case. However, this is not an exact science and is much like analyzing A(a)rt. There will be those who might disagree with our analysis and those who identify aspects of the analysis we missed or purposely omitted; this is perfectly understandable and encouraged! As artists, we know that our life—and A(a)rt—experiences are the foundation of our A(a)rt decision making. Further, we also know that our A(a)rt-making process evolves over time. Therefore, our analysis of A(a)rt (and how we make decisions) should and will evolve as well, as a number of the cases demonstrate.

Lastly, the CEOs and Executive Directors in these Case Sets are describing and relating their critical decisions concerning their companies and organizations. It should be mentioned that they are human and with humanity comes errors, mistakes...and sometimes success. The fact that they are willing to share their experiences with emerging arts entrepreneurs is certainly welcome, but also reflects the courage (and belief in new arts entrepreneurs) they possess in letting the world know about their experiences. While it would be easy to simply focus on the more business-based aspects of these cases, we encourage the reader to pay particular attention to the self-actualization and personal growth of these individuals.

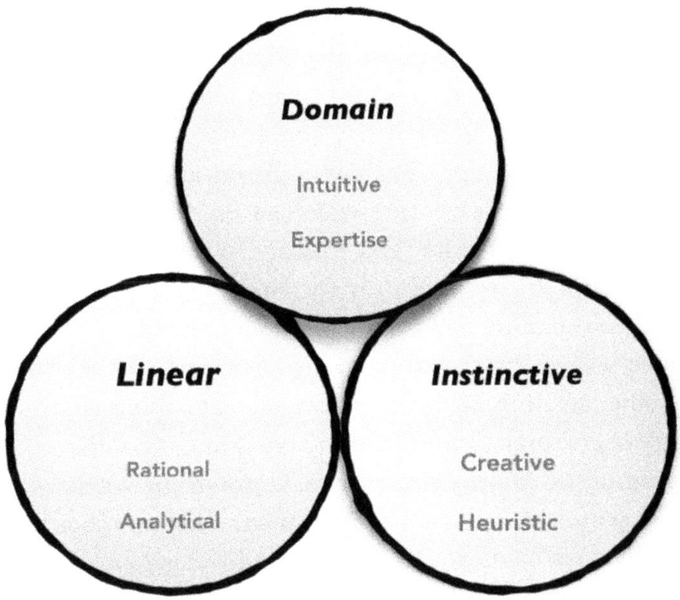

Figure 2.1 Decision Model Groups.

What this Means in the Real World

In our daily life, decisions occur at almost every moment. (Reading this book is a decision, for example.) Simply understanding different decision-making models empowers emerging arts entrepreneurs and suggests more success than one who does not, since knowledge of these models allows *choice*. As a part of that empowerment, one can (if time and circumstance allow) test (at least as an intellectual exercise) how different models can impact a decision. Additionally, it becomes easier to identify one's favorite model, which helps in understanding how one tends to lean when making a decision. (For example, some may be more comfortable with Linear models and suspicious of Instinctive models.) Knowing how we make decisions helps in self-actualization, certainly, but has additional benefits such as: knowing how to create comfort and ease when planning and executing actions, response tendencies during periods of anxiety, crises or opportunity, etc.

As an example, some 2D artists will create art with whatever they have at hand and "see what happens." Others may not feel comfortable with that approach and desire to have all the necessary materials first. Given the section immediately above, we could say the "whatever is at hand" process is more Instinctive-based and the artist might be comfortable launching a venture with less pre-planning, preferring to make decisions in "real-time" and trusting in a positive or unique outcome. Contrastingly, we might say the "materials first" artist finds the Linear decision-making approach less anxiety provoking and feels most comfortable with as much pre-planning as possible. While this may be true for some, creating art is not *exactly* like launching an arts venture. Though there are some similarities (and one *could*, if not *should*, approach an arts venture as A(a)rt), we must make room for a *venture's* context as much as we make room for art's context. Perhaps more simply put, just because one is comfortable creating art by engaging a certain set of decision-making models does not mean one is more naturally inclined to use those models when launching a venture; art creation and venture startup exist in different contexts and *likely* have different goals.

For emerging arts entrepreneurs, the authors suggest keeping in mind two important points: 1) an arts business (for- or non-profit) is not about starting the business, it is about *sustaining a mechanism for the distribution of aesthetic value*, which means there are decisions to be made daily (like any other business) and 2) artists are frequently better equipped and practiced to make these decisions because of their art-making experiences and training. However, to understand and apply our arts-based decision-making skills to an arts venture requires both training and practice. At some level, this book helps to address the former but one cannot escape the latter; artists practice (or rehearse or test) their art with some regularity in an effort to learn, execute and perfect. Sustaining an arts venture requires practice as well.

Linear Decision-Making Models

Going about the process of grouping the models is simply about identifying significant similarities, differences and affinities in each model's step-based process. Table 2.1 compares the Rational and Analytical models in the Linear group.

Table 2.1 Analytical and Rational Model Steps

Step	Analytical	Rational
1	Gather ALL information or relevant data	Identify the problem
2	Verify that you understand the data	Identify the decision criteria
3	Verify the impact of the data	Allocate weights to each criteria
4	Eliminate data irrelevant to the issue	Develop multiple options
5	Objectively decide on the course of action based on the data at hand	Analyze each option
6		Decide best option
7		Implement the decision
8		Evaluate the decision and implementation

Analytical Model

The Analytical model is almost exclusively data driven.[1] An astute reader will notice this is the decision-making process used in the *Entrepreneurial Ecology of the Art's* (EEA) **Steady State Model** tool (SSM).[2] The SSM helps emerging arts entrepreneurs quickly and broadly evaluate relevant data in the four primary ecologies critical to their venture. Benefits of this decision-making model include its explicit use of data critical to the venture *and its market or community served.* The challenge is that it takes time to learn, understand and evaluate the data, in addition to how the data interacts within the venture's ecology. Perhaps the most challenging aspect is the data's potential impact on the venture's market and the venture itself. In summary, the Analytical model takes time to learn but provides a broad view of the data impacting both the venture and the market, much like the SSM, which creates a data-driven platform for decision making.

Rational Model

Arguably, the Rational model is more management-based—and not because it has more steps![3] Specifically, this model is 1) deliberate and 2) demands an evaluation of the decision after it is made. While one could argue this model is based on analytical processes (or uses the Analytical model's "spirit"), it provides a more nuanced—if not more human—view of how one could approach problems. For example, step 3 (Weighting criteria) and step 6 (Decide best option) allows one's experience, research and intuition about potential solutions and desired outcomes to enter into the decision-making process. Obviously then, the advantage of this model is that instead of the Analytical model's if-this-then-that orientation, the Rational model accounts for one's practical knowledge, experience and training about potential solutions for an issue. The downside to this model is the time required to make a decision. Yet as illustrated in a number of Cases in this book, the Rational model can be quite effective despite the time required to make the decision. Further, allowing one's *habitus* to negotiate a more deliberative process can result in a more satisfying, honest and "true to self" outcome, yet requires a certain amount of maturity, clear goal setting and awareness of self.[4]

Comparison

If we were to summarize both models, perhaps the Analytical model would be the "if-this-then-that" model and the Rational model could be the "I need to slow down and think about this because it's an important decision" model. Both models demand data (albeit different types): the Analytical model requiring raw numbers or facts and the Rational demanding "criteria" through observation, goal setting, research, etc. One could consider the Rational model an Analytical model embracing the human experience. Additionally, we could envision the Rational model as a more evolved Analytical model. Interestingly, step 5 of the Rational model (Objectively decide on the course of action based on the data at hand) *is* the Analytical model. Yet what brings these two models together is not simply that one can imbed one into the other but that the mechanical "if-this-then-that" concept is used as a matter of degree: the Analytical is all "if-this-then-that" and the Rational weighs "if-this-then-that" depending on the situation, one's goals and a multitude of other contexts and variables.

What this Means for Emerging Arts Entrepreneurs

While the Rational model contains more steps, variables and consideration of what "data" might mean and the Analytical does not, both models share a common core: get data, analyze the data, make a decision.

The only real difference is how the data is analyzed. An Analytical model can act like a spreadsheet of sorts where one acts only on raw facts, while the Rational model accounts for the human making the decision. For emerging arts entrepreneurs who are more data or deliberation driven and rely on a plan, Linear models provide the same sense of comfort as Google Maps; you can trust the default criteria for the fastest route or set other criteria (such as no highways or tollways) to generate options. These models are especially helpful (or may provide some comfort) when encountering an unknown or unexpected issue.

Domain Decision-Making Models

As seen with the Rational model's relationship to the Analytical model (where it can be viewed as step five in the Rational model), Domain-based models are related as Table 2.2 illustrates.

Table 2.2 Expertise and Intuitive Model Steps

Step	Expertise	Intuitive
1	Observe the problem at hand and make *sense* of it in its domain	Identify the problem
2	*Assess* as many aspects of the problem as possible and determine how it may impact the situation.	Scan the environment for cues to *recognize patterns*
3	Based on one's understanding and experience within a domain, *identify patterns*	Select *one* potential course of action, based on experience, knowledge, and training
4	Based on the domain, goals, issue at hand, etc., determine potential courses of action	Consider potential course of action through to outcome
5	Determine *a single* course of action appropriate to both the issue and the domain	If chosen course of action will not produce desired outcome, alter it and retest
6		If altered course of action still not deemed workable, discard and look for alternative
7		Test alternate course of action until viable option found
8		Implement the chosen course of action

Expertise Model

There are a number of distinct aspects of the Expertise model, yet the underlying core is domain driven.[5] While the name of the model may summarize its five steps, each one is in the context of a certain domain—or for arts entrepreneurs, the venture's ecologies. Interestingly, Step 3 (Identify patterns) could be thought of as a set of "if-this-then-that" scenarios as we saw in the Analytical model. Step 4 (Determine potential courses of action) is clear about determining *multiple* options while negotiating the variables surrounding the problem. Step 5 (Determine a single course of action) requires the entrepreneur to select an option.

Perhaps the most maddening aspect of this model is that pattern recognition (Step 3) is a set of "if-this-then-thats" (Step 4 of the Intuitive model). Bluntly put, if one is launching an arts venture with little experience or understanding of the venture's ecological systems, how can one complete either step? This is typically where one seeks advice, researches or simply scours the myriad of digital platforms in the hopes of finding promising recommendations. While these are admirable courses of action, unfortunately experience launching or sustaining the venture is the only real solution; this takes time, small successes and a few failures along the way.

It must be made clear, however, that the *ideal* benefit of experience is that one does not have to repeat a mistake. The beauty of this model is that it keeps one humble no matter their experience; no one knows everything. For example, effective CEOs, managers and executive directors frequently seek advice from others. In part, this is because one would like to make the best decision possible the *first* time; one person's experience is not another's. The value in understanding other experiences is that one can build a set of "if-this-then-thats" while also gaining vital information about patterns experienced by others; this reduces the time required to make a decision, frequently provides new insights and certainly better decisions.

Intuitive Model

One of the Expertise model's weaknesses is the length of time it takes to arrive at Steps 4 (Based on the domain, goals, issue at hand, etc...) and 5 (Determine *a single* course of action...). For the (sometimes) impatient (or perhaps "more feeling-full") among us, the Intuitive model offers two distinct benefits: 1) it takes less time and 2) it accounts for an aspect of human nature: intuition.[6] We can see the time advantage in Step 2 (scanning for patterns earlier than the Expertise model) and the human nature advantage in Step 3 (Select *one* potential course of action) also occurring earlier.

What we have in this model (at least on the surface) is a reliance on human intuition (an undefinable "sense" of a situation or its context), execution and then evaluating the decision to determine if it addresses the issue. If the decision doesn't produce the desired outcome, repeat Steps 1 through 4. As outlined in Table 2.2, the Intuitive model may seem somewhat similar to other models. What sets it apart from the others is the speed at which this model can operate. Here, there is no "data" to speak of other than recognizing patterns and the analysis aspect tending to occur in short order. Yes, this model may appear as a variation of the "if-this-then-that," but again, this model is about speed and human nature.

Intuition, as we know, is that "gut feeling" many occasionally experience. While it is beyond the scope of this work to examine what human intuition is or isn't, artists are not immune from intuition and, arguably, frequently use it in their art: those "what if I do this" or "this might be cool" moments all artists encounter at one time or another. (Yes, sometimes these moments have wonderful outcomes and other times not). We also have these "gut feelings" every day when meeting new people, assessing a social or new geographic environment, etc., and often, we act on these feelings. For example, if one visits a new restaurant and the "vibe" feels odd or uncomfortable, we typically leave. On the other hand, the "vibe" could be new and enticing, imploring us to stay because it "just feels good." In this example, intuition either saves one from experiencing an uncomfortable situation or encourages a comfortable and engaging experience.

With this model, the human element occurs in Step 2 where one *scans the environment* and tries to *recognize patterns*. (It should be said that "feelings" can be a pattern as well). Additionally, we see that the last half of the model (Steps 5–7) introduces solution testing: a simple "does this work or not?" We could envision this type of testing as sifting through possible outcomes.

Comparison

When comparing these models, we notice a number of similarities. The most obvious (and critical) is understanding the venture's ecological systems. Without this, one tends to make decisions based on incomplete information. To blunt this possibility, experienced entrepreneurs sometimes leverage their networks in search of a better or more timely understanding of their venture's domains, or comprehending what others did in similar situations.

Additionally, there is a subtle "yin-yang" or "complementary" relationship embedded within the two. With the Expertise model, when faced with two options of equal outcome, which do you choose? This is where one's intuition may be used to tip the balance for one course of action versus another. Yet pattern recognition and "trusting your gut" (i.e.: intuition) are (hopefully) better sharpened by an increasing number of experiences. On the other hand, with the Intuitive model, one's experience and knowledge generates the confidence to choose the first workable option.

Lastly, we see the importance of time in using these models to their fullest potential. Gaining the experience of sustaining an arts venture takes time and experience. However, sharpening, being open to, and learning to trust one's intuition can take time as well. One positive aspect of these model's relation to time is that once practiced, they can be quicker to use than Linear models.

If we take a broader view, we see that Domain models mimic childhood development. In an effort not to repeat mistakes and achieve a desired outcome, one needs experience making mistakes. Yet in this process, one's intuition is honed by gaining expertise in a specific domain. *Trusting* one's intuition, of course, is another matter.

What this Means for Emerging Arts Entrepreneurs

Everything takes time. We have all heard this and had varying experiences with the concept. As artists, we have a clear understanding that honing our creative and technical skills will take time, practice, guidance and patience. Yet understanding the various domains of our A(a)rt and our venture (the "art world," band culture, other artists we admire, the recording industry, fast fashion, arts education, etc.) are central to how we make decisions and negotiate success or failure. Artists tend to demonstrate this understanding by working diligently toward an outcome, gaining experience, skills and (sometimes) learning to trust this thing called "intuition."

The similarities of one's arts education experiences to the Domain models should be obvious. It could—and should—be said that despite certain rhetoric and popular-isms, artists tend to possess a certain discipline and patience when it comes to their A(a)rt. Sustaining an arts venture demands (in part) the same skills. Again, this means that an entrepreneur must be familiar with the commitment, humility and discipline it takes to make Expert and Intuitive decisions.

With these two models, understanding a venture's domains (i.e.: its ecological systems) is central to their use. There are no shortcuts. For example, one could learn everything about a specific ecology from a book or a classroom. Yet successful leveraging (i.e.: decision making) requires 1) being immersed in a domain for a time (working with people, making mistakes, building a trusted network, asking questions, experiencing success, etc.), 2) being open to gaining and using experience, and 3) developing an intuitive sense of how a domain might react when stimulated or threatened. This suggests that Domain models demand a similar commitment as an artist throughout their creative life: an investment in time and understanding yields expertise and intuition. This is the fertile ground where creativity nurtures the seeds of both innovative ideas and impact…and, of course, good decisions.

Instinctive Decision-Making Models

Our last grouping (Table 2.3) differs from the previous two in that they are far less data-driven and analytical. Yet the key feature with these models is that they are time-based. The Creative model allows for time to pass before making a final decision while the Heuristic model can be used in situations where a timely response is required. As we shall see, these models leverage both the artist's natural inclinations and humanity.

Table 2.3 Creative and Heuristic Model Steps

Step	Creative	Heuristic
1	Identify the problem	Observe the situation
2	Immersion—Think about the problem consciously and gather information	Identify obvious, critical trigger data and ignore extraneous data
3	Incubation—Set the problem aside and do not think about it for a while	Rely on simple, proven or learned solutions to make a decision.
4	Illumination/Insight—The solution becomes apparent, usually when least expected	Execute decision
5	Verification and Application—Verify the feasibility of the solution and implement the decision	

Creative Model

With this model, we have a more relaxed, yet still deliberate process. In many respects, this model leverages one's unconscious—specifically Step 3 (Incubation).[7] With Step 2 (Immersion), however, there is a conscious effort in solving a problem. In fact, one could make the case that aspects of the previous four models could (or perhaps should) be used in this Step based on one's decision-making style, preference or situation. What sets this model apart from the rest, however, is that in Step 3 there is a purposeful retreat from engaging in a conscious deliberation of the problem. This is where one's unconscious mind is leveraged to generate potential solutions (Step 4—Illumination/Insight).

Though one might regard an unconscious deliberative process (Step 3) negatively, it leverages human biology. In the course of one's daily life, it is frequently impossible to devote conscious effort to one task when needing to accomplish many throughout the day. Distractions, required social, family, personal or work demands, self-actualization goals, etc., are plentiful yet put a significant amount of stress and expectation on everyone. This means the time required for a sustained, conscious effort to solve a problem frequently isn't available. Indeed, the 21st century's demand that we hyper-multi-task as a matter of course has its drawbacks.

However, almost all of us know the experience of "sleeping" on a problem, waking up and feeling that somehow the problem seems not as critical, annoying or as complicated as it was the day before. While there are many reasons for this, one is that the unconscious mind is "working through" the problem, for lack of a better non-psychological term. It is in Step 4 (Illumination/Insight) where the outcome of an unconscious effort (the "working out" of a problem while one sleeps) emerges.

What we see in this model is one suited to our 21st century lifestyle. Instead of making an intentional effort to solve a problem from start to finish immediately, once Step 2 (Immersion) is achieved (as much as possible, of course) this model is purposeful in leveraging our biological assets to solve a problem. Yes, there are many rocks to be thrown at the pace and demands of the present, yet deliberately employing an asset when required is the function of an asset.

Heuristic Model

Perhaps the least time consuming model presented, the Heuristic model is also the least deliberative.[8] As Case 1A details, this model is simply the "knee-jerk" or "fight or flight" model. This is the model some entrepreneurial miracle stories are based upon—the singular, impulsive action that magically produces results. While some of these accounts are true and worth our attention, the fact is that many of these entrepreneurs had previous experience, a vast network, were skilled at analyzing opportunities and possessed a clear understanding of the ecologies, their goals and where emerging opportunities resided.

Note in Step 1 (Observe the Situation) there is a key distinction in the models. In this step, the entrepreneur *observes* the situation. He/she does not go about the process of understanding or identifying the problem. Similar to the first step in the Expertise model, one initially observes, then moves forward in their respective processes. This suggests the Heuristic model demands (or at least benefits greatly from) repeated experiences before its implementation.

Again, we see the use of steps similar to other models. In Step 2 (Identify critical data), there is an explicit reliance on data gathered from either experience or knowledge. Step 3 (Rely on simple solutions), however, is where the model deviates from the others. Note that in this step, there is no analysis of the data, hence the characterization of the model being a "more immediate" reaction to a situation or problem. The trick to successful decisions, then, is to make that "knee" as knowledgeable and experienced as possible before it needs to "jerk."

Comparison

While these models might appear unrelated, they have a "yin-yang" relationship like the models in the Domain group. Specifically, the Creative model relies on the long-term unconscious to do much of the actual problem solving as the conscious is more responsible for gathering information, evaluation and execution. The Heuristic model, on the other hand, relies on a quick, conscious mind to execute the entire process. What unites them is not only leveraging of the "whole" mind but the trust each model demands. In the Heuristic model, the entrepreneur is trusting that a simple and quick response solves the issue (Step 3—Rely on simple, proven or learned solutions). Likewise, with the Creative model, one is trusting the unconscious mind to help illuminate the decision-making process. While one could make the argument that all decisions require a certain amount of trust in their respective processes, trusting oneself is at the core of these two models.

What this Means for Emerging Arts Entrepreneurs

Both of these models are well known by artists: some create art in one sitting, others require some time away from the creative process before completing a work. For example, Jackson Pollock was quite familiar with the Heuristic ideal and its immediacy. Da Vinci, on the other hand, took three years to finish *The Last Supper*. Therefore, A(a)rt can happen immediately or over a long period.

All A(a)rts ventures will have opportunities and problems throughout their life. Some problems will require Linear approaches and others more Domain-based. For those problems where time is not a significant issue, trusting that one's unconscious will solve the problem is as much a test of the model as it is a test of self. Yet the fact remains that when an opportunity presents itself that potentially achieves a goal—yet is time dependent—decisions must both achieve the goal and empower self.

Notes

1 For examples of the diversity and popularity of analytical decision-making scholarship, see Öncü Hazir, "A Review of Analytical Models, Approaches and Decision Support Tools in Project Monitoring and Control," *International Journal*

of Project Management 33, no.4 (2015): 808–815; Joke Bilcke et al, "Accounting for Methodological, Structural and Parameter Uncertainty in Decision-Analytic Models: A Practical Guide," *Medical Decision Making* 31, no. 4 (2011): 675–692; Lennart Sjöberg, "Intuitive vs. Analytical Decision Making: Which is Preferred?" *Scandinavian Journal of Management* 19, no. 1 (2003): 17–29 and Swamidass, Paul M. and William T. Newell. "Manufacturing Strategy, Environmental Uncertainty and Performance: A Path Analytical Model." *Management Science* 33, no. 4 (1987): 427–546. Note the importance of ancillary discussions and implications of data quality and context in, for example, Guiwu Wei, "Grey Relational Analysis Model for Dynamic Hybrid Multiple Attribute Decision Making." *Knowledge-Based Systems* 24, no. 5 (2011): 672–679 and Zhi-Ping Fan and Bo Feng, "A Multiple Attributes Decision Making Method using Individual and Collaborative Attribute Data in a Fuzzy Environment," *Information Sciences* 179, no. 20 (Sept. 2009): 3603–3618.

2 Gary D. Beckman, *The New Arts Entrepreneur: Navigating the Arts Ecologies* (London: Routledge, 2022), 71–74.

3 Models and parameters of rational thinking are one of the primary foci of the decision-making discussion in many corners of management and near-related disciplines. See, for example, Brian J. Taylor, "Risk-Managing Decision-Making: A Psycho-Social Rationality Model," *The British Journal of Social Work* 51, no.7 (2021): 2819–2838; Francis C. Uzonwanne, "Rational Model of Decision Making," in *Global Encyclopedia of Public Administration, Public Policy, and Governance*, ed. Ali Farazmand, (New York, NY: Springer, 2016), 1–6; Hamid Noorani, "Rational Decision-Making" (Bloomington, IN: Xlibris, 2010) and Barry Schwarz, Yakov Ben-Hiam and Cliff Dasco, "What makes a Good Decision? Robust Satisficing as a Normative Standard of Rational Decision Making," *Journal for the Theory of Social Behavior* 41, no. 2 (2010): 209–227.

4 Bourdieu's theory of the "habitus" is used throughout this text. See Pierre Bourdieu, *Outline of a Theory of Practice* (Cambridge: Cambridge University Press, 1977).

5 The concept of "expert" knowledge within a domain is a frequent source of discussion in some corners of scholarship. See Jennifer K. Phillips, Gary Klien and Winston R. Sleck, "Expertise in Judgment and Decision Making: A Case for Training Intuitive Decision Skills," in *Blackwell Handbook of Judgment and Decision Making*, ed. Derek J. Koehler and Nigel Harvey (Hoboken: Wiley, 2004), 297–315; Richard P. Larrick, and Daniel C. Feiler, "Expertise in Decision Making," in *The Wiley Blackwell Handbook of Judgment and Decision Making*, ed. Gideon Keren and George Wu (Chichester: John Wiley & Sons, 2015), 696–721 and Ralph Hertwig, "Decisions from Experience," in *The Wiley Blackwell Handbook of Judgment and Decision Making*, ed. Gideon Keren and George Wu (Chichester: John Wiley & Sons, 2015), 239–267.

6 For a brief survey of intuitive decision making discussions, see Said Elbanna and Yasir Fadol, "The Role of Context in Intuitive Decision-Making," *Journal of Management & Organization* 22, no. 15 (2016): 642–661; Andreas Glöckner and Cilia Witteman, "Beyond Duel-Process Models: A Catagorisation of Processes Underlying Intuitive Judgement and Decision Making," *Thinking & Reasoning* 16, no. 1 (2010): 1–25 and Marta Sinclair and Neal M. Ashkanasy, "Intuitive Decision-making among Leaders: More than just Shooting from the Hip," *Mt Eliza Business Review* 5, no. 2 (2002): 32–40.

7 More creative models of decision making can vary as the scholarship demonstrates. For a diverse view of the topics available, see for example, Simone Ritter and Ap Dijksterhuis, "Creativity—the Unconscious Foundations of the Incubation Period," *Frontiers in Human Neuroscience* 8 (April 2014): 1–10; Arnaud Rey, et al, "Does

Unconscious Thought Improve Complex Decision Making?," *Psychological Research: An International Journal of Perception, Attention, Memory, and Action* 73 (July 2008): 372–379; Carl Martin Allwood and Marcus Selart, "Social and Creative Decision Making" in *Decision Making: Social and Creative Dimensions*, ed. Carl Martin Allwood and Marcus Selart (Dordrecht: Springer Media, 2001), 3–11; George Lowenstein, "The Creative Destruction of Decision Research," *Journal of Consumer Research*. 28, no. 3 (Dec. 2001): 499–505 and Steven H. Kim, "A Formal Model of Creative Decision Making," *Robotics and Computer-Integrated Manufacturing* 8, no. 1 (1991): 53–65.

8 Heuristics are discussed in many of the social sciences. See, for example, Gerd Gigerenzer and Wolfgang Gaissmaier, "Heuristic Decision Making," *Annual Review of Psychology* 62 (2011): 451–482; Carissa Bonner and Ben R. Newell, "In Conflict with Ourselves? An Investigation of Heuristic and Analytical Processes in Decision Making," *Memory & Cognition* 38, no.2 (2010): 186–196 and Elke Kurz-Milcke and Gerd Gigerenzer, "Heuristic Decision Making," *Marketing: Journal of Research and Management* 3, no. 1 (2007): 48–60.

Bibliography

Allwood, Carl Martin and Marcus Selart. "Social and Creative Decision Making." In *Decision Making: Social and Creative Dimensions*, edited by Carl Martin Allwood and Marcus Selart, 3–11. Dordrecht: Springer Media, 2001.

Beckman, Gary D. *The New Arts Entrepreneur: Navigating the Arts Ecologies*. London: Routledge, 2022.

Bilcke, Joke, Philippe Beutels, Marc Brisson and Mark Jit.. "Accounting for Methodological, Structural and Parameter Uncertainty in Decision-Analytic Models: A Practical Guide." *Medical Decision Making* 31, no. 4 (2011): 675–692.

Bonner, Carissa and Ben R. Newell. "In Conflict with Ourselves? An Investigation of Heuristic and Analytical Processes in Decision Making." *Memory & Cognition* 38, no. 2 (2010): 186–196.

Bourdieu, Pierre. *Outline of a Theory of Practice*. Cambridge: Cambridge University Press, 1977.

Elbanna, Said and Yasir Fadol. "The Role of Context in Intuitive Decision-Making." *Journal of Management & Organization* 22, no. 15 (2016): 642–661.

Fan, Zhi-Ping and Bo Feng. "A Multiple Attributes Decision Making Method using Individual and Collaborative Attribute Data in a Fuzzy Environment." *Information Sciences* 179, no. 20 (Sept. 2009): 3603–3618.

Gigerenzer, Gerd and Wolfgang Gaissmaier. "Heuristic Decision Making." *Annual Review of Psychology* 62, no 1 (2011): 451–482.

Glöckner, Andreas and Cilia Witteman. "Beyond Duel-Process Models: A Catagorisation of Processes Underlying Intuitive Judgement and Decision Making." *Thinking & Reasoning* 16, no. 1 (2010): 1–25.

Hazir, Öncü. "A Review of Analytical Models, Approaches and Decision Support Tools in Project Monitoring and Control." *International Journal of Project Management* 33, no. 4 (2015): 808–815.

Hertwig, Ralph. "Decisions from Experience." In *The Wiley Blackwell Handbook of Judgment and Decision Making*, edited by Gideon Keren and George Wu, 239–267. Chichester: John Wiley & Sons, 2015.

Keeney, Ralph L. *Value-Focused Thinking: A Path to Creative Decisionmaking*. Cambridge, MA: Harvard University Press, 1992.

Keren, Gideon and George Wu, editors. *The Wiley Blackwell Handbook of Judgment and Decision Making*. Chichester: John Wiley & Sons, 2015.

Kim, Steven H. "A Formal Model of Creative Decision Making." *Robotics and Computer-Integrated Manufacturing* 8, no. 1 (1991): 53–65.

Kim, Yaeri, Kiwan Park, Yaeeun Kim, Wooyun Yang, Donguk Han and Wuon-Shik Kim. "The Impact of Visual Art and High Affective Arousal on Heuristic Decision-making in Consumers." *Frontiers in Psychology* 11 (2020): 565829.

Koehler, Derek J. and Nigel Harvey, editors. *Blackwell Handbook of Judgment & Decision Making*. Malden, MA: Blackwell, 2007.

Kurz-Milcke, Elke and Gerd Gigerenzer. "Heuristic Decision Making." *Marketing: Journal of Research and Management* 3, no. 1 (2007): 48–60.

Larrick, Richard P. and Daniel C. Feiler. "Expertise in Decision Making." In *The Wiley Blackwell Handbook of Judgment and Decision Making*, edited by Gideon Keren and George Wu, 696–721. Chichester: John Wiley & Sons, 2015.

Lowenstein, George. "The Creative Destruction of Decision Research." *Journal of Consumer Research*. 28, no. 3 (Dec. 2001): 499–505.

Mu, Enrique and Milagros Pereyra-Rojas. *Practical Decision Making: An Introduction to the Analytic Hierarchy Process (AHP) Using Super Decisions V2*. New York: Springer, 2017.

Noorani, Hamid. "Rational Decision-Making." Bloomington, IN: Xlibris, 2010.

Phillips, Jennifer K., Gary Klien and Winston R. Sleck. "Expertise in Judgment and Decision Making: A Case for Training Intuitive Decision Skills." In *Blackwell Handbook of Judgment and Decision Making*, edited by Derek J. Koehler and Nigel Harvey, 297–315. Hoboken, NJ: Wiley, 2004.

Rey, Arnaud, Ryan M. Goldstein and Pierre Perruchet. "Does Unconscious Thought Improve Complex Decision Making?" *Psychological Research: An International Journal of Perception, Attention, Memory, and Action* 73, no 3 (July 2008): 372–379.

Ritter, Simone and Ap Dijksterhuis. "Creativity—the Unconscious Foundations of the Incubation Period." *Frontiers in Human Neuroscience* 8 (April 2014): 1–10.

Schwarz, Barry, Yakov Ben-Hiam and Cliff Dasco. "What makes a Good Decision? Robust Satisficing as a Normative Standard of Rational Decision Making." *Journal for the Theory of Social Behaviour* 41, no. 2 (2010): 209–227.

Sinclair, Marta and Neal M. Ashkanasy. "Intuitive Decision-making among Leaders: More than just Shooting from the Hip." *Mt Eliza Business Review* 5, no. 2 (2002): 32–40.

Sjöberg, Lennart. "Intuitive vs. Analytical Decision Making: Which is Preferred?" *Scandinavian Journal of Management* 19, no. 1 (2003): 17–29.

Swamidass, Paul M. and William T. Newell. "Manufacturing Strategy, Environmental Uncertainty and Performance: A Path Analytical Model." *Management Science* 33, no. 4 (1987): 427–546.

Taylor, Brian J. "Risk-Managing Decision-Making: A Psycho-Social Rationality Model." *The British Journal of Social Work* 51, no. 7 (2021): 2819–2838.

Uzonwanne, Francis C. "Rational Model of Decision Making." In *Global Encyclopedia of Public Administration, Public Policy, and Governance*, edited by Ali Farazmand, 1–6. New York, NY: Springer, 2016.

Wei, Guiwu. "Grey Relational Analysis Model for Dynamic Hybrid Multiple Attribute Decision Making." *Knowledge-Based Systems* 24, no. 5 (July 2011): 672–679.

3
Understanding and Engaging Case Studies

As mentioned earlier, case studies are likely to be new to traditional arts students. We wrote this chapter to make this experience transparent and less anxiety provoking. It should help prepare you to engage with the cases in this book and any classroom.

Arts Learning Methods vs. Case Learning

Young creatives are taught in various settings such as:

- Lecture classrooms for learning the theory and history of your A(a)rt.
- Ensemble rehearsals for dance, theatre and music.
- Private studio lessons, one on one, for musicians.
- Group class for dancers.
- Critique class for visual artists.

Some of what you learn in these settings include:

- The "right answer." For example: facts in arts history and theory classes, the "correct" way to perform something, etc. In these cases, an instructor knows the answers and is there to help you

DOI: 10.4324/9781003414483-4

integrate the answers into either your thinking as a creative or during a performance.

- Technique and the aesthetic boundaries of "good" or "innovative" A(a)rt.
- How to use your "solo" time effectively. For example: practicing a musical instrument, applying paint to a canvas, standing at the barre, writing today's allotment of words as a fiction writer or playwright, etc.

Case-based learning differs from these familiar experiences in *how* you are asked to learn. In the traditional arts class or rehearsal, you are expected to listen to the instructor, respond as needed for clarification or possibly with an answer or two, if requested. However, in a case-based classroom, you are expected to be familiar with (and understand) the case, listen to fellow students, respond with information about the case or with your own questions, and—importantly—offer your solutions to the problems the case presents.

What you are learning is the second area where case-based learning is different. As listed above, in a traditional arts classroom you learn "right" answers, aesthetic boundaries, and individual discipline. Goals for a case-based classroom, on the other hand, can include:

- **Conceptual Models.** These are models for how to think about the world or, less grandiosely stated, your field or discipline. Conceptual models are useful to learn as tools for identifying patterns or generating missing pieces of possible solutions. Sometimes, in pointing out a larger pattern that contradicts existing beliefs, conceptual models make it necessary to change one's beliefs in order for the world or your discipline to still make sense. Thus, keeping one's mind open to exploring conceptual models is a valuable outcome of the case study method.
- **Learning How to Think.** One definition of "thinking" is the act of concentrating on something long enough to develop an idea about "the something."[1] This is different from learning other people's ideas, learning a "right" way of doing something, or memorizing a body of information. Instead, thinking is about developing your own ideas.

How does one learn to concentrate on one thing? How does one learn to develop an idea about something? According to *Project Zero* at Harvard, one learns to think by acquiring tools for thinking.[2] Many of these tools are part of the "what" and the "how" of case-based learning. These include routines for:

- Digging Deeper Into Ideas.
- Introducing and Exploring Ideas.
- Perspective Taking: looking beyond your own perspective and considering experiences, thoughts and feelings of others.
- Considering Controversies, Dilemmas and Perspectives: seeking out and exploring differences and tensions among multiple facets of complex issues.
- Generating Possibilities and Analogies: formulating questions, considering alternatives and making comparisons.
- Synthesizing and Organizing Ideas.

Important other skills are introduced in a case-based classroom, as well, including:

- Practicing decision-making skills. Many cases present a choice an organization is facing, and ask students: what would you decide in this situation? If the readers are given decision-making tools (as in this book), then they can apply them to the question. Some readers will suggest one decision, while others might suggest a different one. Both will need to provide their reasoning, from the text and their own experience. More data may be needed, and some may change their minds and decide differently as a result.
- Learning how to discuss topics in a group or team setting, especially for questions having many possible right answers. A case's decision or other dilemma must be discussed. Then the discussion itself can be discussed, focusing on who said what, how they said it, what was effective, what pushed the discussion and ideas forward, what brought the discussion to a halt or closed down any openness previously achieved.[3]

- Specific skills of starting and maintaining an entrepreneurial venture. This includes skill acquisition, practice with problem identification/analysis, and solution creation for venture startup. Budgeting, pricing, hiring, product development, marketing and sales are frequent discussion points.

Learning about skills in the abstract via lectures and readings becomes, instead, situated in the real world of action and activity by reading and discussing a case. For many students, this context makes the skills more understandable and memorable.

Struggle is Important in Case Method Learning

Throughout most of life, struggle is something we reduce or avoid, if possible. Struggle for food leaves one hungry. Struggle for housing leaves one at the whims of the weather. Struggle to find friends and companions leaves one lonely and isolated. In a college classroom, the struggle to memorize and make sense of what the instructor presents leaves one with learning gaps and, occasionally, a bad grade on the next test or in the course overall.

In case method learning, however, struggle is put at the center and used positively to generate deeper learning. The problem in a case must be identified and solutions both conjured and considered. There are questions to answer, decisions to make and mysteries to solve. In the process of going from questions to answers, it is possible that some unpleasant emotions are provoked, such as anxiety, confusion and frustration. Research shows that these can, in moderation, be helpful for engagement in learning. More pleasant emotions, including curiosity, surprise and enjoyment, can also be a part of case method learning, as students are engaged positively by those same mysteries, missing pieces and problems. These epistemic emotions are correlated to greater learning by students.[4] Curiosity enhances memory for the content that makes one curious.[5] It also creates additional knowledge exploration and better knowledge acquisition.[6]

Case method learning aligns nicely with the experiential learning model developed by David Kolb which has "struggle" at its core (though it does not explicitly say so).[7] The first step in Kolb's learning model is to **experience** something new. Next you **reflect** on that experience, trying to make sense of it by yourself or with other learners. Eventually, you **conceptualize** what you are learning, often with the help of outside sources such as coaching or readings from some expert. Finally, you **apply** your learning and start the cycle again, with a bit more knowledge or skill in hand. Struggle comes in the first two steps, "experience" and "reflect." When having a new experience and reflecting on it, much understanding is missing, many questions cannot yet be answered by you, many problems cannot yet be solved. This makes you ready and eager for outside help in the third step, "conceptualizing."

Let's use Kolb's model to look at case method learning. First you are given a case to read and **experience** on your own. Often there are literal questions the case author provided for you to consider, to help guide your initial experience of the case and help you **reflect** on it to build your initial understanding. Next you bring your thinking to a classroom discussion of the case, joining with others to reflect more deeply on the case and what you can learn from it together. The course leader can help you **conceptualize** from the case by in-class interjections of knowledge and by recommending further readings that build upon the intended learnings of the case. Completing the cycle, you **apply** your learnings from this case in further cases, in other courses, or in your own entrepreneurial ventures.

One other picture we would like to put in your head is about struggle and its usefulness: intellectual struggle can be like certain kinds of physical struggle. In both, there is a different feeling if you struggled and overcame that struggle than if you were simply gifted achievement of a goal without struggle. For example, to arrive at the top of Mount Washington in New Hampshire, the highest peak in the Northeastern United States, you can pay to take a shuttle van ride to the summit (no struggle) or you can hike 4.1 miles from the bottom at about 2,102 feet above sea level to the top at 6,288 feet above sea level (a real, but not impossible, struggle). The view at the top is the same—in some ways—regardless of how you got there. But the view for the hiker includes memories of how the raw spot that developed on her foot after the first 30 minutes felt as it turned into a blister and broke, how delicious the water from her water bottle tasted at the halfway point, how warm the sun was on her face, how loose the rocks were for the final 1000-yard scramble on hands and knees. The physical struggle provides more memories, more learning and a deeper knowledge about that mountain.

Perhaps a mental picture of intellectual (not physical) struggle is helpful, too. If you (one day) get curious about gravity, and REALLY want to know how it works, but only remember something about Sir Isaac Newton and an apple tree, you might be at the start of an intellectual journey. If you decide not to use the Internet, there will definitely be some struggle involved. There might be times in your journey when you experience anguish, staying up all night working on what turns out to be a dead end. Other times, an insight will suddenly arrive, like Newton's apple falling from above! If you eventually (in a day, a week, 20 years?) figure out that the formula for gravity is F = (G*m1*m2)/r^2, your intellectual struggle paid off. Will your *discovery* be any less than Newton's? After all, you both went from not knowing to knowing. Was your *struggle* any less than Newton's? Certainly, yours would be less, since you knew from the start there IS something called gravity! We feel confident that your *understanding* after this process of discovery would be far greater than if we just told you right now the formula for gravity, explained it to you in detail and gave you a written quiz. The "view"—being able to "see" the formula—is the same, either way. But *your* knowledge and understanding will be deeper if you alone determine the formula through intellectual struggle and discovery. Bottom line, struggle is important for the most and deepest learning to occur. As you engage with cases in a case-based classroom, embrace struggle.

How Cases in this Book are Structured

Each case in this book has multiple parts, sometimes separated by reflection questions for you to read, think about and answer. The first part of each case lays out the situation and, typically, the dilemma facing the protagonist in the case. Usually there is a decision required, either between one thing and another, or between more than two options. Should the protagonist continue being a musician full-time, or move to a focus on growing a non-profit, for instance. How to respond to a specific change in public policy? How to get a dream gig?

The second part of each case either tells more about the situation and looming decision, or describes what the protagonist decided and the results. If this section focused on providing more details before the decision, then there is a third part, covering what was decided and the outcome.

A unique feature of this book is that there are multiple cases about each organization or artist. In this way, we provide an opportunity for students to see the cumulative results of decisions over time. This is important because a decision that looks great in one case can become partly the cause of a problem in another and vice versa. No individual decision is likely to be singly responsible for the ultimate success nor demise of an organization. We hope this methodology demonstrates how individual decisions combine to generate the ultimate success or demise of an organization. Relax! There's always another chance for success—or failure—tomorrow.

Preparing for a Case-Based Classroom Session

You know how to prepare for arts classes, you've been doing that for years. For a lecture-based course, you read the assigned chapters in the textbook. Actors run lines for ensemble productions, until they are reasonably memorized. Musicians practice etudes and solos for private lessons, till they are in top form and their teacher can put the final touches on their performance. Visual artists produce artworks, videos and designs to share in critique classes.

To prepare for a case-based class, you must first read the case, including all footnotes, charts and graphs. (If your instructor wants you to read the Discussion section as well, you should follow those instructions). Before you do that, it usually is good to read the reflection questions embedded in the case, as they tend to contain clues about what the author wants you to gain from the case. Once you have read the case carefully, prepare answers to the reflection questions. Your answers are likely to change as a result of class discussion, which means the class is well-facilitated and your fellow students are engaged. Congratulations to all of you.

How to Participate During a Case Discussion in Class

You have some choices and responsibilities as a case discussion participant. These are different from a typical lecture class, where (as a gross generalization) you participate by listening. You can then choose to ask clarifying questions, if you have any and feel they will help you and others understand the material.

In a case-based class, on the other hand, you have the responsibility to:

- Be prepared. Do the reading beforehand and arrive with questions about certain parts of the case, as well as reasoned answers about other parts of the text. Take notes as you read and bring those with you.
- Answer the reflection questions in the case beforehand. Take the extra step to write answers that formalize your thinking. You may decide to change your answers once you hear what others have to say during class discussion, but that's okay. Commit to starting somewhere.
- Contribute by adding your own voice to the discussion. Say something in every session.
- Be respectful of others. Ask yourself, "Is what I want to say kind?" If you want to disagree with someone else, keep it kind and respectful. Rather than saying, "That was wrong," you might instead say, "I did not expect that answer. Can you say more, to help me understand?"
- Watch the instructor. What is she writing on the whiteboard? This provides clues about what she is hoping you are learning from this case.
- Listen to the instructor. What questions is he asking? These questions are trying to push the class in some direction, possibly toward some specific issue or learning objective. Listen, think, then respond with answers from the text.
- Listen to other students. What answers and insights are they providing? Hear what they are saying, then build upon their answers.
- Know the difference between facts and interpretations. Facts are the stuff that can be pointed to in the text, like "On page two, paragraph three, we read they were running out of money." Interpretations are your opinions, even if based on what's in the text: "I think this is what was causing the problem." Too much

interpretation and not enough facts will cause unnecessary confusion and conflict. Likewise for too much interpretation before getting the facts straight and agreed upon by the group.

You have choices to make in a case-based classroom, including:

- When to say something and when to continue listening. One general rule on this is to speak when your contribution will add to/build upon/challenge/offer an alternative to an idea previously expressed.
- How much to say. If you find yourself raising your hand all the time, or giving long answers that nobody responds to or adds onto, you're talking too much. Give others a chance to contribute by keeping your hand down for a while and listening.
- What to say. Don't just say the same thing someone else has said. That shows you have not been listening. If you're not sure your idea is different from what's already been said, ask a question instead: "Can we clarify what Mary just said? I think I have something different to add to that, but I don't want to just say the same thing." On the other hand, don't show you were not listening, or do not care what the prior person has said, by starting a completely new idea.

The Instructor's Role During a Case Discussion

In a case-based classroom, the instructor's role is to facilitate the discussion and guide it towards important learning objectives. Facilitating involves asking questions to provoke, nudge and encourage, which is an artform in itself. You'll hear questions like these to launch the discussion of the case and keep it rolling along and keep students engaged: "What is the problem in this case? How do you feel about…? What do you notice about…? How do you think X felt in this situation? What would you do in this situation? What would be the cost of doing that?"[8] To make sure the instructor and the whole group understands what is said at any point, a different sort of question might be used by the instructor: "Can you tell us more about the reasoning behind your statement? What evidence did you use to determine that? Who else agrees with this statement and why?"

Writing on the whiteboard is the instructor's other role in the case-based classroom. This is not random note taking, so don't expect them to write a note for everything you utter. In many ways, the leader is waiting for someone to identify key concepts they think are embedded in the case. They are also "drawing a picture" to connect various concepts and visualize them as a whole. Such a drawing might include relationships between program design, pricing and financials, hiring criteria versus measurable results.

Notes

1 William Deresiewicz, "Solitude and Leadership," *American Scholar*, March 1, 2010. Available at: https://theamericanscholar.org/solitude-and-leadership.
2 Project Zero, "Project Zero's Thinking Routine Toolbox," *Harvard Graduate School of Education*. Available at https://pz.harvard.edu/thinking-routines.
3 Scott Andrews, *The Case Study Companion: Teaching, Learning and Writing Business Case Studies*.
4 Elisa Vilhunen, Miikka Turkkila, Jari Lavonen et al, "Clarifying the Relation Between Epistemic Emotions and Learning by Using Experience Sampling Method and Pre-posttest Design," *Frontiers in Education* 7 (April 2022). Available at: https://www.frontiersin.org/articles/10.3389/feduc.2022.826852/full.
5 Kang, Min Jeong, Ming Hsu, Ian Krajbich et al, "The Wick in the Candle of Learning: Epistemic Curiosity Activates Reward Circuitry and Enhances Memory," *Psychological Science* 20, no. 8. (2009): 963–973. Available at: https://papers.ssrn.com/sol3/papers.cfm?abstract_id=1308286#.
6 Mary Ainley, "Interest: Knowns, Unknowns, and Basic Processes," in The Science of Interest, ed. Paul A. O'Keefe and Judith M. Harackiewicz (New York: Springer International Publishing, 2017): 3–24 and Shirlene Wade and Celeste Kidd, "The Role of Prior Knowledge and Curiosity in Learning," Psychonomic Bulletin & Review 26, no.4 (2019): 1377–1387. Available at: https://link.springer.com/article/10.3758/s13423-019-01598-6.
7 David A. Kolb, "Experiential Learning: Experience as the Source of Learning and Development. (Englewood Cliffs, NJ: Prentice-Hall, 1984).
8 Scott Andrews, *The Case Study Companion*: *Teaching, Learning and Writing Business Case Studies*.

Bibliography

Ainley, Mary. "Interest: Knowns, Unknowns, and Basic Processes." In *The Science of Interest*, edited by Paul A. O'Keefe and Judith M. Harackiewicz, 3–24. New York, NY: Springer International Publishing, 2017.
Andrews, Scott. *The Case Study Companion: Teaching, Learning and Writing Business Case Studies*. New York, NY: Routledge, 2021.
Deresiewicz, William. "Solitude and Leadership." *The American Scholar*, March 1, 2010. Available at: https://theamericanscholar.org/solitude-and-leadership.

Freeman, Scott, Sarah Eddy, Miles McDonough, et al. "Active Learning Increases Student Performance in Science, Engineering, and Mathematics." *Proceedings of the National Academy of Sciences*, 111, no. 23 (2014). Available at: https://www.researchgate.net/publication/262267588_Active_Learning_Increases_Student_Performance_in_Science_Engineering_and_Mathematics/link/54b7223a0cf2e68eb2800b84/download?_tp=eyJjb250ZXh0Ijp7ImZpcnN0UGFnZSI6InB1YmxpY2F0aW9uIiwicGFnZSI6InB1YmxpY2F0aW9uIn19.

Genin, Delphine. "Why Confused Students Learn Better: Confessions of an Evil Teacher," *Harvard Business Publishing Education*, July 6, 2021. Available at: https://hbsp.harvard.edu/inspiring-minds/why-confused-students-learn-better.

Kang, Min Jeong, Ming Hsu, Ian Krajbich, et al. "The Wick in the Candle of Learning: Epistemic Curiosity Activates Reward Circuitry and Enhances Memory." *Psychological Science* 20, no. 8. (2009): 963–973. Available at: https://papers.ssrn.com/sol3/papers.cfm?abstract_id=1308286#.

Kolb, David A. *Experiential Learning: Experience as the Source of Learning and Development*. Englewood Cliffs, NJ: Prentice-Hall, 1983.

Project Zero. "Project Zero's Thinking Routine Toolbox." *Harvard Graduate School of Education*. Available at: https://pz.harvard.edu/thinking-routines.

Vilhunen, Elisa, Mikka Turkkila, Jari Lavonen, et al. "Clarifying the Relation Between Epistemic Emotions and Learning by Using Experience Sampling Method and Pre-posttest Design." *Frontiers in Education*, 7 (April 2022). Available at: https://www.frontiersin.org/articles/10.3389/feduc.2022.826852/full.

Wade, Shirlene, and Celeste Kidd. "The Role of Prior Knowledge and Curiosity in Learning." *Psychonomic Bulletin & Review* 26, no.4 (2019): 1377–1387. Available at: https://link.springer.com/article/10.3758/s13423-019-01598-6.

4
From Decision Models to Arts Cases

Let's move from theory to cases. Here is a story of two artists we know, Ian and Sharon. Their experiences help us put decision models to work in an A(a)rts context.

In September of 2022, Ian opened his second solo show at a gallery in Chicago. He was 34 years old at the time. By the end of the opening, he had sold 12 of the 16 paintings in the show. It was a great night, but the path to that moment began years before and required many decisions.

Three months earlier, Sharon had opened her second solo show at that same gallery. She was 27 years old. By the end of the opening, she sold all but one of her 24 pieces. Sharon was thrilled, though not surprised. "There are collectors of my A(a)rt. They've been waiting quite a while for my next paintings."

Within these two artists' young careers are examples of some of the six decision models explored in depth throughout this book. Let's examine each story separately. Then, we'll look for our first examples of decision-making models.

Off to Work He Goes

Often, an artist's first relevant career decision is whether and/or where to attend college. When he was that age, Ian longed to be passionate about some direction for his future and wanted a college major reflecting that

 DOI: 10.4324/9781003414483-5

passion. But as a high school senior he hadn't found that passion. So, he did not choose a college based on a specific program. His list of possible colleges included Marquette in Milwaukee, close to his home but also far enough away. Several friends were exploring Marquette as well. High school was fun with this crew, so once his friends committed to Marquette, Ian decided to follow.

Ian chose business as his major. This changed in his sophomore year when the grueling combination of accounting, economics and statistics convinced Ian that business was not for him—at least not to study. He met with the dean of the business school. "What do you love?" the dean asked. Ian thought about the classes he'd taken so far and answered, "History." The dean responded, "Go be a history major, then. I was a history major as an undergrad." Eventually, Ian added minors in theology and criminology, and never took a visual art class.

The next big decision for Ian was what to do after graduation. He decided graduate school was not for him, so he needed a job. A degree in history, criminology and theology does not get you a job…anywhere. Ian caddied at an exclusive golf course each summer since sixth grade, earning him plenty of spending money, but he knew caddying wouldn't provide enough to live. He loved his parents and looked to them as positive role models. (Ian's mother was a successful freelance photographer and his father ran a thriving non-profit). However, college gave Ian a taste of freedom and he knew living at home wouldn't work any longer. In the first months out of college, an acquaintance told him about an entry-level job as an ad buyer in a small advertising firm. He didn't know much about the job, other than it paid a decent starting salary; he took the position.

Ian was an excellent ad buyer given his combination of organizing and writing skills (from college), and ability to communicate (from caddying). After several years, the small firm lost its main client and started laying off staff, so Ian found a new job in another, slightly larger advertising firm, doing the same thing. His plan was to stay in the industry he now knew something about, but to find an agency with a broader roster of clients; more clients means stable employment.

For Ian, work was still just about bringing in money, and he was making more now than ever before. "Be careful," his dad said to Ian, after he got another sizable pay raise, "they're trying to make it impossible for you to leave." Ian was increasingly dissatisfied with work—but enjoying the money—so this comment hit close to home.

According to his post-college roommates, Ian's visual art development started while he was watching football on TV and scribbling on a paper pad. "Ian was always drawing something, while the rest of us were drinking beers and watching sports," his former roommates report. Ian says it went back earlier: scribbling graffiti tags in elementary school, then spray-painting them onto trains with his good friend Pedro.

One day Ian's girlfriend (later wife), knowing Ian liked graffiti, suggested they visit a gallery in Chicago for street artists, Horizontal Gallery. He saw tagging in some pieces, and spray paint pieces displayed in frames as art. This led Ian to attend more shows there and, eventually, to have some long talks with the gallery owner. Gradually, Ian was figuring out how street art—and being a street artist—worked. He started going out at night to post his art on Chicago's walls. Without really trying, he caught the street art bug.

Soon, Ian began organizing and collaborating with other street artists. For example, he once asked five street artists to create painted interpretations of photographs by Ian's mother. The paintings were photocopied onto large sized paper and wheat pasted on walls in the city—one new wall per week. Another project had artists making pieces based on people who are not well known but should be, with the promise that the original artwork would be part of a group show Ian organized for Horizontal Gallery.

These projects were a good way to meet artists Ian admired. Since street artist subculture is notoriously hard to break into, he decided to apply his organizational and leadership skills. He knew other artists enjoyed doing collective projects together, so why not elevate everyone's status in the Chicago art scene, including his own? At the time, he had disposable income to buy materials for these group projects; all the artists had to do was show up and paint.

Ian was being asked to create pieces for group shows in other galleries, too. If his piece sold, the gallery got half the selling price and he got the other half. Price it too low and you barely cover material costs. Price it too high and it doesn't sell. Galleries in Chicago, Portland Oregon, New Orleans and Miami all asked Ian for group show pieces.

Wherever Ian traveled, he would take his rolled-up artwork copies and wheat paste some on the streets in the middle of the night: New York City, London, Portland Oregon, Mexico City, Paris. Fellow artists followed his travels and postings on Instagram, gaining him more than 4,000 followers. Not bad for an unknown street artist.

Ian's biggest decision, after several years of doing street art, was when to quit his day job. They were paying him a pretty penny now, but the satisfaction was missing. He recently married (another big decision) and wanted to purchase a house in the city. Ian could paint more art if he did not have the day job and calculated that making more paintings could mean making enough money from just being an artist. A gallerist in New York, when Ian asked the "when can I quit my day job" question, gave him this formula: "You can quit when you have $50,000 in the bank as a safety net, a year's worth of shows on the calendar, and a year's worth of commissions."

The tipping point came when Ian was asked to do a solo show at Horizontal Gallery in four months. His first solo show was at a warehouse gallery in the suburbs several years before and sold only a few pieces. Ian accepted the invitation at Horizontal, then realized he could not make enough paintings to fill the walls of a solo show with the time he had available. He knew, by that point, how long it would take to create the pieces. There simply was not enough time in his schedule to make that many paintings by the opening if he was just painting at night and weekends. Could he quit and paint full time for the next four months? Would that give him enough time, or was he sunk, even without the day job?

Ian thought about the criteria for quitting your day job. $50,000 in the bank: almost. A year's worth of shows scheduled: yes. A year's worth of commissions: yes. Then he thought about his upcoming show. Was there enough time to create 16 pieces by the opening: yes, if he paints 60 hours per week from tomorrow till opening. "I'd rather be painting art 60 hours a week instead of doing a job I hate." That was it; time to become a full-time artist. Obviously, this was a big decision.

His last day on the day job was early May and the solo show opened September 3. The final piece for the show was completed and hung the night before. By the end of the opening night, 12 of 16 pieces had sold, with sales totaling over $20,000.

Sharon Gets Her Start

Sharon started drawing in the 8th grade, and hung out at galleries during high school, asking lots of questions. The more she learned, the more she wanted to become part of the scene. Sharon never thought about going to college, until one showed up at her high school in her sophomore year and wanted to see her portfolio. They offered her a spot, if she spent two more years in high school. However, she didn't like school and thought she would simply get a job with the fire department, like her dad.

Art school was a whole new idea. She researched several art schools, learning everything about their offerings, professors, tuition, costs and even studying the students' art. In the end, she went to the place that asked first, The American Academy of Art in Chicago, because of their strong illustration department and reasonable tuition. After Sharon took her first painting class, she stopped her illustration studies and took every painting class offered over those four years.

Her parents were supportive but had no contacts to help after graduation. Sharon's father was a lifelong fireman in Chicago. Her mother worked as a financial advisor, though she had been an artist in her first years of college. Sharon knew she was on her own as a working artist. During college she worked part-time at an art framing shop. In her senior year, Sharon started her own business framing other artists' work (for less cost than a frame shop) and built canvases as well. Her dad had some tools she borrowed and learned by trial and error.

After graduation, Sharon only wanted to be an artist, but she also knew there were many talented painters. She painted full-time, had her framing and canvases business, and did installations plus other support tasks at Horizontal Gallery. Eventually, the Gallery gave Sharon an exclusive framing contract for artists visiting Chicago from out of town. This helped her framing business become sustainable almost immediately. Combining all her efforts, Sharon could pay the bills. She was also learning many things about the visual art business…from every angle.

Very soon after starting the framing business, she was introduced to a different product she could offer artists. It was an aluminum surface mounted on a wood frame. Some artists who tried it—including both herself and Ian—liked the texture more than a traditional surface for how it took and held paint. However, most artists still came to her wanting canvases, based on both cost and functionality. To encourage more to try aluminum panels, she curated a show at Horizontal, who gave over 80 artists one 11" x 14" aluminum panel to use and a spot for each panel in a group show.

Quickly, space became an issue as Sharon was working out of her basement. With miter and table saws, saw dust and her own artworks in varying stages of completion, the basement was becoming cramped. Happily, a collector had an old shoe store he was willing to let her use for a few months at no cost. Eventually, Sharon and several other artists agreed to terms with the collector and leased the 3,000 square foot space for multiple studios.

Sharon was now juggling her own art, framing other artists' work, and helping run a thriving art gallery. Did this make her a part-time artist, part-time art framer with business expenses to cover, and part-time gallery employee? Was this the definition of "portfolio career?"

This Year's Model(s): A Brief Analysis

Let's stop for a moment and make note of the decisions both of these young artists made along the way to their second solo shows, and the decision-making models they represent. Here's a list, as the authors see them:

Ian's decisions:

Go to college where your friends are going: heuristic.
Major in business: heuristic.
Switch major to history: heuristic.
Get first post-college job at advertising agency: heuristic.
Move to second and third ad agencies: expertise/intuitive.
Make drawings, post them on walls on the streets at night: expertise/intuitive.
Decide to walk into Horizontal Gallery for first time: heuristic.
Organize collaborative projects with other street artists: expertise/intuitive.
Do first solo show at suburban gallery: expertise/intuitive.
Get married: expertise/intuitive.

Buy house: heuristic.
Quit day job and become full-time visual artist: expertise/intuitive.
Do second solo show at Horizontal Gallery: expertise/intuitive.

Sharon's decisions:
Decide in HS you want to be an artist: heuristic.
Choose to go to art school for college: heuristic.
Start framing business to bring in money: expertise/intuitive.
Get part-time job in art gallery during college: expertise/intuitive.
Do first solo show at gallery: expertise/intuitive.
Do second solo show at gallery: expertise/intuitive.

Ian starts his decision making with some **heuristic model** decisions: he chooses the college where his friends are going. He chooses a major, then switches majors, seemingly based on others' influences. After graduation, he takes a job totally outside anything he studied in college. When that agency becomes less stable, he switches to another in the same field. Perhaps this is his first decision using knowledge he's accumulated, putting it into the domain models grouping. Several larger decisions are looming.

Next, he must decide whether to get married or not. After dating the same person for years and living together—plus going to friends' weddings—Ian finally decides. We could say he built up some expertise in the domain of relationships by this point, studied his options and went with the one that made the most sense. Perhaps it seems crass to think in decision-model terms about such an important personal decision. But, we can see that Ian did not just jump into this decision like he did for others before it, so there must have been more going on—consciously or subconsciously. Let's call this using the **expertise model** of decision making.

Ian must then decide when to quit his well-paying day job in order to pursue his passion—making visual art—full time. He is given criteria for this decision by an expert he meets and uses it as a metric to guide his decision making. When he comes to a crossroads (i.e.: the moment of determining how to get enough time to create all the art for his second solo show by the show's opening date), he quits his day job and plunges into life as a full-time artist. At this point, he is using the **expertise model** for this very important decision as a young artist.

For Sharon, after a few youthful **heuristic model** decisions, she moves to **expertise/intuitive models** for decision making, as she gains experience and knowledge of her chosen fields of artist and framer. She decides by the end of high school to become an artist and sets about making that happen, beginning with deciding where to go to college and what to study based on her goals. During and after college (rather than taking a day job in an unrelated field), she works part-time both in a framing shop and then a "street art" gallery. Sharon then launches an arts business framing other people's art and building traditional canvases. To differentiate her business, she finds a new framing method that works for her as an artist, then gradually invests in the space needed to make it happen.

Thus far, both artists arrived at a similar place—a successful second solo show—but by making strikingly different decisions in their lives and careers. Sharon arrived there at age 27, while Ian was 34. Certainly, decisions about college propelled Sharon there sooner. But Ian caught up after a late start. Have they both built solid foundations for future success? Or has one set of decisions prepared one artist for greater future success than the other?

As we see from these two simple examples, an artist's life involves many decisions, especially early on. This fact alone demonstrates that decision making is an important skill. You are going to do it frequently, so better to be good at it, apparently. Furthermore, there are good decisions and mediocre decisions. A good decision can get you to your goal more quickly or more fully. A mediocre decision may slow you down, though very few decisions will thwart you entirely. Paying more attention to the process of making decisions can generate the outcomes you desire. Knowing which of those decisions are taking your attention, time and skill is critical. Being aware of and using the models in this book is *one* way to make sure you pay more attention. This helps you systemize the decision process and gives you formal tools.

Ian's and Sharon's stories have just begun, and their endings are in no way certain. Will both continue to paint? Will one or both decide being a full-time artist is not for them? Perhaps Ian will decide he cannot make enough money to survive and pay a mortgage while painting full-time.

Will he feel pressured then to move on from art making? Or will Ian find ways to increase the revenue from his art making? Perhaps Sharon will become exhausted from running her growing framing business and continuing to make her own art. Or will she find ways to balance these dual activities?

Throughout this book, we examine cases having more detail and depth than the two brief examples above. By using sequences of cases from the same artist or organization (i.e.: sets), we will see how some decisions lead to—or influence—other decisions over time. We will also see how many of the decisions in the Case Sets turn out as intended. Some will produce remarkably positive results, and some partially negative results, usually in unanticipated ways.

Case Set 1

A Rural Videography Business

5
Case 1A: Freelancer or Agency?

Chantel Aspesi wanted to make more money. For the five years since she'd earned her undergraduate degree in International Studies, it had been fun and exciting to be a video freelancer. Now marriage, a mortgage, and a baby at home added up to new levels of financial responsibility and worry. What had been enough no longer was. An option presented itself but would it change her fun into drudgery? Could she afford this solution?

Chantel Gets Her Start

Raleigh, North Carolina was Chantel Aspesi's hometown. There, she imagined her International Studies major at college would be a step toward traveling the world. She minored in Spanish so she'd have the language skills to engage with people in many other countries. Her double minor in Arts Entrepreneurship gave her a taste of the skills she'd need to start her own business someday. Internships in her junior and senior years introduced her to using social media to generate sales leads and boost event attendance.

After college, Chantel took a temp job at the North Carolina Community Foundation in Raleigh. That temporary job as administrative assistant lasted more than two years. It started with event coordination but eventually gave her a taste of many of the tasks that make a nonprofit, or any organization, run smoothly.

 DOI: 10.4324/9781003414483-7

Her next job gave her lots of the experience she would soon use to begin her video freelance work. Being a client advocate and event manager at the Valley Women's Clinic doesn't sound like it would have anything to do with video production. Yet it was there Chantel learned Adobe Premiere Pro for video production. Chantel also continued to learn skills valuable in any business situation. She wrote copy and produced marketing videos, in addition to being client counselor, volunteer trainer, donor outreach assistant, event manager, public speaker and event volunteer supervisor.

In her personal life, things were changing. She married in 2016, moved three and a half hours away from Raleigh to rural Virginia for her husband's job, and bought a house. By 2018, they were preparing to welcome their first child. The plan was to go back to part-time after the birth. "We wouldn't make ends meet, otherwise."

Just one day before the baby was born, their daycare plan fell through. Suddenly, the couple was confronting the scenario of Chantel staying home with their new baby, lacking a part-time job to help with the family's finances. Her husband's job was full-time at the local university. "It paid fine for a single guy, but not for that guy and a wife and a new baby," Chantel says:

> That's why we started the business. The baby was born in May, 2018, and the business was born in June, one month later. We looked at each other when our childcare fell through and I said "What can I do?" I knew how to make good videos. I'd taken arts entrepreneurship courses. So, I figured I'll just wing it and see if it works.

Launching her own small business, which she called Lily and Gems Media (LGM), would use all the skills she developed: video production, arts entrepreneurship, social media marketing, sales lead generation. Her clients would be businesses that, as her website says, "are changing the trajectory of people's lives."

Looking for Leverage

By April of 2019, nearly one year after starting her own business, Chantel knew some things needed to change. "Clients were treating me just like

I was one of their employees," she said later. "Plus, I needed to be making more money. We were profitable, but not profitable enough." Her initial clients included a cement company, a small law firm and a social service agency. She knew not all of them were "changing the trajectory of people's lives."

One of her clients was a larger video agency. She knew the client was taking advantage of her, including not setting clear scope for projects; this typically resulted in far more effort than her typical fee covered. Then, that client was not paying her on time. Several times she sent her husband to their offices to ask for the checks they promised were mailed. "There were a ton of really toxic issues with that client relationship." At one point, that client told Chantel: "If you want to get paid on time, you should go into a different business."

Clients were not treating Chantel like a valuable partner for their marketing efforts. "They would just say, 'Go shoot this video,' and I would do whatever they said to do. It was like going into a McDonald's. Whatever you order, they give it to you. I needed more leverage in that negotiation."

She sought advice from colleagues and joined a Facebook group called "How to sell Video at Higher Rates." It was hosted by Dynamos Video, a company offering courses in running a video business. Chantel quickly came to value the support she received from this group and reached out to them whenever she had questions.

Doing Nothing was not an Option

Something needed to change on the revenue side, too. Lily and Gems Media had generated $5,344 in its first year. That was a start, but it was not enough. Chantel said:

> My husband and I were just kind of clawing to get by. It was very stressful. I had a one-year-old at home, so I was full-time at home with her and full-time bootstrapping this business. We just knew something had to change.

One option they discussed was for Chantel to get another job, like she'd had before the baby came. "We were getting desperate," she says. She researched using her film industry skills as a way to make enough money for her family's needs. "There's not much film industry work in this geographic area," she determined. "I also realized there was going to quickly be a ceiling on how much I could charge just to be a videographer. There's not that much demand in this area." So, another job would have to be outside of video and film.

Chantel did not do any research into the local chamber of commerce and what kinds of businesses were in her area. She regrets not identifying businesses, to target how to meet them and grow LGM. "I should have done that research. I knew better."

"I process things through conversation," Chantel says. As a result, she spent time with her husband, friends, family and anyone immediately around her, conversing about what to do to alleviate her family's financial desperation. They helped her think about her few options, along with best and worst case scenarios for each. "We talked about doing nothing, too. It became very clear that doing nothing was not an option. We had to do something."

Through her Facebook videographers' group, she heard about Dynamos Video Academy. It was a training program for videographers. Other members of the group had taken their courses and said they were worthwhile. Chantel also heard stories of their success at closing deals for amounts she could never imagine. They made the Dynamos Video system sound simple, too. Chantel had not found any other education option. "The university near us had some courses, but those were all about film industry jobs," she says. Chantel decided the education route was either Dynamos Video or nothing.

Dynamos Video Academy's initial course was called Zero to Dynamo. The course focused on moving from being a freelancer to becoming a video agency. Content included lead generation, sales technique, pricing and accounting. There were six weeks of live sessions, plus pre-recorded content to watch between sessions, as well as lots of bonus content. If you liked that, there were more course modules you could purchase later.

Cost was the hitch. For the initial intensive six-week course, tuition was $2,000. It promised a deeper level of access to a network of colleagues all over the United States who could help you change your business. This was a lot of money to Chantel and her young enterprise. She could only afford to pay half upfront. If she decided to do this, she would need a payment plan.

The promised result was a solution to her problems of 1) not having enough revenue coming into her video business and 2) providing the income her growing family needed. People who took the course increased their incomes significantly. Course participants learned how to charge more for each video project, and how to generate more video projects. Would that be the result for her, too?

Chantel began to consider what else moving from freelancer to agency might mean. "I wonder if I'm ready," she said to herself. She would be changing her professional identity. No longer would she be a freelancer, doing whatever the client requested. Instead, she could launch a video agency, finding clients by meeting with business owners, listening to their business issues, then pitching them on strategies and products she determined they needed. "This is going to be telling business owners what to do," Chantel thought. Did she have the nerve to do that? Would it be any fun, or was making videos suddenly going to be more like work?

Doing nothing was not a viable option. Her family was struggling financially. She could get another job, outside of video. Or she could take this course and change her business from freelance to video agency. Were there other options? Should she invest money she didn't have and put her trust in Dynamos? If it did not work, she'd probably be broke and out of business.

Reflection Questions

1. What would you do if you were Chantel?
2. How would you decide what to do?
3. Has Chantel done enough research to decide what to do?

Doing Something

Chantel decided to take the course. Looking back, Chantel understands that she did not really explore other options. Her process then was simple: this opportunity presented itself, she got positive feedback about it from her Facebook group, she talked to family and friends about the pros and cons, and could it produce the results she needed? Chantel decided it was worth the risk and enrolled. Her main criteria was that it needed to give her a way to generate more income. After six weeks of taking the course, the promise was that she'd be getting better-paying projects. Her back was against the wall to make more money. She spent her last $1,000, plus $1,000 she didn't have, on the only option she had found.

Just three weeks after Chantel started the course, she was at a local conference for women in business in her part of Virginia, and met a woman who worked for the local transit agency. She found herself talking at length to this new contact. Using some of the sales skills she just learned, Chantel pitched her on a $7,000 project—the largest she ever proposed. The transit agency representative agreed. Chantel says it was the confidence she'd gained from the course that made this happen. A few months later, this same client hired Chantel for another project at $3,000. Since then, the client has hired Chantel for $50,000 of additional projects.

For Chantel's business at that early stage, the financial results from the course were significant. Before the course, her revenues were $5,344 for the year. The year she took the course, revenues jumped to $25,857. Half of that new revenue was from one client—the local transit agency. Chantel was closing much larger deals than ever before, thanks to the confidence and techniques she learned from Dynamos course.

Additionally, Dynamos taught Chantel about a wider variety of video products. One of those was "video business cards," which she now says are very basic but she had no experience with these before the course. "They are a one-size-fits-all kind of video asset that every business needs. So, they are easy to sell, and relatively quick and easy to produce."

This was an extension of the question that scared Chantel a little before the course: she'd be changing her basic model, yet would she be ready and able? Now, beyond just closing bigger and more deals, she was closing a different kind of deal. In this model, she had video "products" she knew how to do and could confidently recommend as the solution to a potential client. Chantel was building a repertoire—a portfolio she could draw upon. She evolved from one-off videos to products she could more easily pull off the shelf and repeat. Where might her product evolve next?

Chantel also built a larger community of fellow video producers from the course, for hands-on mentorship. "When I started, I was completely in a vacuum. I didn't know any other entrepreneurs. I didn't have any kind of specific video education. This was such a big jump for me." She was learning that education—taking courses in skills needed in her new field, specifically—was one way to achieve the increased revenue she wanted and needed for her growing family's financial needs.

Had it been fun, or had it felt more like work? Chantel says now her job has changed, but in a good way. She realized her unique contribution to her video "agency" was to be the one person who could pitch new work to potential and repeat clients, calculate the right pricing, close those deals and shoot the video. This meant hiring others (i.e.: contractors) for the time-consuming task of editing the videos, which was just fine with her. She enjoyed what she was doing now.

There'd been real excitement, as well, harkening back to Chantel's interest during college to one day travel the world. One client needed a year's worth of new videos for her luxury travel business, and wanted to shoot them all in Italy. She hired Chantel and a small team to accompany her to Italy, paid for all their video work plus all expenses paid and luxury accommodations. "I wouldn't have had the courage and confidence to do that if I hadn't taken that course and all that came after it," Chantel says now. Dream come true.

At the age of 27, Chantel achieved a few dreams with LGM's \$25,857 in revenues. Still, she had plenty of room to learn and grow. Just staying in business a few more years could provide those opportunities.

Discussion: Case 1A — Freelancer or Agency?

Summary

This Case Set focuses on a common question posed by emerging arts entrepreneurs: if I start an arts business, what should I expect during the first few years? At the outset, we should say that what happens during the startup period is unique to the individual and circumstances of the venture's startup environment (i.e.: arts product, market, ecological makeup and conditions, etc.). One's *habitus*, context and circumstances play a role in this context and can take time. Launching an arts business is both invigorating and humbling. It is exhilarating being a CEO—you really *are* your own boss. Yet realizing you *alone* are responsible for what's in your bank account may be intimidating for some.

Before we get into the Case, the reader should know that 1) not everyone is an entrepreneur. To be frank, if one decides not to launch simply because they do not feel ready or are daunted by the work involved, there is no shame in that decision. It *does* take a certain *je nes sais quoi* to launch a business.[1] Some of us have "it"—whatever these possible traits, orientations or attitudes may be—and some do not. (We could say the same about entering any profession: some have "it," and some do not.) However, if you've taken arts entrepreneurship courses during your college years, most businesses *value* this experience and will likely see you as a creative asset. If you are ready to launch, 2) consider the value of doing it slowly. As mentioned in *The New Arts Entrepreneur*, the arts market is flooded with A(a)rt and artists. Making the decision to launch and expecting instant success is not a reasonable assumption for most; many make this mistake and fail almost immediately. Lastly, 3) if you are on the fence about launching, this is not a bad position to occupy. Fence sitting, however, can be problematic: one can sit for decades and lament their indecision or keep the idea of launching an arts business frontmost in their minds waiting for the right circumstances.

Case 1A is rather typical of recent college graduates: a few internships during college, a few jobs after graduation, a move, a marriage and a family. Though much of this Case concerns factors forcing Chantel's decision (discussed below) and the immediate aftermath, a critical aspect is ensuring Lily and Gems Media's (LGM) sustainability. (One should note the financial risk she and her family are assuming in this decision).

One of the most beneficial aspects of the Case narrative for emerging arts entrepreneurs is this quote appearing during Chantel's deliberations about the Dynamos Video course:

> "This is going to be telling business owners what to do," Chantel thought. Did she have the nerve to do that? Would it be any fun, or was making videos suddenly going to be more like work?

This highlights another seldom addressed aspect concerning the launch decision: authority. In this quote, Chantel comes to terms with her role not only as an entrepreneur, but the responsibility she has to her soon-to-be clients. Her concern is about not only her knowledge and creativity in service of her market, but whether her ideas to assist other businesses are originating from a place of expertise, which could be viewed as… authority. This means Chantel would be providing video solutions, based on the experiences she possesses (education, internships, previous jobs and video experience), which when combined, gives her the "authority" to tell "…business owners what to do." We should note this sense of authority in these serviced-based value exchanges is embedded in what is referred to as a "product solution," where companies propose a portfolio of products or services to solve a client's problem based on their expertise (read: authority) in a particular field.

Lastly, we learn in this Case that Chantel "process(es) things through conversation." Knowing this pattern is helpful as we move through the Set. Therefore, we should 1) expect Chantel to have a significant network by the end of the Set, and 2) see her leverage this network. We see bits of this in the narrative where she consults with family and friends about being in difficult financial circumstances. Another example of this is leveraging her Facebook videographers' group to find Dynamos Video.

Factors Forcing the Decision

The primary reason Chantel launches Lily and Gems Media is financial. With childcare evaporating a day before she delivered her first child and having to stay home as a result, Chantel didn't have many choices since she couldn't go back to her previous job. For readers without children, raising a child is an expensive endeavor. A 2023 Brookings Institute analysis suggests it costs over $300,000 to raise a child to 18 years of age.[2] Starting a family without both parents working is almost impossible, especially when just daycare for the first five years of a child's life averages over $66,000.[3] Again, Chantel's choices were few. But in some respects, she was lucky as there was a reasonable basis for the decision. We see this when she says: "…'What can I do?' I knew how to make good videos. I'd taken arts entrepreneurship courses. So, I figured I'll just wing it and see if it works."

The most interesting aspect of this Case, however, is not Chantel's decision to start LGM, but what she did after the first year: her engagement with Dynamos Video. The factor forcing her decision to take the classes was financial, yes, but centered more specifically on two issues: 1) being treated like an employee by her clients and 2) her clients were not those who were "…changing the trajectory of people's lives." The former issue is a matter of LGM's relationship with the clients and the latter concerns LGM's mission as a company. Arts businesses (regardless of for- or non-profit status), can establish missions beyond pure profit or community betterment. In this Case, Chantel established a mission—an *ethical* mission—when she launched LGM.

Her decision to engage Dynamos Video demonstrates Chantel building and leveraging her network. As the Case narrative describes, one of the first things she did was to join their Facebook group. Then, she spent time with family and friends gathering their opinions of various options to "alleviate her family's financial desperation." Finding Dynamos Video's educational opportunities was a promising option, but we also see Chantel taking the initiative to get more data on the classes and the potential outcomes for her family. Though stating her research was lacking, this is likely hindsight after a number of successful years being the CEO of LGM. Chantel's experience and "process" serves as a lesson: when making a significant decision, a network's perspective on your internal deliberations is valuable. They can offer objectivity, new ideas and ways of thinking—as we'll see in other Cases. Again, Chantel teaches us to use our network when making big decisions.

Decision Model

Before our discussion concerning the decision model used in this Case, we remind the reader again that Chantel "…process(es) things through conversation." To be clear, this is not a decision model, it is (among many things) more of a technique or style. For example, gathering data (experiences, prior results, opinions, suggestions, raw data, etc.) can occur in many ways: alone, online, community conversations, libraries, speaking with experts or trusted sources, etc. Chantel, then, is what some would call a "verbal processor." This (broadly speaking) is a *technique* she *employs* as a part of her decision-making process—not necessarily a stand-alone decision model.

With the caveat above firmly in mind, Chantel is speaking with many people regarding these two decisions (i.e.: launching LGM and classes with Dynamos Video).

> "I process things through conversation," Chantel says. As a result, she spent lots of time in conversation with her husband, first, then with friends, family, anyone immediately around her, talking about what to do…. They helped her think about her few options, along with best and worst case scenarios for each.

The quote above is helpful as it not only confirms her decision-making technique/style, but it also provides a significant clue as to which decision models she is using in this Case. What we see in the last sentence is Chantel gathering data: options, pros/cons and scenarios. Note that she is *not* searching for similar answers, recommendations or opinions. This suggests we eliminate the Domain group models since she is not *explicitly* trying to recognize patterns in this data.[4]

Decision 1: The LGM Launch

From the Case narrative we understand Chantel's financial pressure to launch LGM, and her indecision about what to do after its first year. Launching LGM was time-critical and Chantel was speaking with many people about the Dynamos Video decision; both involved time. This suggests Chantel is using models from the Instinctive model group for both decisions—both explicitly and implicitly.

With the decision-making group identified, we simply have to identify how Chantel made her decision to start LGM. From what we learn in the Case narrative and knowing her decision-making style, it is clear that she's gathering data with both decisions. Beginning with the LGM launch decision, let's examine the following:

> Just one day before the baby was born, their daycare plan fell through... They still needed some income to be coming from Chantel, however... "That's why we started the business," said Chantel. "The baby was born in May, 2018 and the business was born in June, one month later. We looked at each other when our childcare fell through and I said 'What can I do?' I knew how to make good videos. I'd taken arts entrepreneurship courses. So I figured I'll just wing it and see if it works."

As mentioned in the Factor's section above, launching LGM was a financial decision. The inset immediately above is proof. Since there was only one month between both "births," time is a factor. With a quick decision required after they received news of their daycare falling through and the financial pressure of a new baby, Chantel had almost no choice but to launch LGM. This suggests she was using the Heuristic model, given her time constraints. After observing the situation (Step 1), Chantel ignored all extraneous data as she focused on the singular issue of no available daycare (Step 2—Identify obvious, critical trigger data and ignore extraneous data). The simplest solution (Step 3—Rely on simple, proven or learned solutions to make a decision.) was launching LGM (Step 4—Execute decision).

Decision 2: Dynamos Video

Concerning the Dynamos Video decision, the quote immediately above helps tremendously. If we examine the Analytical model, Step 1 (Gather ALL information or relevant data) is clear given the number of people from whom she sought guidance. It appears that Chantel *understood* the data from these individuals (Step 2—Verify that you understand the data) and understood the *impact* of the data as well (Step 3—Verify the impact of the data), which we see here: "They helped her think about her few options, along with best case and worst case scenarios for each." Since Chantel appears quite focused on this decision, Step 4 (Eliminate data irrelevant to the issue) is not an issue. It appears that she executed Step 5 (Objectively decide on the course of action based on the data at hand), except when we read:

> Looking back now, Chantel understands that she did not really explore other options. Her process then was simple: this opportunity presented itself, she got positive feedback about it from her Facebook group, she talked to family and friends about the pros and cons, and could it produce the results she needed? Chantel decided it was worth the risk and enrolled. Her main criteria was that it needed to give her a way to generate more income. After six weeks of taking the course, the promise was that she'd be getting better-paying projects.

Here, we see that she was not objective since other options may have been available. Additionally, she still needed to bring in more money, which is the desired outcome from the decision. Interestingly, this criteria identification is Step 2 of the Rational Model (Identify the decision criteria). However, Chantel didn't execute Step 4 (Develop multiple options) of the model since Dynamos Video was the only option she examined. So…which model did she use?

Let's reconsider Step 1 of the Analytical model and ask two simple questions: is data an "option?" Or, are options separate and each option has its own data set? The Analytical Model is *implying* the latter and the Rational model is explicit in the latter. Therefore, we could say that each option has its own data set, suggesting that Chantel *did* gather information about a *single* option. Now, did she objectively decide based on this information about a single option? Yes. Was she objective about options? No. What we have then, is a decision based on the Analytical model, which has an aspect of the Rational model (Step 2). Because Chantel did not seek out other options, we cannot say that she used the Rational model.

Note, however, that with her Dynamos Video decision, she clearly has time, which suggests that (as mentioned above) the Creative model from the Instinctive group is in play, specifically, Step 3 (Incubation—Set the problem aside and do not think about it for a while). While it is true this specific decision took some effort, what we do not see in the narrative is Chantel "setting the problem aside" and instead, read that she is actively gathering data for roughly a year. It is unreasonable to think that she either spent a year devoting her time to gathering data or "setting the problem aside" exclusively; she could not do both. Therefore, we could make the case that given the time required, Chantel employed a number of models to create a hybrid: primarily Analytical with *aspects* of the Rational and Creative models.

Chantel's use of multiple decision-making models is common, especially with new arts entrepreneurs. When one is new to any situation (especially with consequences concerning family economics) making decisions is more of a learning experience. Of course, we would like to think our prior experience creates easier decision making and this is true to some extent. However, in new roles, decision making is typically a learning process where early decisions are based more on prior experience and preparation rather than precise modeling. Therefore, young or "new to the game" decision makers tend to use aspects from other models in making decisions.

Hybrid model decision making *can be* a sign of inexperience. Yet on the other hand, there are many successful decision makers who use hybrid models quite successfully throughout their career. This suggests one should not necessarily strive to be model-specific when making decisions. Rather, that models are helpful in leveraging one's decision-making technique/style and should serve to be both suggestive and models in the truest sense. In short, one should be aware that models exist and borrowing aspects from other models like Chantel has done is not necessarily good or bad, though it *could* show some inexperience as an entrepreneurial decision maker. Yet like many things, this depends on factors unique to the decision maker, the context of the decision and the decision itself.

Ecology Discussion

The video ecology below broadly describes the environment in which Chantel finds herself. She is in a common position where her new arts startup sees some initial success yet can generate more income. While

Chantel has a solid understanding of the Video Ecology and LGM's place in that system (given her video production experience, arts entrepreneurship education and post-college work experience), she also needs LGM to achieve its potential for both clients and her family (Figure 5.1).

In order to achieve her company's full potential, Chantel embraces a more holistic approach. Obviously, her decision to pursue the Dynamos Video opportunity lies outside the Ecology, yet her decision is common among entrepreneurs of all kinds: get more education. She is also applying her arts entrepreneurship education in this decision as she knows that (broadly speaking) arts education creates—and can sustain—arts professionals. The targeted arts business education Dynamos Video provides certainly helped LGM but will also help Chantel become a better and more effective decision maker, both as an artist and a business leader. This, however, requires her to move outside of the Video Ecology.

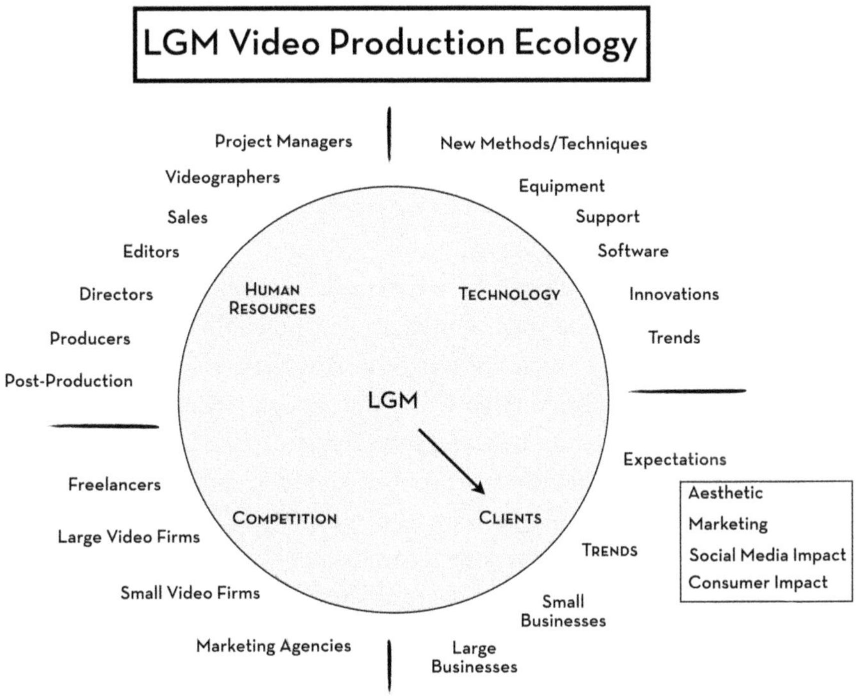

Figure 5.1 LGM Video Production Ecology.

Chantel's decision to engage another ecology is typical. When a CEO decides to move out of their ecological system for one reason or another, it is common to leverage familiar ecologies. In this Case, Chantel moves to the Arts Education ecology with the hopes of bringing new information back to the business so it can reach its potential. The Arts Education Ecology is one of the advanced ecologies in *The New Arts Entrepreneur* and appears as one ecology in *The Creative Ecological System*.[5] With Chantel being a recent college graduate, it is not surprising she would engage this familiar ecology (i.e.: leverage) to help her reach her business goals.

In Figure 5.2, *The Creative Ecological System* appears above the Video Ecology. Between the two is LGM's ecology (not articulated) and Chantel. This illustrates not only Chantel's role in this decision, but also the topography she is negotiating. In this Case, Chantel is acting as an intermediary between the *System* and LGM (who participates in the Video Ecology). This figure illustrates not only the interconnectedness of *The Creative Ecological System*, but also Chantel's role.

Obviously, moving between different ecologies may not be a conscious effort while making or executing a business decision. Certainly, when one needs to gain information or react to a business need, one simply acts. However, by knowing that other ecological systems exist, it at least provides the knowledge that these grouped landscapes exist, even if one is not creating a hybrid ecology.[6]

Yet if we examine Chantel's opportunities embedded within the *System*, she clearly has options. For example, she could attempt to solve the problem by simply engaging with the Aesthetic Ecology. (In other words, developing an innovative video framework better suited for her present small client market needs). However, she gained a new aesthetic framework with the video postcards when she took the Dynamos Video course. Interestingly, since she wanted to position LGM as a video service to provide marketing strategy and business consultation services (using video as a part of the strategy), she was actually developing a new experience for her clients. While she may have been able to create this by engaging with the Experiential Ecology, the amount of research required to support her vision would have taken far longer than simply taking the Dynamos Video course. LGM was already participating in

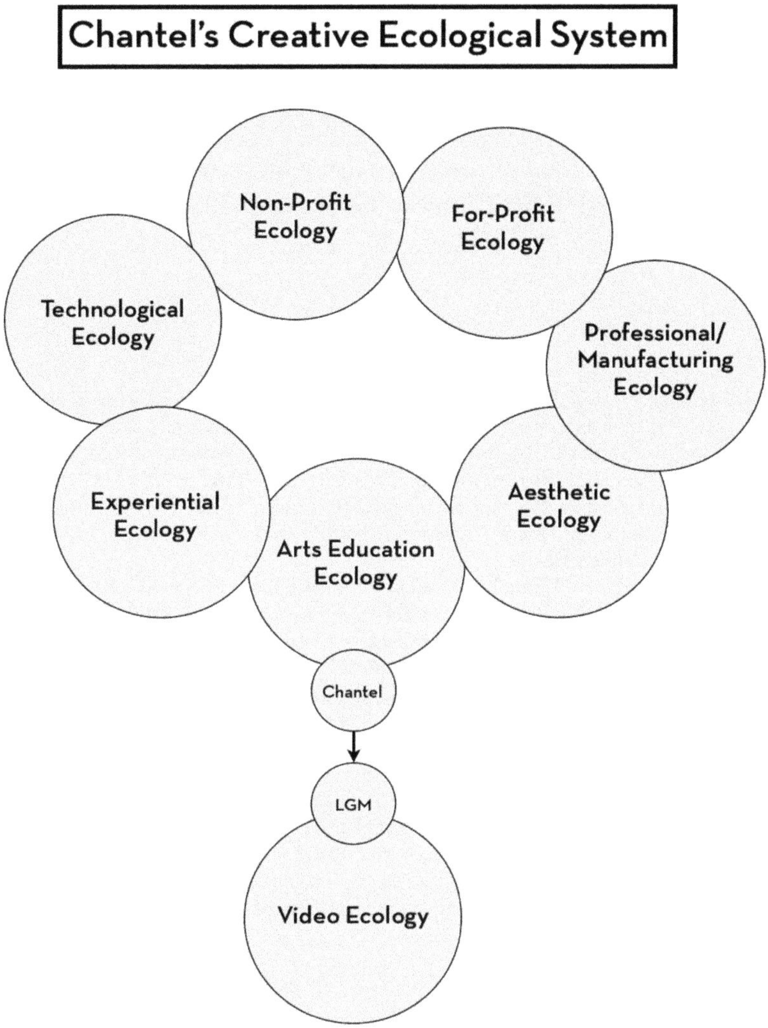

Figure 5.2 Chantel's Creative Ecological System.

the Technology Ecology by virtue of its aesthetic medium and neither the Professional/Manufacturing Ecology or Non-Profit were engaged for this venture.

Dynamos Video was a risky decision financially, but also paid off financially since Chantel was able to increase her revenues by almost 400% the next year. While she still needed to contribute more to her household, this was clearly movement in the desired direction. Ecologically speaking, Chantel's decision to engage the Arts Education ecology also saved a significant amount of time as Dynamos Video engaged with the Aesthetic and Experiential Ecologies in their courses. Clearly, this was a good decision to solve a financial issue in the immediate term. The remaining Cases in the Set will tell us if this was a good long-term decision.

Notes

1 Scholarship concerned itself for some time about entrepreneurial "traits." For a survey of recent examples, see Sari Pekkala Kerr, William R. Kerr and Tina Xu, "Personality Traits of Entrepreneurs: A Review of Recent Literature," *Foundations and Trends in Entrepreneurship* 14, no. 3 (2018): 279–356.

2 Abha Bhattarai, Dan Keating and Stephanie Hays, "What does it Cost to Raise a Child?" Available at: https://www.washingtonpost.com/business/interactive/2022/cost-raising-child-calculator.

3 U.S. Department of Labor Blog, "New Childcare Data Shows Prices are Untenable for Families." Available at: https://blog.dol.gov/2023/01/24/new-childcare-data-shows-prices-are-untenable-for-families.

4 If Chantel was "looking for answers" from this group, it is plausible that she could be looking for patterns in responses. The Case narrative, however, is clear she is looking for "data."

5 Gary D. Beckman, *The New Arts Entrepreneur: Navigating the Arts Ecologies*, (London: Routledge, 2022).

6 The purpose of *The Creative Ecological System* is to create a hybrid ecology. Instead of monitoring the broader Steady State Model for an arts venture, one can better articulate an arts business' ecological environment by creating a more systems-based ecological model using *The Creative Ecological System*. See Gary D. Beckman, *The New Arts Entrepreneur: Navigating the Arts Ecologies* for a description of how to create hybrid ecologies.

Bibliography

Beckman, Gary D. *The New Arts Entrepreneur: Navigating the Arts Ecologies*. London: Routledge, 2022.

Bhattarai, Abha, Dan Keating and Stephanie Hays. "What does it Cost to Raise a Child?" *The Washington Post*, October 13, 2022. Available at: https://www.washingtonpost.com/business/interactive/2022/cost-raising-child-calculator.

Kerr, Sari Pekkala, William R. Kerr and Tina Xu. "Personality Traits of Entrepreneurs: A Review of Recent Literature." *Foundations and Trends in Entrepreneurship* 14, no. 3 (2018): 279–356.

U.S. Department of Labor Blog. "New Childcare Data Shows Prices are Untenable for Families." Available at: https://blog.dol.gov/2023/01/24/new-childcare-data-shows-prices-are-untenable-for-families.

6

Case 1B: Fall on your Sword or Blame the Client?

When Chantel Aspesi launched her video business in 2018, she knew she could make good videos. She admits she didn't know much about running a video business, though, and just figured she'd "wing it and figure it out." A year later, she evolved the business by taking a course in how to become a video agency, not just a freelancer. The result was growth, from $5,344 of revenue in her first year to $25,857 in the year she took that course. Now it was year three, 2020, and she was on her way to record revenue of $36,000 for the year.

Taking specialized courses wasn't the only way Chantel was learning to grow her business, though it was one that worked. She also was learning by asking colleagues in her Facebook group of videographers. Fellow CEOs with business experience often had good advice for those younger in the field. Of course, Chantel was also learning from every client and every new project she tackled. The projects were getting bigger, stretching Chantel and her team, showing them where their boundaries were as a business.

Now the biggest project of her young business was falling apart and Chantel knew plenty of reasons why. What she didn't know was what to do about the situation. A client was making the project nearly impossible

 DOI: 10.4324/9781003414483-8

to finish, let alone by the deadline. But Chantel's own team was causing problems, too. Should she admit failure, make sure the client knows everything the client did to cause that failure, and return the client's money? Or should Chantel admit her own role in the failure, reset and complete the job? Admitting failure and returning the client's money was not a lesson Chantel could afford to learn. If she chose to invest in doing the job right, her profit would be spent on additional labor costs. Either way, Chantel's finances would take a significant hit.

Biggest Job Ever

In the first two years of Lily and Gems Media (LGM), Chantel created several videos for this client, a business coach in New York City. "She's awesome. So easy to work with, great on camera." They established a good working rapport, resulting in professional videos that satisfied the client. When the client decided to pivot her own business model from one-on-one coaching to offering a series of video-based courses for executives, she naturally came to Chantel to see what she could do to create the 40 videos she would need for the first run of her new courses.

This was the largest project yet for Chantel's young business. She was confident that she and her team could manage the project and be proud of the results. The contract stated the client would shoot all the footage themselves, because of the pandemic's restrictions on travel and in-person...anything. Chantel's team would then edit the footage, "add some captions, make it look just gorgeous." Even without shooting the 40 videos, it was a huge project.

Chantel had been building a stable of freelancers on whom she could rely. For this project, she would need three video editors. Happily, she knew three who had done solid work for her on past projects. It would feel good to give each of them part of this project to employ them over the coming months. This was mid-2020 and the pandemic had made work scarce for many in the video production field—at least in rural Virginia where Chantel lived and located her business. She needed projects like this to keep her freelance team busy and committed to her, as her business—hopefully—continued to grow.

Problems, so many Problems

The situation began with the client. A first batch of videos were not as expected:

> Completely out of focus, like really bad. So, we're like, can we fix this? Or do we have to ask her to reshoot it? We really didn't want to ask the client to reshoot it, so we fixed it. But that took so much more time.

Problem number two was a lack of clear communication at the beginning of the project, and no written guidelines. "It was like we were two people who are too similar. So, there were some missed signals. We thought we'd been communicating clearly, but not so much." Then the client began missing agreed-upon deadlines. All these issues were slowing down the project and making it increasingly more difficult.

A third challenge came from Chantel's team. Midway through the project, two of Chantel's three editors could not continue. One had a major family crisis, and the other suffered a fall and broke her arm. Chantel and the remaining editor looked at each other one day and said, "Wow, we are not going to make the due date. There's no way."

Chantel did not have other editors she could trust to simply step into this project mid-stream. Finding new editors, then getting them up to speed on the particulars of this project, would slow things more. Chantel could do some of the editing herself, but she needed to be selling and closing deals, so there'd be work for all after this big project was done. She felt she was the only one who could do that sales work. Could the one remaining editor put in more hours? How much would that cost? Added costs for any solution would kill the profit margin on the project.

This was all very upsetting to Chantel. A promising project was falling apart. Yes, part of it was a result of real disasters in the lives of two of her three team members. Chantel considered these two her friends, not just freelance helpers she could call at will. That made her especially upset, as she wanted to be angry at them, but knew it wasn't really their fault.

What upset her even more was that the client contributed to this mess and yet was likely thinking everything was fine. As far as she knew, the project should be arriving on her desk soon. The client had no idea she had made this nearly impossible, even before the two editors quit. It was like the client set up Chantel to fail, and she wanted to tell the client exactly how she felt: "Here, you can keep your money. This is not worth it."

Reflection Questions

1. If you were Chantel, what would you do?
2. What process would you use to determine what to do in this situation?
3. Can you think of any other options, besides the two Chantel is considering?
4. What can Chantel do to avoid this dilemma on future projects?

Looking for Solutions

Chantel took a deep breath and paused before she did anything. Then, she reached out to her colleague group on Facebook, who she came to rely on for questions and problem-solving. They were all trying to succeed in the video production business and many had several more years of experience. Her Facebook colleagues were supportive and had a mix of opinions about Chantel's situation. There was much to think about, but no clear consensus on a decision.

Next she talked with her dad about this problem. He didn't know much about the video production business, but he'd given her sound advice in the past on general business matters. His advice this time was that she should own her part in the problem, not just blame the client. "Take responsibility," he told her.

Chantel met with her one remaining editor to get her opinion. Could the project be completed on time, somehow, maybe by the remaining editor and Chantel putting in some superhuman effort and hours? If she didn't have her last editor onboard, there was no way *that* option had any chance of succeeding. So, better ask. The remaining editor thought the two of them could finish the project nearly on time. However, the extra hours would cost Chantel much more than she'd originally budgeted.

Father Knows Best

Once she had a plan to complete the work, Chantel decided to take responsibility for the problem. Her father's advice was key—own your part in the problem. Chantel knew he was right. It was how she was raised and was advice he gave many times.

Chantel wanted to finish the project and do a great job for the client, even if it meant she made nothing on the project. Better to keep a good client than lose one over a single contract. As soon as she decided on this course of action, Chantel called the client. She was honest and said there was no way LGM could meet the deadline but said this in a way that didn't blame the client for the entirety of the project's delay. "The project is behind schedule and here's why." The "why" included the two editors leaving, but Chantel also gently but directly shared the difficulties the client had caused the project.

"I'm not mad, I'm disappointed," was the client's response. This was hard for Chantel to hear. This person trusted her, and she was letting her down.

Chantel says, "I fell on my sword. I told her 'This is on me. We did not plan properly. We were not prepared for this. And now we're going to make it right.'" She explained her plan moving forward: Chantel and the other editor were going to put in the time to get the video done by a slightly delayed deadline. The client agreed this was realistic.

Surprisingly, the client expressed how much she appreciated Chantel's candor and that the conversation made her trust Chantel all the more. "When everything's going great, everyone feels great. When things are going bad, it tells the client if this person is trustworthy," Chantel explains.

"We worked our asses off and we got it done," Chantel says now. She invested her own time and it was her money that paid for the freelance editor. "Honestly, I probably lost money on that project," Chantel says. She made the new deadline and kept the client. The trust Chantel earned resulted in many more projects with the client in the years to come, including putting Lily and Gems Media on retainer for a number of years.

Discussion: Case 1B — Sword or Blame?

Summary

Case 1B describes not only the interactions and choices an arts entrepreneur may encounter, but also the first steps in venture sustainability. Chantel had a number of choices to consider in the situation. She could put the blame squarely on the client's video production skills or have LGM shoot the raw footage. Additionally, she could simply edit the footage as it was given to her, submit the final product to the client without any explanation and demand payment. Yet with the number of options at hand, Chantel chose a course of action that integrated her ethics (both personal and business) into the decision-making process.

Perhaps the most important aspect of the Case is how Chantel is making this decision. The three critical issues Chantel is focused on (out of focus raw footage from the client, a lack of communication and availability issues with project editors) are more extrinsic and discussed in the next subsection. However, if we look at the more intrinsic aspects, we might see this decision in a different light.

As established in Case 1A, part of Chantel's decision-making technique is to speak with trusted colleagues, friends, family and other trusted individuals. We see this again in the narrative:

> Chantel took a deep breath and paused before she did anything. Then, she reached out to her colleague group on Facebook, who she had come to rely on for questions and problem-solving. They were all trying to succeed in the video production business and many had several more years of experience.

This is valuable information since it helps us understand that Chantel not only has a decision-making *technique* established, but she continues to rely on this technique. At this point, the result of this continuity helps us see Chantel as a reliable decision maker in *how* she makes her decisions. We see this again when she uses a suggestion offered by a family member:

> Next she talked with her dad about this problem. He didn't know much about the video production business, but he'd given her

> sound advice in the past on general business matters. His advice this time was that she should own her part in the problem, not just blame the client. "Take responsibility," he told her. …Once she had a plan to complete the work, Chantel decided to take responsibility for the problem. Her father's advice was key—own your part in the problem. Chantel knew he was right. It was how she was raised, and was advice he gave many times.

The two paragraphs above describe an ethical basis Chantel is using to *guide* her decisionmaking. Specifically, an entrepreneur should take responsibility for their product—despite the circumstances—in order to preserve the business/client relationship. Implicitly, this also suggests that taking responsibility in this context is an honorable and dignified act. Yes, this is a philosophical point, but an important one. Ultimately, an entrepreneur is expected to act ethically. However, one also has a responsibility to the A(a)rt product as well. Chantel knew from the start that the client's video was not shot well, which put the quality of her product at risk; it was this first issue causing Chantel's concern about the project.

As the Case shows, Chantel not only has an established decision-making technique (or style), but her ethics also play a role in *how* she weighs her decisions. Certainly Chantel—like all of us—may have a favorite decision-making model, but models are just models; they evolve over time through varied means and are only one part of a decision. For Chantel, continuity of process and personal ethics also played a role.

Factors Forcing the Decision

The subsection above discussed the more intrinsic aspects of the Case. What follows is an examination of the extrinsic features of Chantel's decision. From the narrative, we see her struggling with three factors forcing this decision: 1) poor quality raw footage from the client, 2) a lack of communication with the client and 3) two of the three project editors leaving the project.

Let's organize these factors by categories. Table 6.1 is one way to arrange the issues.

If we work with these categories, Chantel's decision factors are both art and business-based. Note the art category initiated the decision since

Table 6.1 Extrinsic Features of Chantel's Decision

A(a)rt	Out-of-focus Raw Footage
Business	Insufficient Communication w/ Client
Business (Human Resources)	Project Editors Leaving

the quality of the client-supplied footage impacted not only the art product but created an additional time component Chantel didn't anticipate. The time required to fix the client's footage wasn't just time, of course, she had to pay the other editor for his extra time on the project and *not* pay herself for any of her additional time. Obviously, this one artistic factor not only effected the final project's quality, it negatively impacted the amount of time required to complete the project and LGM's profit.

As many experienced entrepreneurs and business owners will attest, communication is crucial when working with clients and negotiating contracts. In this Case, Chantel admitted her lack of communication with the client. While one could fault her for not immediately addressing the raw video's quality issues, we should remember that Chantel clearly valued her relationship with the client and likely had little experience in similar situations. As someone with barely a year under her belt as an arts entrepreneur in a rural area, unique and varied business experiences were likely not as prevalent as in other areas. Here, we have a situation seldom discussed in this context: an arts entrepreneur (like anyone else) needs decision-making experience to sustain their venture. Since LGM has cleared the startup phase, we could consider this communication aspect more of a sustainability factor that forces the decision.

Chantel's last factor is clearly a human resources issue and perhaps the easiest to understand. Again, however, this relates to time. Without her team of three editors, Chantel couldn't deliver the project on time. While this may seem to be the easiest factor to address (i.e.: just hire replacements) there is an A(a)rt component to this suggestion. Chantel is not only clear that LGM has a mission, she is also clear that the product must be high quality. For this to occur, she needs to see an editor's portfolio, evaluate it and be confident that she can create a good working relationship with this editor (i.e.: building trust). This takes time; in some cases, a lot of time. Chantel didn't have time to establish this relationship with a new editor, given her looming project deadline.

We should also note that with two editors leaving, she had their pay to help buttress any extra costs. Indeed, this is true, but she was also in a position where she needed to pay the one remaining editor for their extra time covering the work of the two who left.

What we have according to the categories in Table 6.1, is a group of mixed factors forcing this decision (arts and business). Obviously, with this set of factors, any solution is going to be either complex or costly. Chantel chose to forego the complexity of another possible solution and instead, risked losing money on the project to retain both the customer and her ethics.

Decision Model

When it comes to the decision-making model in this Case, we see an evolution in Chantel's decision-making process. In the previous Case, she was a new arts entrepreneur and like all new arts entrepreneurs, had little experience with the kinds of decisions she would confront. So, Chantel did what many new arts entrepreneurs do: make the best decision possible. This Case, however, is slightly different since LGM was in its sustainability phase.

Before we continue this section, let's briefly address what one *should* expect in a decision-maker's evolution. For a company in the early stages of its sustainability phase, we should expect a CEO to have experience in making basic, day-to-day decisions and some experience with more unique and perhaps more difficult decisions concerning a variety of aesthetic and business issues. Further, we should also expect that when more difficult decisions arise, this experience would be used to inform the decision. What we have then, is an *expectation* of an evolutionary component in a CEO's decision-making process.

Moving on, the Case narrative is clear that Chantel gathers data for her decision using her network—similar to her process in the previous Case. (As a reminder: in the last Case, she seemed to favor the Analytical model, but used a hybrid model). To work through this decision, Chantel 1) engages her FaceBook network, 2) speaks with a family member and 3) discusses the situation with her remaining editor. There are reasons for her speaking with these three sources.

Chantel's relationship with her FaceBook group was established in the previous Case. Her reliance on their input was crucial and we see that she continues to leverage this aspect of her network. Additionally, we see the importance of her father's input about the decision. Lastly, Chantel speaks with the remaining editor to receive confirmation on her thinking and on her plan to move forward with the client.

Since Chantel "process(es) things through conversation," leveraging these first two network sources should not come as a surprise. This is both a critical data point in her decision-making evolution and proof of a maturing decision maker and leader. Specifically, Chantel is meeting the *expectations* one should have about a CEO guiding an arts business through the sustainability phase. What further supports this point is that she engaged with her remaining editor to verify her thinking; this is indicative of the trust she had in the editor's artistic skills. However, it also indicates the establishment of a strong working relationship with this individual—who Chantel was comfortable enough with to be honest about the situation. This is more proof of Chantel's increasing maturity as a CEO who is clearly embracing the evolutionary process of becoming a skilled decision maker.

In this Case, Chantel is showing a clear preference for the Analytical model. Additionally, she has refined her decision-making process with this model when compared to the previous Case. Her leveraging of Step 1 (Gather ALL information or relevant data) improved as she focused her data gathering on established, trusted sources (Facebook and family). Yes, the sources were few, but she had previous experience with them and trusted both. Step 2 (Verify that you understand the data) appears clear given her lack of confusion about the situation. (Specifically, Chantel understands the issue and does not appear to struggle with her network's guidance.) Where she excels is her engagement with Step 3 (Verify the impact of the data). Chantel is crystal clear about the impact of not only the issue at hand, but also the data she is receiving from her network and the implications of this data. She appears open to different solutions as well and does not seem to favor one scenario over the other. Her verification strategy is not mentioned specifically in the narrative, though given the Case as a whole and the manner in which she is speaking about it, her understanding about the impact of the data she is receiving appears solid.

We do not see Step 4 (Eliminate data irrelevant to the issue) as the narrative is not reporting specific solutions from the network, nor

Chantel needing to sort through a series of these solutions. Lastly, Step 5 (Objectively decide on the course of action based on the data at hand) is evident as she engages not only her network, but her ethical principles in making her final decision.

One of the most valuable aspects about this Case is how experience with prior decision making creates *continuity* in decision making. While some may describe this as "predictability," in the early stages of a business' sustainability phase, establishing continuity in the decision-making process or comfort with trusted decision-making models is vital. Without establishing either, an arts entrepreneur will lose the benefits of this continuity and risk putting the venture in jeopardy. Perhaps the best way to envision this is to think of a CEO not solely as a decision maker, but as a *leader*. Even in a sole proprietorship, an individual is a leader of an organization. As a leader, one will make decisions frequently and the quicker one develops and becomes comfortable with making decisions, the more time is available for product development. (i.e.: making A(a)rt products). Therefore, arts entrepreneurs are not simply CEOs of arts businesses, they are leaders whose responsibility is not only to sustain a venture through continuity in decision making, but also to sustain the *artistic integrity* of the business.

Ecology Discussion

Chantel is experiencing issues with two aspects of the Video Ecology: clients and human resources. With the latter, she has two freelance editors (from a team of three) who withdraw and with the former, a small business client providing less-than-adequate raw footage, which will negatively affect LGM's Consumer Impact Expectations element. Ecologically speaking, this is an obvious identification, though the potential ramifications of a bad decision on Chantel's part could echo throughout LGM.

The primary concern about this decision—ecologically speaking—lies in the Client quarter of the Video Ecology. Specifically, if Chantel inadvertently loses the client because of this miscommunication, there is a possibility the client will make the situation known publicly. If this occurs, LGM would likely suffer from negative press, which *could* impact both prospective clients and any marketing plan Chantel had in progress. Further, it could also impact future Small Business customers, particularly if any negative press mentions that a dissatisfied customer was a small business. Given LGM's rural location and likely small potential client base, making a haphazard decision could prove detrimental to much of LGM's future sales efforts.

Secondarily, the Human Resources side of the issue is more than simply two people needing to leave the editing team. Rather, having this critical resource reduced by two-thirds eliminated any chance of the project meeting its deadline. This resulted in Chantel having to do some editing herself, which took away time she would typically spend on sales. Ergo, human resource issues beget human resource issues.

While Chantel's primary focus appears to be keeping the client while still being in the position to complete the project, she is actually using the Video Ecology as it was intended. Obviously, she didn't need an ecology to understand the issue at hand, nor does there appear to be any way she could predict what transpired via the Ecology. Chantel is acting like a responsible CEO of a small arts business and trying to retain a client; one doesn't need to know an ecology to act in this manner. However, understanding an ecological system also demands that one act when the ecology experiences stress. The potential negative consequences of a bad decision on Chantel's part would stress LGM's ecology. By this, we mean that LGM is a part of the Video Ecology and LGM has its own ecology as well. If there were negative social media comments about LGM initiated by the client, *LGM's ecology* would be stressed and potentially at risk. The larger Video Ecology could survive this by her competition picking up the project and by default, the client.

This Case describes keeping a client and the responsibility to "tend their own yard." Specifically, by tending to LGM's ecology, Chantel is keeping it healthy so it operates as she intends. Otherwise, a larger system (the Competitors in the Video Ecology) will subsume the remains of LGM's ecology: human resources, clients, etc.

Bibliography

Beckman, Gary D. *The New Arts Entrepreneur: Navigating the Arts Ecologies*. London: Routledge, 2022.

7

CASE 1C: WIND DOWN OR RAMP UP?

In 2022, her fifth year running Lily and Gems Media (LGM), Chantel Aspesi had her most profitable year ever, generating gross revenue of $57,855. She had just five clients that year, which was fewer than the year before, when she grossed $61,227. However, her business was more profitable than ever, due to a focus on containing costs and doing more projects with each remaining client. Her projects included a trip to Italy to shoot a batch of videos for a new and fun client in the luxury travel business. Not only was she paid for her video work on that trip, but she stayed in luxurious accommodations alongside the regular paying guests and all her trip expenses were paid. This project fulfilled one of Chantel's long-held goals: to travel the world. It was the kind of dream trip that usually happens when you're right out of college, as a graduation gift from generous parents and family. (Or you wait till you're retired). It's not usually a trip you do ten years out of college, with two young children at home.

As soon as she returned home from Italy in October 2022, after weeks on the road, Chantel started feeling something was physically wrong. She felt great in Italy, but when she got home, symptoms began. Chantel was sometimes unable to stand and walk from a reclined position without becoming dizzy. She had what she described as brain fog. Additionally, she was anxious and her heart was racing despite feeling fine some days. Other days she couldn't focus on anything and was

 DOI: 10.4324/9781003414483-9

completely debilitated. On the Friday of her first week back, Chantel went to her family doctor to see if he could figure out what was wrong. After some tests, he determined she had a version of long-COVID, called Postural Orthostatic Tachycardia Syndrome, or POTS for short. He told her this ailment was likely affected by stress, such as the traveling from which she'd just returned, or maybe the stress that comes from running her own small business. The doctor gave Chantel a prescription he hoped would help quiet the symptoms. When she took it, she felt no better, possibly worse.

Until this health shock, Chantel was thinking about taking LGM to the next level. The individual who referred Lily and Gems Media for the Italy project, Reggie Hampton, told Chantel about a video product LGM could offer that could greatly increase her revenues. LGM would create a video business card for a client, build them a landing page and put the video on that page. Then, LGM would create quarterly video ads. Reggie would teach Chantel how to place those ads on the most successful platforms and use the best keywords for her brand (LGM). All of this would drive potential clients to her client's website. The client would give Chantel a budget for running video ads and she would make them happen.

All Chantel had to do was take another course, which Reggie's company would provide, costing her $7,800. It would change LGM's business model to digital advertisement creation and management. Though she still had a strong dislike of digital ads, she felt she could justify creating and managing the advertisements, considering how positive they could be for her clients. Chantel told herself she had a unique talent for eliciting and telling a business' story via video. Using that talent in this way could produce powerful outcomes for her clients.

Reggie, who knew her current business and capabilities well, projected she could increase her revenue from $50–60,000 per year to more like $200–300,000 per year, in 12 months. With this larger revenue stream, she'd finally have enough money to do what she wanted in other areas of her business and supply the net income her family needed. Chantel found this all very exciting. She was eager to talk with her team and Facebook colleagues to think it all through as soon as she got home.

But now what happens if she can't get out of bed on any given day? What if there's a meeting scheduled with a potential or a current client on one of her bad days? Do those opportunities wait for her good days? Or do they silently disappear? Chantel knew she was not the only videography company, but also knew she was the only person at Lily and Gems Media who could find clients, negotiate pricing and close deals.

Unfortunately, another complexity arose. After a few months of thinking about and trying to adjust to her new health issues, Chantel's largest client called and told Chantel her business was pivoting its marketing strategy; they no longer needed a YouTube channel. This meant Lily and Gems Media—who created the business's videos and maintained the channel—would no longer receive that content generation revenue. Combine this news with the potential change to an ads-based business model and Chantel's health issues…well, this felt like a turning point.

There were so many options crashing about in Chantel's head. Perhaps she needed to put LGM on hiatus until she could get her health issues in order. However, she still needed to produce income to help pay the mortgage and keep food on the table at home. Maybe she could find some kind of day job to generate a paycheck, but without the stress of running her own business. Then there were her as-yet-unresolved health challenges.

One other option Chantel had ready was to produce a video documentary series. She had one in pre-production, about a set of social-impact founders. It was exciting for Chantel to interview inspiring leaders who created their own dynamic organizations.

With sales season coming up, Chantel found herself trying to organize the many options, in overlapping layers and possible combinations:

- Stop the business for a short time to focus on health issues?
- Take a part-time job to earn some money?
- Change her current business model from making videos for clients, into creating video documentaries about social impact, for broadcasting on various platforms?
- Or ramp up the business as a lucrative ad-serving agency?

Her trip to Italy gave her a taste of traveling the world. She wanted more of that, but how could this be happening to her so soon after she got back from that dream? It was painful to consider passing up any new opportunity for increased revenue, telling people's stories and, potentially, more world travel.

Prioritizing Physical Health

There were several criteria Chantel and her husband set out for thinking about this decision. At the top of the list was to prioritize her health. Balancing her family's finances was a close second. With these two priorities firmly atop the list, Chantel had to stop and think about whether there were any other priorities to consider in making this decision. A third issue came to her eventually—her mental health. She needed to be around people on a regular basis. In fourth place—after more thought—was the vision she'd written for Lily and Gems Media: changing the trajectory of people's lives, restoring humanity by capturing people as they are and in their own words. "Grandiose, right?" she said to herself. However, it reflected an idealism she valued.

Getting her health back was unpredictable. COVID was a new disease and so much was still unknown. Since the first waves of the disease washed over the population and then vaccines arrived to reduce the number of hospitalized patients, the whole world was studying a new affliction: long COVID. POTS was one of its related ailments. At that point, the world didn't know how to treat long COVID. So, there was no predicting how long it might take for Chantel to get her health back. This could be a lifelong issue.

Her mental health was a fairly concrete issue for Chantel. She needed to be with people. While running her business from home, she noticed how isolating it was to work remotely and only occasionally see people in-person. This was especially true during the first two years of the pandemic, until vaccines became available and people started gathering again in person. She considered joining a co-working space—if only to see people more regularly. Thinking about running an internet advertising business—with fewer and fewer meetings with live humans—was not appealing. She had to stop and seriously consider how this choice would affect her.

Chantel knew she still cared about changing people's lives through her work, whether that be video production or something else. But if she couldn't reliably get out of bed each day, she had to consider other options to provide income for her family.

Too Many Options?

Perhaps Chantel had too many options. "I've angsted (sic) over this decision hundreds of hours, more than any other business decision so far," she admitted. Let's dive deeper into each.

The first option she considered was to halt Lily and Gems Media entirely (for at least a while) and take a day job. She knew a day job would not pay $200,000 per year, like the business model change promised. But she was sure it would not entail the levels of stress she currently experienced while doing sales and everything else to run LGM. Less stress might address her top priority: her physical health. Receiving a steady paycheck could reduce stress as well. Of course, this addressed her second priority: helping to keep her family financially solvent. Working daily with others at an outside job would help her third priority: her mental health.

One *variation* on this option was to halt LGM and start doing freelance video work again. She could do this for other video agencies she already knew. Agencies would, essentially, hire her to do their projects, whenever she was available. There'd be no sales to worry about and no managing other people, which eliminates some stress. Additionally, it would be energizing to interact with others on video shoots.

Yet another variation was to continue LGM, but only do projects with current clients, with no sales work to generate new clients. Her largest client was ending their relationship with LGM, meaning a drop in revenue from current clients. Thus, pausing LGM in this way would still—financially—require finding some kind of low-stress part-time job. She did not have such a job lined up, but the nightly news said there were plenty of jobs available at that point. Looking online at job listings, Chantel saw plenty she was qualified to do, now that she had more experience. For instance, a local construction firm was looking for an account manager for their marketing department. "I've managed plenty of accounts now," she said.

The second option Chantel considered was to ramp up her business one of several ways. She could, for instance, take the $7,800 course to become an ad-serving agency, creating video ads for clients and managing where those ads got placed and how often. Another way to ramp up her business would be to turn it into a "production house," creating documentaries for broadcast. Could she manage either of these two options with her current health concerns? Becoming an ad-serving agency promised financial returns that satisfied her financial criteria. What about the production house option? How did the money work for that one? How did either of these look, in terms of her need for socialization?

Chantel got excited thinking about the ad-serving option. $200–300,000 per year was enticing. Building that size of business motivated her. After five years of running her own video business, growing it, experimenting with different products to bring in more clients and learning some important lessons, she felt ready for that kind of business challenge. Some of her *Facebook* group colleagues reached that level and she had heard them talk about the advantages as well as the disadvantages. Chantel wanted to prove she could do it, too.

One concern about the ad-serving option was getting from here-to-there. Chantel was told it would take about a year to take the course, implement it and change her business model. Once it was established and working, it meant stable income—not the feast or famine cycles she experienced now. She would also be able to delegate more of the work to others, so she could be doing less and reduce stress. Of course, shooting videos for clients' landing pages and quarterly ads would be back to what Chantel loved most, but setting it up and finding clients who would buy this, would take a full year. Could she put in the work now, to get to that easier and more lucrative place? If her health would let her do that work, could she afford to do it financially (i.e.: paying $7,800 upfront and waiting most of that year with little revenue until new customers for this business model surfaced)?

Another consideration—for any of the options—was where to live. Rural Virginia was isolating for Chantel and she had felt this way for a while. Her parents and other family were in Raleigh, North Carolina and it would be good to see them more often. Now that her health was an issue, the better medical care in Raleigh was frontmost in her mind. For whatever business she might be running, or whatever job she might wish to apply for, there were more and bigger businesses in Raleigh—and those businesses were also more entrepreneurial. Lastly, Chantel had a better network in Raleigh.

Her final concern: if Chantel wound down the business, what would happen to her team?

> If I don't bring in work, they're not getting paid, then they're struggling financially. There's a sense of responsibility for them. Some of them do freelance on their own. Some will probably look for other employment. Some of them already have their own businesses, as well.

Chantel talked to her Facebook and Video Dynamos colleagues. Then she took a trip to Raleigh to meet with her former professors and advisors. Nobody said, outright, "Do this option."

Looking on the bright side, almost any option she chose would mean learning something that could help her later. Take the ramping up options, for example. "Ad-serving and paid media are a huge gap in my understanding," she says. "Even if I don't like ads, I recognize they're important in the whole system of getting videos in front of eyeballs of people it should be in front of." She would learn things by getting an outside job, too. Working in someone else's business and getting paid by them could be a chance to learn on the job. Chantel could learn how to target B-corps and social impact businesses, which would fit her stated mission. "I feel strongly that video has a place within social impact marketing. There's been some use of it with brands like Patagonia, but I feel strongly it's an untapped market."

Those are positive signs. She has plenty of options. Now she just has to decide which way to go next.

Reflection Questions

1. Based on her priorities, what path do you think is best for Chantel now?
2. Should Chantel consider other options?
3. What are some ways that Chantel might "pilot" (try out on a limited basis) any options with which she is less familiar?

Discussion: Case 1C — Wind Down or Ramp Up?

Summary

In this last Case in the Set, Chantel confronts a number of complexities, including a concerning health issue. While the Case narrative describes this interwoven array of data and potential decision outcomes, let's briefly review where *Lily and Gem Media* (LGM) is at this point. First, it is five years old and clearly making a profit. Second, it has reliable, steady clients, suggesting it is solidly in its sustainability phase. Lastly, while LGM's profit is helpful, Chantel is still concerned about her household financial contribution.

The first and most important aspect of Chantel's decision in this Case is her physical health. She has a supportive family who agrees her health is the first priority. Next, she has an opportunity to change her business model and focus on creating video advertisements and managing aspects of a client's marketing plan. However, this requires 1) more education, 2) more money and will have to wait one year before the promised six-figure income emerges. She also just lost her most profitable client due to a change in their marketing strategy. With these three issues emerging almost simultaneously, Chantel is considering how to respond. We see her now as a mature decision-maker.

Let's prioritize Chantel's stress level and use it as a frame before we continue. We see this explicitly in the narrative:

> The first option she considered was to halt LGM entirely (for at least a while) and take a day job. She knew a day job would not pay $200,000 per year, like the business model change promised. But she was sure it would not entail the levels of stress she currently experienced while doing sales and everything else to run LGM. Less stress might address her top priority: her physical health. Receiving a steady paycheck could reduce stress as well. Of course, this addressed her second priority: helping to keep her family financially solvent. Working daily with others at an outside job would help her third priority: her mental health.

To be clear, most entrepreneurs experience heightened stress levels. After all, when one is the sole decision maker in any organization, there are bound to be stressful situations—and making difficult/complex decisions can be stressful. This said, difficult/stressful decisions are part of life, regardless of one's position in the world. Likely, the reader has experienced a number of these "life moments" already. However, when stress becomes something one experiences day after day, it can become overwhelming—and for some, debilitating. While likely not debilitating, Chantel's stress level appears at least elevated given the inset above. However, she is also a full-time parent and must be a contributing partner in her marriage. Obviously, she has far more on her plate than the business issues she's considering. Hopefully it's easy to see how stress is becoming a legitimate issue for her. The point about this part of the conversation is not just that stress is part of everyday life, but that without a plan to deal with stress, it can become a serious quality-of-life issue. In this Case, Chantel recognizes that running LGM in the way she has previously is causing her stress level to increase, which is impacting her quality of life. Therefore, this aspect is also in the mix.[1]

Next, is Chantel's mental health. As the narrative outlines, Chantel is a "people person" and needs personal contact. We are, after all, social beings and with the isolation that COVID wrought on the world, many suffered this lack of personal contact in silence. Her struggle is clear in the narrative:

> Her mental health was a fairly concrete issue for Chantel. She needed to be with people. While running her business from home, she noticed how isolating it was to work remotely and only occasionally see people in-person. This was especially true during the first two years of the pandemic, until vaccines became available and people started gathering again in person. She considered joining a co-working space—if only to see people more regularly. Thinking about running an internet advertising business—with fewer and fewer meetings with live humans—was not appealing. She had to stop and seriously consider how this choice would affect her.

Chantel needs a work environment with strong social contact and for her to know that in the midst of this Case is laudable. Both knowing, respecting and prioritizing this aspect says much about her maturity and self-actualization.

Lastly, there is always the "money" issue—seemingly the problem with many arts ventures. Certainly, Chantel's contribution to her family's financial health is a valid concern and should not be discounted. It is true that money is important and even in the 21st century, many collegiate arts students are still not taught about its importance or how to handle money when it graces one's palm. However, in the Case, we see Chantel not "chasing" money, but knowing that her financial contribution to the household (i.e.: money) is an ethical act; yet "how" she contributes to her family is critical. (We see this as she considers operating an internet advertising business). Again, we see Chantel aware of not only her ethical stance on issues related to her business—and her A(a)rt—but accepting and acting on these beliefs.

Factors Forcing the Decision

There are five factors forcing this decision. In Table 7.1 are the factors, their possible responses and outcomes.

As we can see, Chantel's decision is both complicated and interwoven given the number of factors, possible responses and consequences. In the Case, Chantel does not make a decision, as she was still in the

Table 7.1 Factors Forcing the Decision

Factor	Possible Response	Outcome
Chantel's Physical and Mental Health	Put LGM on Hold Video Documentary Series Freelance Video Work Focus on Current Clients	No Income from LGM Aligns w/ Chantel's Vision Less Stress—Health permitting Less Stress—No Sales Effort
Potential Business Model Change	Advertisements Video Documentary Series	$7800 for Class, wait one year for greater income Aligns w/ Chantel's Vision
Losing a Long-term Client	Focus on Current Clients	Less income for LGM and requires more effort to replace
Financial Household Contribution	Part-time Job	Contributes less to Household
Desire to Move		Better Health Care What happens to her Team?

decision-making process at the time of her interview. Additionally, with these factors being so impactful for her and her family, it's not surprising.

What is important about Table 7.1 is not just how complicated the decision is, but the fine line between 1) being overwhelmed with the decision, 2) too much data to analyze, 3) too much analysis and 4) trying to "make the right decision the first time." As many who confront complex decisions like these know, it's easy to cross at least one line if not all…sometimes simultaneously. Let's take a look at all four individually.

First, being overwhelmed with a decision this complex is natural. There are so many factors and outcomes, that even keeping them organized can be a problem. Some decisions with emotional consequences or factors—as we see with Chantel's concern about her health and her team—can seem overwhelming. In this Case, Chantel has a number of emotional consequences to consider and concern about her health likely leads the list—with her team a close second. However, though she likely experienced emotions around these factors, we see nothing in the Case indicating that she is overwhelmed with the decision. Rather, we again see a maturing decision maker wrestling with decisions by 1) realistically embracing the consequences of any decision, 2) being responsive via her decision-making strategy, and 3) remaining calm and deliberate.

Second, while there is much data to analyze, Chantel is keeping track of not only what is occurring, but potential options and possible outcomes as well. Typically, when we encounter decisions with too much data, it is easy to become blind to potential outcomes, much less the possible consequences of a decision. Again, Chantel is in control of her decision making despite the many data points and is accepting the data (i.e.: understands the data, its potential outcomes/consequences and is not biased when considering facts as they emerge). We could say then, that (in part) being uncomfortable with- or not accepting the data, *could* lead to becoming overwhelmed when making complex decisions.

Third, for some, "over analyzing" can be a trap. It's far too easy with our present focus on STEM education (for example) to over-analyze. Without putting blame on STEM education entirely, personalities and decision-making styles play a role. Though this "paralysis by analysis" situation occurs, it can occur for the wrong reasons and *not wanting to make a decision* can be routine for some. Complex decisions involving family or friends—especially those decisions with emotional components—are not pleasant experiences typically, and putting them off to a later date under the guise of "still thinking about it" is not only common, but convenient when the outcomes are difficult. While one could say the Case narrative describes Chantel in this way, there is a fine line between this and being deliberate with your decision. While it's true that Chantel is taking some time with this decision, it is also true that her family, both immediate and extended, will be impacted by her decision. Taking some time in this situation seems warranted, especially when there are children involved.

Lastly, trying to make the right decision the first time is also common. Inevitably, with some years of decision-making experience, when one gets into a decision as complex as this, one wants to "do it right." Unfortunately, this leads to obsessing about the decision, which can further lead to each of the three previous issues mentioned above. This is perhaps where Chantel finds herself. While there are many reasons for wanting to make the right decision the first time—many of them reasonable and responsible—there comes a time when the decision must be made, or the consequences of not making one take over; this leads to making a reactive decision instead of a controlled decision.

There are strategies for making complex decisions. Sometimes making a decision with the least impact first is helpful. For example, since LGM lost their most important client, they could simply focus on the remaining ones as Chantel suggested. Yes, the revenue would be lost, but likely this decision also means hiring a smaller team, which should not impact her household financial contribution significantly. Another strategy entails making the decision with the most impact first. The idea is that making a big decision reveals smaller decisions you did not initially envision. For example, Chantel and her family could just move to Raleigh. Granted, her husband would need to find a new job, but other options and consequences could emerge in a much larger city.

Whatever Chantel decides to do, however, she understands what is happening, the factors and consequences of the decision and is in control. Likewise, she also understands this is not simply dominos falling. This is not a Case where one decision leads to a series of other decisions. Rather, it is one where once her decision is made, she must anticipate the consequences and prepare for the multi-dimensional outcome of those consequences.

Decision Model

Previously, Chantel either used or favored the Analytical model. It was argued this consistency was a part of her evolution as a decision maker, resulting in a certain continuity and predictability in her solutions to problems. Case 1C clearly shows Chantel's preference for the Analytical model, but also for the Linear model group as she is using aspects of the Rational model as well.

Where she excelled in her decision making is in Step 1 of the Analytical model (Gather all information or relevant data), and much of the narrative describes this process. Additionally, Chantel is clear in both understanding the data and its impact—Steps 2 and 3. While the Case does not identify her final decision (Step 5), the narrative describes two options mentioned above: putting LGM on hold and transitioning to documentary making. The fact that Chantel is thinking about options to address the decision demonstrates her use of the Rational model. (Step 4—Develop multiple options). Note that gathering data and developing options are two different things. Developing options requires an amount of creativity (amongst many other skills) and gathering data requires research. While both will eventually involve analysis after the fact, these are two different things.

Now would be a good time to discuss why both this and the first Case in the Set have Chantel using aspects of two different models. As mentioned in Case 1B, decision makers typically evolve and test different decision-making techniques as a part of this evolution. These experiences prepare them for decision making outside of the typical day-to-day and help prepare them for novel situations. Of course this doesn't mean all decisions require hybrid approaches. Decision makers in later Cases use a combination of decision-making models.

To be clear, there are two critical points. First, *there is no "right" decision making model* for every situation, arts business, decision or decision maker, as we previously mentioned. Second, sticking to a specific decision model for all decisions is likely not a good strategy. Given the number of potential decisions an arts entrepreneur will make during the course of their venture's life, it needs to be said that one can favor a specific decision-making technique, but (as Chantel demonstrates) evolving, testing and experimenting with different techniques should be part of any decision maker's growth. Without this growth, arts businesses are at risk; we are artists, not management majors constantly studying business decisions. Sustaining our businesses means sustaining our A(a)rt, the impact it has on our markets and most importantly, ourselves. Being a nimble decision maker helps keep all of this thriving.

Ecology Discussion

Since the thrust of this Case concerns Chantel's health and how to negotiate LGM within that parameter, there is little to analyze in this context except for the fact that if LGM shuts down, the Video Ecology would balance the loss, as outlined in the Case 1B discussion. However, beyond putting LGM on pause, Chantel's two options described in the Case narrative would have an ecological impact.

Perhaps the first option to note is Chantel's proposed changing of LGM's business model and converting it to an advertising agency; this would change the context of LGM's ecological system. Specifically, LGM would then have to interface with an Advertising Ecology, which would require Chantel to learn that Ecology and negotiate how LGM operates within the Video Ecology in this proposed (new) context. Though this option may be somewhat complex, it could generate new opportunities—and perhaps the promised rise in income.

When comparing the two options, one (social impact documentaries) does not require Chantel to leave the Video Ecology explicitly (since she is not changing her business model), while the other (the ad agency option) requires her to negotiate with a new, unknown ecology she doesn't want to engage with for (what appear to be) ethical reasons. The documentary option, however, is something Chantel appears to ethically (and perhaps passionately) support. What is interesting about the ad agency option is that Chantel would have to return to the Education Ecology of *The Creative Ecological System* to gain this information and then learn an Advertising Ecology.[2] In addition to a significant learning curve, there would be quite a bit of movement between these Ecologies to make this work: pulling information from one, filtering it creatively and ethically, then finally fashioning it in a manner Chantel can support. With the documentary option, she simply applies the Video Ecology in a more creative manner.

Yet the astute reader should opine that Chantel would have to engage a Social Impact Ecology in order for the documentary option to work as she intends. This is true; she would have to learn that Ecology. Further, it is likely she would have to engage with an entire *Social Impact Ecological System* since social impact covers many, many realms: economic, social justice, climate, gender, food, cultures, etc. It is likely that a single ecology simply wouldn't come close to describing the breadth of a social impact universe.

These two options are certainly undertakings with different learning curves, ethical considerations, risks and rewards, etc. What we can say is that with these two options, there is no clear winner, as the variables list briefly described immediately above indicates. However, what else can be said is that each option has a different outcome for both Chantel and LGM based on the necessary understandings of the different ecologies and potential ecological systems.

Notes

1 The authors suggest that before starting an arts business, one should create a self-care strategy in a way they see fit. Following this strategy will not only help to prioritize one's mental, physical and emotional health, it can provide the focus and clarity of thought one needs to make the best decisions possible.

2 *The Creative Ecological System* was discussed in the Ecology Discussion section of Case 1A.

Bibliography

Beckman, Gary D. *The New Arts Entrepreneur: Navigating the Arts Ecologies*. London: Routledge, 2022.

CASE SET 2

THE CASE OF THE ENTREPRENEURIAL ACTOR

8

CASE 2A: READY FOR THE BIG LEAGUES?

If a young actor is lucky, one day the "big call" comes: one of the most prestigious theaters in town wants to cast you in a show on its mainstage. Since stepping into an acting class as a teen, Michael Flowers was waiting for that call. Now, here it was. A top theater in Chicago just called to offer him a role in its next play. Why was he hesitating to say yes? First, there was the money: not as much as he expected, not as much as the steady day job he'd have to quit in order to do this show. Second, there was the nagging question of whether he felt ready for this big step in his young acting career. He had done plenty of live theater shows for audiences of 40–50 people per night. This would be audiences of 700–800 per night with actors possessing national profiles and credentials. Was he ready for the same stage as these professionals?

The Artist as a Young Man

Michael grew up in a suburb of Chicago and took acting classes as a teen. He didn't major in theatre or any of the arts in his two years at the University of Illinois in Champaign-Urbana. Instead, he was an English major.

Back in Chicago, he got a job as a performer with a touring children's theatre, adapting and performing children's writing for shows promoting writing and creativity. From there, eager to have more direct contact with students in classrooms, rather than just on a stage performing for them,

 DOI: 10.4324/9781003414483-11

Michael joined Whirlwind Performance Company. For Whirlwind, he used his acting skills to engage K-8 students in creative drama games. He enjoyed this work, with its direct, one-to-one interactions with energetic youth. Going into many of Chicago's most under- resourced neighborhoods, full of black and brown faces, he could see himself in his students.

Michael was amazed when he learned about the full-time job at Whirlwind. It required his theatre skills, came with good pay and health insurance. At that point in his life, he was elated.

The Whirlwind job gave him the flexibility to do live theatre in the evenings. Even with a 30-hour week in the schools, this was possible. Michael was not in the Actors' Equity Association union, where shows rehearsed during the day and performances were at night. The theaters he typically performed in were smaller and paid little or (at worst) nothing. He could afford to act because his day job paid well enough to cover living expenses.

Michael was gaining experience on Chicago stages. While much of what he was learning was positive, one experience was not. He'd been cast in the leading role. At the first rehearsal, the director quickly determined Michael did not adequately prepare and was not ready for the role. He took Michael aside and demoted him to a lesser role. Though this stung, Michael knew the director was right. He was given a chance to move from bit parts to a leading role—even if in a small theater—and didn't put in the time. This lesson would stick with him.

At that point in his career, Michael's life was a balancing act. On one side was his day job: enjoyable, creative and paid the bills. Acting gigs were on the other: artistically satisfying and where he wanted his career to go. To spend more time acting and preparing for roles, he needed more hours in his acting day, but he knew his employer wouldn't agree to shorter hours.

Perhaps Michael did not yet feel fully invested in acting as a career? Yes, it was his dream, but how realistic was it? Would he be happier if he was spending all his time acting? That demands putting oneself on the line: going for lead roles, preparing for auditions and risking rejection. More time was needed for memorizing lines and working on the characters he was playing created new artistic choices. This would mean establishing a daily regimen of studying plays in which he wasn't yet cast, and doing acting exercises for his body and voice. If he changed nothing, he could do the lower level of preparation he was accustomed to and perform at the (lower) level he was currently performing. Michael could keep his day job by maintaining this status quo, too, while lead roles would continue to go to others. He couldn't help but think that, if he wasn't ready, maybe that was okay.

Let's Talk about "The Goodman"

Goodman Theatre is one of the top two or three stages in Chicago. Formed in 1922, the Goodman is the city's oldest currently active non-profit theater. As one sign of its quality, the theater was recognized in the 1990's with a Special Tony Award for Outstanding Regional Theater. Major names from Broadway, television, and movies helped create this reputation over the years.

Any role on that stage would be a significant opportunity for Michael. Casting directors from other Chicago theaters would see that performance, and being seen was important at this point in Michael's acting career. Hopefully, Michael thought, they might remember him next time they needed a tall, African American male with a deep voice and commanding presence for their next play (or season). Until now, Michael could barely secure a slot at a general audition call for the other top theaters in Chicago, like Steppenwolf, Court and Chicago Shakespeare.

Goodman typically casts experienced actors in lead roles but is interested in discovering new talent for supporting roles. Michael saw a number of local actors get their first big break in smaller roles on the Goodman stage and watched them go on to bigger roles over time. It was fun to follow other actors' careers—actors a few years older than him—and watch their success. There were no guarantees, but any role in a Goodman play held promise.

Michael was unsure how actors were paid at the Goodman. He knew actors who secured more important roles were paid more. So, how much did actors in smaller roles get paid per week? He knew some roles were advertised in audition announcements as union roles, while others could be filled by non-union actors. For non-union roles, you were paid less than the other actors who were in union roles. How much less? Michael was not sure.

Shortly after an audition, Michael received a call offering a small role on the Goodman stage. The caller confirmed it was a non-union role. Since Michael was not yet a member of Actors' Equity, so this was not a surprise. What was a surprise was the weekly pay rate; he investigated and it was about one-third what a union actor would make in that same production.

A Little about the Actors Union

Joining the actors' union is no simple matter. You must meet certain criteria. One route to membership is to do enough work in union theaters, but in non-union roles, so that you accumulate 25 points in a two year period. An actor can get one point for every week of employment on a union theater stage. Being cast in a role designated as a union role is a second route to union membership. This is a sign that you are good enough to be in the union and, thus, can join immediately. In fact, you are required to join at that point, in order to do the show. Then it is time for the actor to weigh the benefits and drawbacks to joining the union and decide.

The benefits to joining the Actors Equity Association union are several. First, you get paid more for any show into which you are cast. In the case of shows in union theaters like the *Goodman*, as Michael found out, you are paid about three times the non-union rate. Some auditions are open only to union members. There are work rules protecting you when you're working, including length-of-day restrictions, breaks, days off and safety rules. Actors Equity offers health insurance and retirement plans, as well.

Drawbacks to joining the union include tales of actors who worked all the time in non-union theaters but who never worked again once they joined the union. In Chicago, there are many more non-union theaters than union theaters. These are often storefront or church basement operations where recent theatre school grads stage shows; the pay is meager. Union members are not allowed to perform in these theaters, so joining the union suddenly and significantly reduces your number of opportunities to perform. Additionally, the quality of actors in the union is higher than non-union actors, so the number of high-quality actors competing for the fewer roles in union theaters is usually greater.

One other factor in joining the actors union is cost. Along with basic dues of $176 annually, there is an initial $600 application fee. Then there is an $1,800 initiation fee, which can be deducted from weekly paychecks when the actor is working in a union show. Finally, actors see 2.5% of gross earnings deducted from each paycheck whenever they are in an Equity show, as working dues.

For Equity actors, minimum pay levels vary according to the seating capacity of the individual theater. In other words, theaters with more seats—and thus more potential to gain revenue from tickets—must pay actors more. The 2019 Chicago Area Theaters (CAT) contract between union theaters and Actors' Equity set pay for actors from $134 per week for Tier One theaters to $574.50 per week for Tier Six, the largest theaters. Of course, these are minimums, with lead actors and nationally-known names able to negotiate higher weekly amounts.[1]

Exciting, or Scary?

Michael thanked the caller for the offer of a role, asked for time to think about it, then politely hung up. He sat quietly and thought. This was an offer of a role at one of the top theaters in Chicago. It would require weeks of daytime rehearsals, then eight performances per week, including some matinees. He would need to quit his day job to take this opportunity.

Suddenly, he caught himself. Think about it? Here was the chance he'd been dreaming of getting someday, and that day had come. Why was he hesitating? Multiple thoughts were jamming his brain at that moment:

- How exciting it would be to perform on that prestigious stage.
- How scary it might be onstage next to actors who had been doing this for 30–40 years and on Broadway, on TV and in movies.
- He had always battled stage fright, despite his experience. Could he keep that in check with 700–800 people watching each night?
- Would this be the big break his career needed?
- Was he ready for this opportunity?
- How would he pay his bills if he had to live on the non-union rate he was offered?

Reflection Questions

1. Should Michael take the role at the Goodman Theatre or not? Why?
2. If he takes the role, how will he pay his rent and other bills once he quits his day job?

The Iron ain't Always Hot

Michael decided to take the role. At that moment, he prioritized the future of his acting career above the amount of pay he would receive. Performing at this level was something he felt ready to do. He was optimistic that the money side of his life would somehow work out.

Several weeks later (right before rehearsals were scheduled to begin), the producer told Michael the role would now be a union role, not the non-union designation originally presented during the audition and casting offer. Michael initially thought this meant he would no longer be eligible for the role. Instead, they still wanted him in the role, which required him to join the actors union. This meant his weekly pay would be about three times what he originally thought when he took the role.

Michael was not told why the theater changed his non-union role to a union role. They didn't need to change it to convince him to take the role, as this change occurred after he accepted. Perhaps the theater had some ratio of union versus non-union roles on its stage that it needed to meet for the season as a whole? Or perhaps they cast more non-union actors than expected and needed some to join the union? There were more questions than he had answers about how this union thing worked.

Whatever the theater's reasons for their decision, Michael had a new decision to make: should he stay in the role and join the actor's union? Or should he turn down the role in order to *avoid* joining the union. He had friends who joined and never worked again, as explained above, leading to great bitterness and regret. Michael was collecting points toward his union eligibility but was still a few shows away from having enough. He had assumed there was time before he needed to make that decision. But now, Goodman could grant this opportunity with this one show. He needed to do some thinking in a hurry…now.

Michael had others he could lean on for advice at that moment. He called a veteran actor friend and mentor to seek his guidance. "Strike while the iron is hot, because the iron ain't always hot," was his friend's advice. Michael also discussed this opportunity with his girlfriend (now wife), who reminded him this was a big opportunity. She echoed his mentor's counsel.

For a second time, he decided to take the role.

A Little Something Every Day

In the first year after joining the union, Michael made about one third the total wages he had made in his day job the year prior. That was challenging, but he was, from the moment he took the Goodman role and joined the union, optimistic it would all work out. "There's a certain freedom when you're younger, where you don't have car notes, house notes, or mouths to feed. You know what you need to earn to get from month to month," he says. He took on other gigs—like being a runner for movies shooting in Chicago. It wasn't acting, but it was flexible, paid some bills and fit with whatever acting gigs he got called to do. He also did some "bus and truck" tours of Shakespeare plays in the South, sponsored by the National Endowment for the Arts.

Michael recounts:

> That first show at the Goodman was so positive. The actors that I worked with were not new to the business. Some had many TV and movie credits. I remember thinking, "If these guys can do it, they're a great example for me, as a black actor." They gave me the inspiration to believe that this was not only possible, but that I could probably do it, if I dedicated myself, if I gave it the attention these guys gave it every day.

Michael learned much from his first experience at the Goodman:

> Until that, I don't think I was giving it everything that I could. I wasn't doing a little something every day or every week—reading a play, taking a class, doing workshops. These are the things that keep your edge. Sometimes I was failing, because

> I wasn't preparing. So, I took that on myself. Now I was prepared and getting cast let me know this preparation was working.
>
> "I also saw there was more than one way to do this," Michael says. "I watched during rehearsals and kept my mouth shut. One actor would come in memorized, while another was maybe not all memorized but used the blocking to seal their memorization. The questions they would ask about their role, all of this was so interesting to me."

"The choice to follow my heart and take a role that I thought was very neat and a lot of fun, in a great theater, ended up paying off," Michael says. "Things worked out, as they often do."

Discussion: Case 2A — Ready for the Big Leagues?

Summary

In an artist's career trajectory (or in a business' life cycle), there are unique processes and decisions that define movement towards a goal. This Case Set outlines one almost never discussed: transitioning from the startup to sustainability phase. Obviously, these transitions vary between arts disciplines and businesses, yet what typically marks the journey is an element of risk, a financial "cost" to fund the transition, leveraging one's network and requiring assets not presently in the entrepreneur's control.[2] In Case 2A, we see a number of these elements in action.[3]

Like most artists, Michael had the desire and—with his position at Whirlwind—was luckier than most working restaurant gigs to pursue their art after hours. This allowed Michael to immerse himself in his art—with the added benefit of gaining improvisational experience in a classroom.[4] Additionally, he earlier made a decision to pursue English as an academic major, which is not remarkable for those drawn to theatre. What unifies both of these decisions is a conscious desire for education; one decision provided a literary context for his passion (English) and the other allowed him to practice an aspect of his passion (Whirlwind). As we will see throughout this Case Set, Michael's desire for knowledge is unflinching.

When Michael started getting roles, things progressed quickly. However, he needed more time to prepare for these roles and Whirlwind was taking this time away. Michael makes the decision to pursue his professional goals and the narrative describes how he intends to achieve them. Broadly speaking, Michael's response was to leverage self-discipline—something most artists can muster at will when required. Clearly, he is making decisions like any serious, emerging professional artist who both acknowledges and responds to their passion.

At the core of the Case is Michael's decision to join the Actors' Equity Association (AEA). This decision transitions him from an emerging artist (the startup phase) to a "union actor" (the sustainability phase—at least potentially). As he weighs the risks with union and non-union roles, his decision process is both deliberate and informed as he considers pay, educational benefits and potential future opportunities. In an effort to gather information, Michael engages his network to learn about the union. He learns that it's risky, yet the career benefits could be significant. And yes, there were going to be some financial risks, as well.

Yet before we go to the next subsection, we should ask if Michael is a business? No, not in the traditional sense since (at this point) he is operating like a typical pre-professional artist: learning the craft, observing those with more experience, practicing and testing technique, trying to pay the bills, etc. However, he is making (broadly) similar decisions as any entrepreneur or sole-proprietor when transitioning from the startup to the sustainability phase. Additionally, he is clear that money is important for sustainability, knows acting is the value he provides an audience (a.k.a.: market) and is comfortable with taking an informed risk for future gain.

However, an astute reader will ask if he is "behaving" like an entrepreneur. If innovation is an aspect of entrepreneurial behavior, then perhaps not yet. Entrepreneurial action does not spring forth fully formed as entrepreneurs typically need experience or knowledge to establish the basis for entrepreneurial action within a domain. This said, Michael is demonstrating opportunity recognition by first learning about the theatre ecology and is willing to assume the financial risk in order to act full time. We note, however, that some would say he is innovating his *life* by pursuing this passion as opposed to staying with Whirlwind.

In summary, if Michael is going to act entrepreneurially according to the traditional definition, he needs experience or knowledge of *what* to innovate *before* he innovates. He is well on his way as he accepts risk, is recognizing opportunities and can develop a network. The only question in the remaining Case Set is whether or not he innovates according to a more traditional definition.

Factors Forcing the Decision

The "meta" factors Michael encounters are those recent arts graduates know well: 1) the desire to make a passion a career and 2) securing enough money to sustain a reasonable existence. One could argue, however, that joining Actors' Equity is not necessarily the real decision. Perhaps Michael is encountering a decision about himself?

He was already—with Whirlwind—using aspects of his acting skills during the day and securing acting roles after hours with the "big stage" in mind. While many artists would like to perform to larger audiences, both parties have expectations. Audiences expect better performances and, *typically*, artists expect more of themselves. Michael admits his preparation for certain roles was lacking, which (at least in part) put his goals at risk. While this may be due to a myriad of reasons, he acknowledges a lack of self-discipline.

The decision to join the union had risks, certainly, but there was also a risk of Michael not living up to his own expectations. A union card means little unless you do something with it and for Michael, he chose self-discipline *through* the art. This action would make him a better actor, certainly, but would likely create a greater sense of dignity. Specifically, he needed to work on his art in a more structured manner to achieve his envisioned success. Absolutely not an easy task but one emerging artists and art entrepreneurs know well. Indeed, the risk of not meeting your own expectations can be more debilitating than a catastrophic stage performance.

Philosopher Emmanuel Kant characterized "dignity" as follows:

> In the kingdom of ends everything has either a price or a dignity. What has a price can be replaced by something else as its equivalent; what on the other hand is raised above all price and therefore admits of no equivalent has a dignity…but which constitutes the condition under which alone something can be an end in itself, has no merely a relative worth, that is, a price, an inner worth value, that is, dignity.[5]

Without getting into a philosophical discussion, Kant suggests that dignity is both intrinsic to human action and its highest ideal. Therefore, to recognize the dignity within others—and one's self—is an ethical, dignified act. While there may be many reasons why Michael decided to exercise a greater sense of self-discipline, we should note his dignity both in purpose and in pursuit of his goals. We are mentioning Kant's thesis primarily because some readers may not think of art making or entrepreneuring as a dignified pursuit in the context of self-actualization. To be clear, one of the most revered philosophers of the western world suggests that artists and entrepreneurs possess dignity, simply because they are human…acting humanly.

Decision Model

If we consider this subsection as only pertaining to Michael's decision about joining Actors' Equity, we would assume he favors a single decision-making model. Perhaps the most efficient way to identify this model is to determine if he is observing or identifying a problem. In this Case, Michael understands and can identify the issue—joining the union or not. This eliminates four of the six models and we are left with two models where one *observes* the problem: Expertise or Heuristic.

Since the Heuristic model is one where quick decisions are required, we should ask if Michael is in a position where the speed of a decision is critical. It is not in this circumstance, thus leaving the Expertise model as our only option. While it is true that decisions do not *require* one to follow parameters, Michael is very close to engaging all the steps in the Expertise model. For example, Step 1 (Observe the problem and make sense of it in its domain) is quite clear. Michael is trying to get information about the Actors' Equity Association (not unions in a broad sense) in the context of the Theatre Ecology. Step 2 (Assess as many aspects as possible) is also clear. He engaged his network of Actors' Equity colleagues and was trying to gain information about membership. Additionally, he was informed about the fundamental differences between union and non-union roles. So far so good.

It is with step 3 (Based on one's understanding and experience within a domain, *identify patterns*) where we encounter Michael's inexperience. Since the Expertise model is in the Domain-based model group, understanding one's domain (i.e.: which ecology they find themselves) is critical. Given Michael's journeyman status as an actor, there appears to be little time for him to grasp the entire Theatre Ecology, though he clearly understood some aspects. For example, he knew there were differences between union and non-union roles. Likewise, he knew some actors were better at their craft and thus, generated better results. He also knew that theatre pay varied in different geographical regions. Certainly, Michael should be applauded for observing these distinctions and leveraging what was possible with very little professional training.

We see Michael engaging in and taking responsibility for his decision-making process—Step 4 (Based on the domain, goals…determine potential courses of action). He was clear about his professional goals (better roles and larger audiences), knew that money was important to exist and was aware that getting a union card could result in either lower annual pay due to fewer roles or the complete opposite. The choices were simple: join the union or not and accept the consequences of either decision. He chose to join Actors' Equity—Step 5 (Determine a single course of action).

Ecology Discussion

One of the benefits of the arts ecologies is its malleability. Since Michael is not a business in the *traditional sense*, one can create an ecological system articulating the collective elements and organizational patterns of live theatre. Figure 8.1 illustrates one way to position this ecological system. Here, there are two adjustments: 1) the For- and Non-Profit ecologies are removed and replaced with a Theatre Ecology and 2) we see the Geography Ecology informing the Theatre Ecology—as shown by the upward arrow.

The Broader Economic Ecology remains in its standard position since 1) economics is critical to producing theatre and 2) disposable income is required for an audience in order to pay for tickets; both are required to support the economic sustainability of a Theatre Ecology. Additionally, the upward arrow indicates that (more so in this discipline than some others) geography plays an important role in theatre, as seen in the geographic distribution of US venue growth.[6] With the number of venues expanding (particularly in urban regions), the market for live theatre becomes an important cultural tourist sector. We could say the same about professional sports as this market will also travel more than 50 miles to attend a sporting event. However, the aesthetic argument points to the importance of New York City's theatre district and, especially, works with the word "Broadway" in the marketing. Some would disagree, however, and suggest Theatre itself influences arts geography. For example, the number of rural, summer-only theatre venues: actors

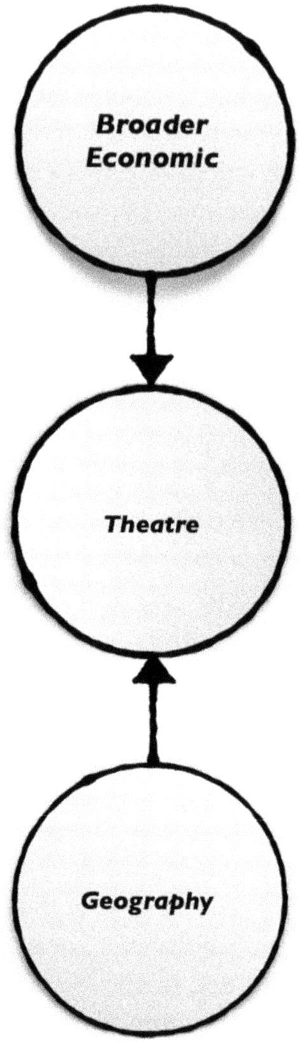

Figure 8.1 Theatre Ecology EEA Orientation.

are resident, perform and prepare for the upcoming season. An equally important argument is the impact of Theatre in communities.[7] Given these meritable views, one could envision the arrow in either position or even inserting a double arrow between the Theatre and Geography ecologies.

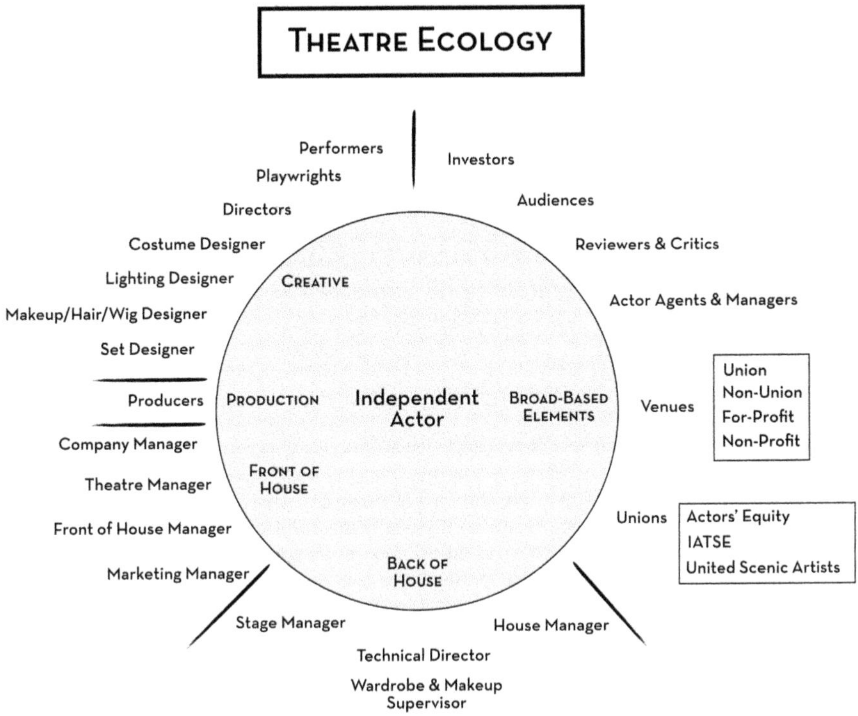

Figure 8.2 Theatre Ecology.[8]

Regardless of one's position on the issue above, it is clear that Michael appears to make his decision concerning Actors' Equity based on both the Theatre Ecology and how this ecology must be leveraged to reach his professional—and life—goals (Figure 8.2). For emerging artists, this is a reasonable and logical way forward. In the arts, we are seldom trained to look beyond our discipline's training priorities (technique and skill development, medium exploration, etc.) and unfortunately, much of our professional education occurs when things are upended in some way. For example, in public universities, the relationship between state sales tax revenue, annual higher education appropriations and university budgets are only brought to our attention when classes or other student opportunities are curtailed.

One is hard pressed to see how differently Michael could be thinking. Unions—beyond what's been discussed—would appear in any Theatre

Ecology as they would in a Film Industry Ecology. However, one could consider this decision from another perspective. If Michael expressed concern about audience disposable income or an investment group's financial return over the long term impacting the funding of union or non-union shows, then considering the Broader Economic and Geography ecologies is appropriate. In the final analysis, Michael used a reasonable—if not the most logical—decision-making strategy (i.e.: considering the entire Theatre Ecology in the context of his professional goals).

Notes

1 For comparison purposes, theaters on Broadway pay union actors a minimum of $2,439 per week.
2 For an asset analysis tool, see Gary D. Beckman, *The New Arts Entrepreneur: Navigating the Arts Ecologies* (London: Routledge, 2022), 142–143.
3 It should be said that in some arts disciplines (or genres) there are well-worn paths to sustainability—however one defines the term—that many artists follow with varying success.
4 For those unfamiliar with leading a classroom, student groups are unique from class to class. Since small groups invariably develop their own group culture, Michael responded dynamically (i.e.: adjusting his "teacher" persona to "fit" a class' "microculture"). This is somewhat similar to improvising a performance on stage.
5 Emmanuel Kant, *Groundwork of the Metaphysics of Morals*, trans. M.J. Gregor (Cambridge: Cambridge University Press, 200), 42.
6 Luke Steffen, "The Development of Resident Professional Theatre in the USA, 1913-2013: A Geographic Perspective" (Poster presented at the Spring Student Symposium, Ohio Wesleyan University, 2016).
7 Amanda Rogers, "Geographies of the Performing Arts: Landscapes, Places and Cities," *Geography Compass* 6, no. 2 (2012): 60–75.
8 The authors acknowledge this is a somewhat less-detailed ecological representation than some theatre professionals would suggest.

Bibliography

Beckman, Gary D. *The New Arts Entrepreneur: Navigating the Arts Ecologies*. London: Routledge, 2022.

Bikart, Joseph. *The Art of Decision Making: How we Move from Indecision to Smart Choices*. London: Watkins Publishing, 2019.

Kant, Emmanuel. *Groundwork of the Metaphysics of Morals*. Translated by M.J. Gregor. Cambridge: Cambridge University Press, 2006: 42.

Rogers, Amanda. "Geographies of the Performing Arts: Landscapes, Places and Cities." *Geography Compass* 6, no. 2 (2012): 60–75.

Steffen, Luke. "The Development of Resident Professional Theatre in the USA, 1913–2013: A Geographic Perspective." Poster presented at *the Spring Student Symposium*, Ohio Wesleyan University, 2016.

9

Case 2B: How to Get the Dream Gig?

If Goodman Theatre is the most prestigious stage in Chicago, Steppenwolf is the hippest. Maybe it's the cachet of major movie stars in Steppenwolf's acting ensemble. Or maybe it's the celebrities showing up for events: actors Steve Martin and Anthony Hopkins, chefs Wolfgang Puck and Rick Bayless, and comedian Chris Rock, to name a few. Perhaps it's all the shows that started at Steppenwolf, then moved to Broadway or all the Tony Awards they've won. Or perhaps it is the rags to riches, church-basement-to-Broadway story of its founding and growth.

Whatever it is that gives Steppenwolf its cachet, Michael Flowers longed to be an actor on that stage. In high school, he wore a Steppenwolf t-shirt, telling people he'd be on that stage one day. Performing there would be a sure sign he had made it. However, five years after getting his big break on the mainstage at the Goodman Theatre in Chicago, Michael felt no closer to getting cast at Steppenwolf. The Goodman show went well and his work there brought roles at other professional theaters in Chicago. At Steppenwolf: many auditions, no jobs.

"We Just Kind of Wail on Each Other"

Steppenwolf Theater Company began in 1976 in a church basement in Highland Park, Illinois, founded by a group of high school and college buddies. From the start, the emphasis at Steppenwolf was on ensemble

 DOI: 10.4324/9781003414483-12

theatre, a group of actors doing intense, intimate, visceral theatre As co-founder Gary Sinise explained later, "We just kind of wail on each other."

The ensemble concept was formalized through a selected, continuous set of actors. Over the years, this included many who worked regularly in TV and movies: John Malkovich, Joan Allen, Gary Sinise, Gary Cole, Laurie Metcalf and John Mahoney to name only a few. Starting with just nine actors, the group has grown to 46 actors, writers and directors.

Steppenwolf's approach has been good for the company, sending multiple productions to Broadway, including *True West*, *Balm in Gilead* and *Grapes of Wrath*. *August: Osage County* garnered five Tony Awards. Its author, Tracy Letts—also an ensemble member—won the Pulitzer Prize for Drama in 2008.

Casting for the plays in Steppenwolf's season gives preference to its ensemble members. Roles not taken by them are offered to actors seen in general auditions. If you are an actor who has not yet worked at Steppenwolf, there are several ways you might get cast. One is through their Equity auditions, which are held each January for the next season that starts in the Fall. You can pursue this route only if you are an Equity member. If you're not a member, you can "crash" their Equity auditions. You are not guaranteed to get an audition this way, but there's a chance you might. The final way to get cast is through the non-Equity auditions, held each year. Representatives from Steppenwolf and other professional companies in Chicago attend. You might get noticed.

Michael tried these avenues both before and after he earned his Equity membership. No go. Steppenwolf was not calling.

What "Being Prepared" Really Means

Working with experienced actors at the Goodman, watching them in rehearsals and every night on stage, was an education for Michael. He was learning what "being prepared" meant and how to achieve a higher level on a consistent basis. Additionally, he was learning what clues casting agents and directors were looking for in an actor.

For example, during auditions for stages like the Goodman or Steppenwolf, directors were looking for signs that the actor prepared, such as: had the actor memorized the two or three pages they'd be asked to perform during the audition? Or, better, had they studied the 50 or 60 other pages they'd been sent? Those additional pages held clues about the character they'd be portraying—clues to inform the choices an actor might make about how to play that character for the audition. Is the character mean-spirited or kind on those other pages, for instance? The directors were looking for choices informed by that knowledge. Preparation like that tells directors that, if they cast this actor, he or she is ready to do the work. It went back to being "fully in" as an actor, which Michael was thinking about since deciding to quit his day job.

From Actors Union to Marital Union

After Michael's first show at the Goodman Theatre in 2000, he was an active actor, performing mostly at smaller spaces, like Journeyman Theater. During the next five years, he also did multiple shows at one of Chicago's other prestigious theaters, *Chicago Shakespeare Theatre*. Initially, his roles there were "third soldier on the left," as he typifies them with a chuckle.

Shows Michael was doing in those five years were mainly "Tier N" contracts with smaller theaters. Those productions might hire one Equity actor and the pay was meager. He supplemented his income by working as a runner for Jam Productions, a concert promoter in Chicago. In this job, he met many established artists, as he drove them around to the gym or the grocery store. Occasionally, these artists—Harry Connick Jr, Donny Osmond, Kenny Loggins—engaged in conversation with Michael:

> These were people who had been doing it for a long time. It was a chance for me to see how they moved through the world, and the preparation they gave, even at that well-established level. I found those conversations informative.

Michael got married in 2002. This meant new responsibilities, as well as new stability. His wife had a steady job, which eased some of his full-time acting career financial challenges.

A Foot in the Door?

In 2005, Michael was offered a role in *Take Me Out*, a play produced by About Face Theatre Company. The role offered to Michael was not one of the leads, but it was important to the narrative arc of the play. It was a chance for Michael to shine.

The play had been a success in London and then off-broadway in New York. Its author had a longstanding relationship with Steppenwolf, who produced several of his plays in the past. Steppenwolf was letting About Face use its Upstairs Theatre space for performances, but this was not a Steppenwolf production. Rehearsals wouldn't be in the Steppenwolf building. Rather, they'd be rehearsing several miles away in a church basement. In that way, it was like early-Steppenwolf: happening in a church basement.

As Michael considered whether to take this role or not, he went through some of the pros and cons. How might this role lead to other opportunities in his career? Could the role lead to a Steppenwolf job? Michael knew Steppenwolf staff could easily walk upstairs to catch a performance. Opportunities can happen because they are convenient—then again, this was not on the mainstage, and it was produced by an outside theater company. Maybe Steppenwolf casting directors looked down on anything occurring in their upstairs space. Perhaps actors in that space and outside companies got pegged as "not ready for the Steppenwolf Mainstage." Or maybe Steppenwolf was hipper than that, looking everywhere for talent.

Reflection Questions

1. Should Michael take the role? Why or why not?
2. What other options might Michael consider in his quest to perform on the *Steppenwolf* mainstage?
3. How should Michael analyze and determine his best option?
4. How could Michael test alternative courses of action to see if they were viable?

"A Really Neat Stairway"

Michael decided to take the role in *Take Me Out* and try to make the most of the opportunity. He knew he'd enjoy being in the Steppenwolf building and planned to invite Steppenwolf casting directors and other artistic staff to see the performance—they just had to walk upstairs. He would also invite casting and artistic staff from *every other theater* in Chicago. Michael now knew this type of self-promotion was part of his job.

His marketing as well as his acting paid off. After doing *Take Me Out* from March to May, 2005 Michael was offered other opportunities at Steppenwolf. One of their casting directors saw Michael in *Take Me Out* and invited him to audition for a specific play she was casting. From that, Michael was cast for his first mainstage role at Steppenwolf, in Bruce Norris's *The Pain and the Itch*, which ran from June to August in 2005. A little more than a year later, in October, 2006, he was asked to join the cast of *The Bluest Eye*, which was extending its successful run. This adaptation of a Toni Morrison story was officially part of Steppenwolf's Theatre for Young Audiences program. When *The Bluest Eye* transferred to New York (off-Broadway) the following month in November of 2006, Michael went as well. Playing in New York for four weeks at the Duke Theater, "three or four doors east of the actual Broadway," as Michael tells the story, "it was the first time I could literally say I went to New York to do a show." He liked the sound of that.

In less than two years, Michael went from being ignored at general auditions for the Steppenwolf mainstage to performing in New York City in a Steppenwolf play. "It was a really neat stairway that was set up at Steppenwolf," Michael reflects. "With each production, I could step up my work and skills and build my confidence."

Around that time, in December, 2006, Drury Lane Theatre cast him in the musical *The King and I*. The lead actors were veteran actors Michael admired:

> That was another opportunity for me to watch people who had been doing this for a long time and see how they navigated the rehearsal room. It was as far from a Steppenwolf mainstage rehearsal as you can imagine. It was musical theatre, for one. The rehearsal process was a lot shorter. You have to pick things up in a hurry. I learned a lot in that room.

In the last days of 2006, Michael received an email from Martha Lavey, Steppenwolf's artistic director just as *The King and I* production work began. "I'd love to meet with you right after the New Year," she said and gave him several dates. Michael asked if he should prepare a monologue or in some other way be ready for this meeting. "No, just come and meet."

This was an intriguing set-up. Maybe she wanted him for another project. Michael was anxious and eager. He first performed in a Steppenwolf space not quite two years before in March of 2005. This was immediately followed by his first Steppenwolf mainstage show. He waited 14 months to get cast in another show there, in October, 2006, which led to a trip to New York City in November, 2006 for his first off-Broadway Steppenwolf performances. Going in through the side door had worked.

At the January, 2007 meeting, Martha Lavey was joined by Anna Shapiro, Michael's director for *Pain and The Itch.* Ms. Lavey told Michael she was inviting him to join the acting ensemble at Steppenwolf. "Once I picked my jaw up off the ground, I said yes," Michael recounts. A big announcement followed a few days later on January 29, 2007 on the theater's mainstage. The world now had five new members added to the Steppenwolf ensemble and one was Michael Flowers.

"I'm not going to say things skyrocketed from there," Michael said. "I was still doing plenty of regular theater. But people looked at me differently now. I looked at myself differently, too."

Discussion: Case 2B — How to Get the Dream Gig?

Summary

Case 2B describes Michael's transition to a sustainable career. While it may not seem as if much is happening (till the end, of course), Michael makes a decision that may fly under the radar for some. In this Case, we see how smaller decisions accumulate to create sustainability.

Michael uncovered a risk before his decision to join the union in the previous Case: it may be difficult to secure *only* union roles as a new union actor. He accepted the risk when making the decision and certainly experienced this result. Michael was securing roles during the five years after his Goodman debut, yet the poor yearly pay was creating a financial challenge. However, his determination to get to the Steppenwolf stage—and what it could potentially mean—did not wane.

While it would be easy to write off Michael's desire to become a Steppenwolf member as only a professional goal having nothing to do with entrepreneurship, we *could* envision this desire as a stepping stone to sustainability. An interesting aspect of sustainability (either in an art performance career or in a non-art business) is that it typically appears as a plateau one reaches through a series of steps. For example, to be an engineer making $150,000 a year (a wage most consider suitable to create a comfortable, sustainable lifestyle), one needs to earn 1) a bachelor's degree and 2) likely a master's degree, then 3) find a job that pays that wage 4) in an area where that income level has at least average buying power. "Sustainable," however, is both subjective and context dependent.

In this Case, we see Michael's continued dedication to educating himself both about the discipline and the Theatre industry. For example, learning what directors wanted during auditions, and what it communicated, helped Michael gain a different perspective about the audition process. We also see this in his choice of jobs to supplement his income during these five years. He could have secured jobs unrelated to the arts but did not. Instead, he took a position with a concert promoter, providing him the opportunity to continue his informal arts industries education.

Additionally, performing in the Steppenwolf building (and rehearsing nearby) gave him the opportunity to practice the "marketing oneself is *your* responsibility" lesson—and he embraced the challenge. Michael's physical proximity to Steppenwolf decision makers was crucial as it both articulated his target market (in a sustainability context) and increased the size of his network. This could generate potential opportunities and Michael clearly capitalized on this proximity. For example, he accepted his role in *The Bluest Eye* as a part of Steppenwolf's Theatre for Young Artists Program in Chicago, and then for adults and youth a few short blocks from Broadway.

Obviously, this Case ends on a happy note for Michael. However, we can outline how this occurred. Michael planned to pursue a goal—theatre acting—and realized that solid preparation communicated many things during an audition. In pursuit of this goal, even though being a new union actor potentially meant less roles initially, Michael chose to supplement his income by taking a job in a related arts industry as opposed to (for example) the restaurant industry. And of course, making the decision to accept the *Take Me Out* role, which put him in physical proximity to Steppenwolf, gave him the geographic opportunity to directly market himself. What we have then, is a series of what appear to be smaller decisions that not only helped achieve his goal but also increased the chance for professional sustainability.

Factors Forcing the Decision

Since this Case outlines a series of small decisions over the course of seven years from when Michael joins the union (2000) till he achieves a professional goal (joining the Steppenwolf ensemble in 2007), we should be able to easily determine why these decisions were made. As mentioned above, one of the risks Michael accepted was that *new* union actors may have a difficult time getting union roles. Since he was confronting this very situation, we might also expect Michael to experience increasing financial pressure, which he did initially. This, however, was not the case after he married in 2002, which "…meant new responsibilities, as well as new stability. His wife had a steady job, which eased some of his full-time acting career financial challenges." Financial stress, then, *appears* not to be a driving factor for *some* of these smaller decisions.

Without trying to get into a psychological analysis of Michael's actions during the time period in the Case (2000–2007), we can 1) defer to the ecology discussion below or 2) return to the dignity discussion in the Case 2A analysis. Perhaps a way to approach this is to accept these two items as playing a part in a larger equation Michael is using to make these decisions. Let's leave the former for the discussion below and briefly address the latter.

Michael had been married for three years when he received the *Take Me Out* offer in 2005 and, according to the Case, financial stresses became more manageable after the marriage. This meant he now had *a bit* of self-managerial freedom with his career. It would be easy for the more cynical among us to simply say that Michael was being financially supported by his wife so he could go off and occasionally "play actor." The Case proves this is not true. If it *were* true, then Michael would not be *executing* the series of small decisions the Case outlines, nor would the outcome of his marketing efforts result in being a new Steppenwolf ensemble member. Clearly, Michael *had* a plan, he was *executing* that plan and he had *support* for that plan.

Yes, Michael was fortunate that his marriage offered some easing of financial stressors—an *easing*, not an abdication of responsibility. As many readers know, couples negotiate their relationships uniquely, as do married couples, though with greater potential rewards and consequences. While we have no idea how their relationship was negotiated or what they valued as a couple, it is apparent that 1) Michael had some support for his professional goals, 2) he was making a purposeful effort to continue working on his career, which was slowly, though increasingly, paying off and 3) working for Jam Productions shuttling celebrities around town was an effort to both supplement household income and continue his arts industries education.

The authors make the argument that Michael and his wife were both acting in a *dignified manner*. Supporting a spouse can mean many things and Kant suggests that *recognizing* the other party's dignity is fundamental. The question becomes: what is Michael's *dignified response* to this *dignified* act of support? What we can say is that Michael was pursuing his goals by drawing on *his own model* of dignity *in service of the marriage*, which was likely recognized by his partner as *dignified*—an ethical act by both parties according to Kant. We can ask an opposite question: If Michael were not putting in the effort to reach his goals despite some financial support, is that *dignified?* According to Kant, likely not because we have a responsibility to both define dignity uniquely and *act* on our definition. If Michael was not putting in his best effort, Kant suggests that is *not* an ethical act because he would be denying the dignity embodied in his marital relationship. Dignity and trust, it seems, begets dignity and trust.

Decision Model

In this section of the Case 2A analysis, we saw Michael's likely use of an Expertise model step appeared incomplete (Step 3—Based on one's understanding and experience within a domain, *identify patterns*). To a certain degree, this was due to his inexperience and lack of formal collegiate training in theatre. If we assume he is continuing to use the Expertise decision model, Case 2B suggests he is working on Step 3 throughout. Michael's decision to accept the *Take Me Out* role can be viewed as a response to the marketing patterns he observed with other actors and saw the role primarily as a location-based (or geographic-based) opportunity. Likewise, his decision to supplement his income by being in proximity to other, more successful artists, allowed him to ask questions about the *patterns* of success. And in part, we also see a continuation of Step 2 (Assess as many aspects as possible) where a lack of domain knowledge (i.e.: the Theatre Ecology) did not allow him to analyze the domain effectively, hence dedicating himself to learning this ecology when he could.

What we are likely seeing then, is not a different decision model used in this Case, but a continuation of the Expertise model since the problem (or goal) is not yet solved (or achieved). If we accept the previous sentence, we could even make the argument that Michael is putting a significant amount of effort into Step 3 so he can determine Step 4 (Based on the domain, goals…determine potential courses of action) to execute Step 5 (Determine a single course of action). This thinking may have validity since his decision to accept *Take Me Out* had a significant proximity component, similar to a band accepting an offer to open for a headliner: people who can impact a musical career are surrounding a band they've impacted already…perhaps the headliner can *further* advance the opening band's career?[1] We should note a small difference in the examples immediately above, however. In this Case, those who could impact Michael's career *could potentially* witness rehearsals first just a few miles away—in addition to—the performances upstairs in the Steppenwolf building. This strategy would allow Steppenwolf decision-makers to see Michael's progress as an actor, gain more reliable data and assume less risk if they brought him on as an ensemble member. It's a brilliant—if not entrepreneurial—strategy.

Ecology Discussion

One of the most interesting aspects of this Case is that Michael is continuing to work on Step 3 of the Expertise decision model *in addition to* leveraging the Theatre Ecology—the ecological system in which he finds himself. In this Case, we see him using a more local Geography Ecology by choosing to accept the *Take Me Out* role since the performances were in the Steppenwolf building. Additionally, since About Face Theatre was putting on a Chicago-first production of an award winning, off-Broadway and London play, Michael again leveraged a Geography Ecology (Figure 9.1). Given this pedigree, the Steppenwolf administration would likely want to see the production as well.

From what we can see in the Case, Michael appears to have little concern for the Broader Economic Ecology or how productions were funded. We have no proof that Michael lacks concern, but with the stock market doing well during the first decade of the new century (sans 9/11 and a very light recession in 2001 that barely received a news report), the availability of investment monies seemed unlimited. In this respect, there was virtually no reason for concern with this Ecology when engaging with the Theatre Ecology and working on Step 3 of the Expertise model during this period.

What we see in the ecological aspect of Case 2B, is a continuation of Case 2A. In essence, Michael was working primarily in the Theatre Ecology and knew that in order to make good decisions, he needed to immerse himself in that ecology and learn everything he could about its operation. Then he was able to leverage what he learned, including how a Geography Ecology could influence the Theatre Ecology and vice versa. After all, if *Take Me Out* wasn't an off-Broadway, London hit performed in the Steppenwolf building, would he have considered this role as seriously?

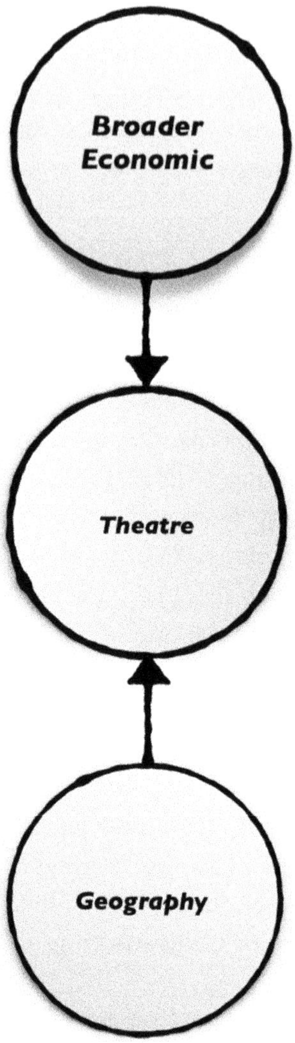

Figure 9.1 Theatre Ecology EEA Orientation.

Note

1 This is similar to the impact some 2- and 3d artists experience when their work is shown publicly; other gallery owners, artist managers, buyers, etc., attend the show and could further the artist's career through networking, commissions, offers, etc.

Bibliography

Beckman, Gary D. *The New Arts Entrepreneur: Navigating the Arts Ecologies*. London: Routledge, 2022.

Kant, Emmanuel. *Groundwork of the Metaphysics of Morals*. Translated by M.J. Gregor. Cambridge: Cambridge University Press, 2006: 42.

Takemura, Kazuhisa. *Behavioral Decision Theory: Psychological and Mathematical Descriptions of Human Choice Behavior*. 2nd edition. New York: Springer, 2021.

Trenton, Nick. *Think in Models: A Structured Approach to Clear Thinking and the Art of Decision-Making*. Self-published, Nick Trenton, 2019.

10

CASE 2C: GO FOR THE MONEY OR THE ART?

In the 12 years from 2007 when he joined the Steppenwolf ensemble to 2019, Michael Flowers settled into his acting career and his mid-life. In addition to doing live theatre as often as possible, he also picked up some television and movie roles.

He was cast in the Chicago production of *Book of Mormon* in December, 2012. The show had won nine Tony Awards in 2011, including best musical. The show ran for nearly ten months in Chicago before heading out to cities across America.[1] Michael was in the touring production until December, 2015. In addition to acting, Michael's role requires significant movement skills and some singing. He performed approximately 1,200 shows with *Book Of Mormon* over that three year period.[2] "Steady work like that is literally life-changing money," Michael shared. "It allows you to get a car loan, a house note." When Michael left *Book Of Mormon* in 2015, the family returned to the western suburbs of Chicago and settled into their new house.

Gradually, Michael increased his work on television and movies. With most roles being shot in the Chicago area, this fit into his family life. Some were one-episode opportunities, but several were multi-episode endeavors. These included 16 episodes for *Boss* in 2011–2012, and eight for *Chicago Med* in 2017–18.

The television and screen actors union, SAG/AFTRA, sets the minimum rates actors must be paid. Plus, there are levels of pay based on

DOI: 10.4324/9781003414483-13

whether an actor will be in one episode or appear in multiple episodes. Adding one more layer of complexity, an episode might take one day of an actor's time to shoot, while another may take six, due to the complexities of the episode or a particular role. The producer might want to pay the actor a "day actor" rate for the one-day shoot and a "guest star" rate for the 6-day shoot, depending on which rate saves the producer the most money. For an actor's agent and manager, it's a huge math puzzle to negotiate with the producers. Obviously, it's advantageous for the performer to get as many episodes as possible. More work is more money and more exposure. Exact pay rates above the union-set minimum are always negotiated.

Stage work is less lucrative per week than TV and movie work, but there is a guarantee of more weeks for the run of a show. A play at Steppenwolf might run five and a half weeks, plus almost as many weeks for rehearsals. Doing a show at Steppenwolf is, basically, a ten-week gig, according to Michael. Actors' Equity, the union for stage actors, sets guaranteed minimum weekly pay rates. Here, as with television and movie work, agents and managers can negotiate for more than Equity minimums.

On Broadway, minimum weekly compensation rates are much higher. This is one reason Chicago actors love when New York picks up their Chicago show. Runs are often longer there, also, which provides steadier work along with the higher pay.

To expand and diversify his portfolio of revenue-generating options, Michael created a professional-quality studio in his basement, where he could do voice-over work. With his deep voice and experience using it to express meaning and emotions, this was a good source of additional income. Michael is best known for his work on the video game *Crysis*, which began in 2007. It was followed by more versions in 2008, 2011 and 2013. He has also voiced characters for a *Star Wars* video game and others. Rates for voice over work for SAG/AFTRA actors are hourly, paying better per hour than stage or screen, but usually for only a few hours per project.

In these activities, there was always the balancing of art versus commerce. "Is it something to feed my spirit, or to pay the rent?" Michael asked. "There have been choices that were opportunities for me to stretch as an actor, roles that I might not have been ready to play at the Goodman." Doing *Othello* was an artistic challenge Michael had been eager to try. He got that chance with the small Journeyman Theater. "I remember thinking 'I don't have any business taking this role. But I should try it. Why not? My mind is agile, my memory is agile. I think I can soak up all this language.'" The same could be said of a role in Athol Fugard's *Master Harold and The Boys*, which Michael performed in a small space in downtown Chicago:

> I was thinking, 'I'm not making a lot of money off this role, but people may see it. I hope they see it. I could do really good work in this role.' In the end, it was a really rewarding experience.

Michael clearly thought about this balancing act. "A lot of artists will tell you that you take the commerce roles so you can do the artistic roles." He began taking smaller roles at big theaters so he could afford to take something at the much-smaller Journeyman to stretch himself as an artist.

Too Much Opportunity

In late 2019, two opportunities came into Michael's acting life at the same moment, directly pitting art versus commerce. The first was the chance to go to Broadway again, to remount the successful Steppenwolf production of *The Minutes* by Tracy Letts. It premiered on Steppenwolf's mainstage in the 2017–2018 season and Michael was in that production. Rehearsals would begin in January, 2020, with previews starting February 25, 2020 and opening night scheduled for March 15, 2020. The contract would be for nine months of performances.

At the same time, Michael's agent called with an offer to be in three episodes of *Fargo*, which Michael thought of, adoringly, as "an iconic television show." Shooting dates would conflict with rehearsal and preview dates for *The Minutes* on Broadway. He could not do both.

Weighing the Options

To help him think through this decision, Michael set out a list of pros and cons for each of these opportunities.

Do *The Minutes* on Broadway:

Pros:
a. Get to perform on Broadway again.
b. Nine months of steady work and income.
c. Know the show, minimal memorization work needed.

Cons:
a. Already did this show, so artistically less-appealing.
b. Already performed on Broadway.
c. Away from family for nine months, except for breaks and visits.
d. Contract length on Broadway is not guaranteed. Shows may open on Broadway but close a week later. Others go through previews and never make it to opening night.

Do three episodes of *Fargo* shooting in Chicago:

Pros:
a. Iconic TV show. It would be fun to be part of that!
b. Shoots in Chicago, so I can be home at night with family.
c. Pays well per week of shooting.
d. Only takes three weeks to do, so I can do other gigs around it.

Cons:
a. Total income will be significantly less than *The Minutes*, so I would need to find more work.

Reflection Question

1. Which opportunity should Michael take? Why?

Show me the Money

Michael told his agent to tell *Fargo*'s casting director he could not take their offer if it was just three episodes. He had another offer, for nine months of work on Broadway, which would pay significantly more and he needed to make the extra money. Michael was sorry to miss the opportunity. "I told my agent 'I hate to walk away from such an amazing show.'" But he had "a house note, a car note, and mouths to feed." He told his agent to see if there was any way he could get more money for *Fargo*, by (for example) doing four episodes instead of three.

Who would have known, even a few short years before, that Michael would one day get to choose between such great opportunities. He was fairly sure the *Fargo* counter-offer would be rejected and he'd be appearing on Broadway again. That wouldn't be the worst thing. "Actually, it would be amazing," Michael concedes. "The consolation prize wasn't so bad."

An Offer You Can't Refuse

Michael's agent called him back the next day. "Are you sitting down?" his agent began. "They're going to offer you ten episodes!" The money would be significantly better than originally offered, as he would be a regular, rather than a day player. The pay rate per episode for a regular is higher than a day player. Plus, he'd be doing seven more episodes.

His income for *Fargo* would now be more than nine months on Broadway. He says:

> This made the choice so much easier. If I had not held out—if I had not said I think I'm worth more than that—I might still have chosen to do that critically acclaimed TV show. But financially, it would not have made any sense.

About that Pandemic…

Michael did ten episodes of *Fargo*. He shot seven of them from October, 2019, until the pandemic shut down everything in mid-March of 2020. The final three episodes were shot in August and September, 2020, (with masks on between every scene and COVID testing daily).

While Michael was working on *Fargo*, the pandemic closed *The Minutes* before opening night, though it got through most of the preview performances. Production was suspended for two years, then opened on April 17, 2022. It ran for 108 performances on Broadway, closing on July 24, 2022.

Michael eventually went to Broadway again, to do a different show, *Skin of Our Teeth* by Thornton Wilder, at Lincoln Center. It ran from

April 1 to May 29, 2022, overlapping with the pandemic-delayed opening of *The Minutes*. As shows began to re-open on Broadway, eight weeks at Lincoln Center was a respectable run after a pandemic. After *Skin of Our Teeth*, Michael took a short rest, then went into *The Minutes* on June 25, 2022, for the final four weeks of its run, replacing an actor who was leaving to do a movie.

In the end, he appeared on an iconic television show and performed on Broadway in two different plays. Two opportunities he considered back in late 2019 had morphed into three actual jobs. "In this world," Michael reflects, "if you say 'My way or the highway,' you have to be ready to walk. Luckily, it worked out." In the tussle between art and commerce, at least this one time, both won.

Reflection Questions

1. What metrics could Michael use to evaluate his decision-making in this Case, starting with his decision to hold out for more money to do *Fargo*?
2. If you were Michael, what results would you show on the metrics developed in number 1 above?
3. Was Michael successful at implementing his decisions, given the fact that a world-wide pandemic interrupted much of what he planned?

Discussion: Case 2C — Go for the Money or the Art?

Summary

In this last Case of the Set, we see Michael fully engaged in the sustainability phase of his career. He is getting roles on stage and now on television and movies. Additionally, he has a voice-over business on the side. Obviously, his decisions in the previous Cases worked out well.

Given his efforts, we should not be surprised Michael finds himself with a decision between two compelling (for different reasons) roles. Michael's initial decision to take *The Minutes* was based on pay. Yes, the *Fargo* role would be a fantastic artistic opportunity, but given Michael's career priorities outlined in the previous two Cases (join the union to make better money, get into a famous acting ensemble for steady money) and the length of the run (more money), taking *The Minutes* was a no-brainer. The only issue was not being with family for nine months.

When the counter-offer arrived for *Fargo*, the pay was much better and with more episodes. Again, we shouldn't be surprised by his decision. It seems Michael has everything going his way. When COVID hits, it seems he made an even better decision by taking *Fargo*. Before we simply assume that "good luck" was responsible for Michael's success, we note that he was working towards this outcome the entire Case Set. A desire for education, passion, effort, raw talent, networking and a certain amount of dignified actions created this fortuitous situation. Certainly "good luck" isn't a bad thing (and one cannot take this for granted) but in many respects, Michael made much of this occur himself.

Yet the core of this Case lies in the decision between two opportunities and we see Michael's pro and con list for each. Getting a glimpse of how he negotiated this decision in the sub-section below is helpful. But here, we'll briefly examine the tension professional artists negotiate between artistic opportunities (i.e.: something new and challenging) and those keeping the refrigerator full.

To begin this discussion, we identify a similarity between the two; A(a)rt that aesthetically feeds us (and others) does not have a universal formula, and neither does "commercial" A(a)rt. As we know, everyone has opinions on what A(a)rt is and is not, so judging the two is not the point; recognizing A(a)rt's role in the life of an artist *is* the point. If we consider the example below as part of a venture startup experience, we may find some clarity.

Let's say a 2D Fine Artist launches a typical originals/print business with 25 original pieces, which includes five that are "good," but not necessarily as innovative, creative or technically difficult as the other 20. And let's assume it is these five that sell the most prints and were the first originals to sell. Most artists would *at least* be somewhat surprised at these sales results. Now, let's say that less than 10% of the remaining 20 pieces sold and none of these originals. Likely, the artist would be surprised—or perhaps disappointed—but perhaps in a different way.

At this point the artist needs to make a decision about his selection of original pieces for sale and their prints. Consider these five options:

1) *Take the money and run.* Create only more pieces like the ones that are selling and have a fat bank account.
2) *Take the art and run.* If the market isn't recognizing the "more creative" A(a)rt, then focus on these innovative works with a new marketing strategy.
3) *Split the effort.* Create more pieces like the ones that are popular, because they obviously sell. This minimizes the pressure for sales and the artist can be fed artistically by also working on other "more creative" pieces. With this strategy, the dollars keep coming in and the artist retains some artistic satisfaction.
4) *Forget it.* If the market can't recognize "good A(a)rt" then what's the use?
5) *Ignore it and follow the market.* Just make more prints to replenish stock.

These are typical options artists consider when faced with this decision. We should also note the many permutations of these options—based on circumstances, contexts, one's habitus, etc. There is never a "perfect" decision in these situations. However, what we can say is that a decision must occur. While it's true the potential directions forward in this example are many, there is one overarching truth: the market is (likely) being aesthetically impacted by the A(a)rt. This generates a few questions:

A. Does the artist have a responsibility to the market and if so, what is it?
B. If the artist selects option 1 or 5, are they now a "commercial" artist simply because they are following market desires? Or are they "selling out?"
C. If the artist selects options 2 or 4, are they making a decision to *not* be a "commercial" artist just to prove that their A(a)rt is not "commercial" A(a)rt?
D. Why does "commercial" A(a)rt have a bad connotation? Just because A(a)rt is popular, is that a bad thing? If markets are being aesthetically impacted, isn't that the point?
E. Who started this "money and popularity is bad" idea anyway? The classical composers we study in music history classes were constantly having their works printed and sold despite their lucrative positions in European courts. If Bach could do it and not be labeled "commercial" what's all the fuss? Besides, no one labels Bach a "commercial" composer just because he had a side hustle.

While the example above may be redundant to some, distinctions between "commercial" and "non-commercial" A(a)rt persist into the 21st century. As Michael notes:

> "A lot of artists will tell you that you take the commerce roles so you can do the artistic roles." He began taking smaller roles at big theaters so he could afford to take something at a much-smaller Journeyman to stretch him as an artist.

The quote above is simply an artist's reality—and it's been this way for centuries. Artists need money to eat. Popular A(a)rt can allow an artist to eat but can become tedious when that's all you do. When artists are bored, they want to stretch themselves artistically. The problem is this: A(a)rt that stretches a typical artist *tends* not to be as popular (i.e.: doesn't allow them to eat). We see this with regional rock bands: playing covers to pay the bills while trying to sell original music that markets struggle to accept.

In the Case, Michael is making a distinction between "commercial" A(a)rt (*The Minutes*) and *Fargo*, presumably not "commercial" A(a)rt. This distinction, however, is subjective. The authors see this distinction as simply an expression of the paragraph above. Michael already knew the play and it was nominated for eight awards—a testament to all those who put it together, certainly—but he felt something more aesthetically fulfilling about *Fargo*. For Michael to subjectively consider *The Minutes* "commercial," is understandable as its popularity makes it reasonable to assume so, even (if not especially) for an artist. And for Michael to subjectively consider *Fargo* less so, is also reasonable. To say the quiet part out loud a bit more clearly: sometimes performing the same A(a)rt day after day can jade how we think of those works. Likely, this is human nature. For Michael to choose a more rewarding artistic experience with A(a)rt he respected *and* more pay, is human nature as well.

Factors Forcing the Decision

Of course, having the luxury to choose from a few great opportunities is enviable and it seems Michael's efforts during this Case Set are yielding results. As a part of this work, we can determine (at least in part) his priorities: long term runs that pay well (i.e.: financial security), "artistic roles" and family. His use of the Expertise model is working well, his understanding about the Theatre Ecology and nearby ecological systems (i.e.: Film and TV) appears clear and leverageable.

If we look deeper at the opportunity, we have two distinct options from which Michael could choose. The first (do *The Minutes* on Broadway) was based on 1) pay, 2) prior experience with the art, 3) duration of the run and 4) being on Broadway again. The second (do *Fargo* for three episodes) offered 1) the art, 2) an improved resume and 3) he could be with his family during shooting. Initially, he felt compelled to choose the first option—do *The Minutes* again—because of the pay. Once his counter-offer was accepted, making the pay roughly the same for either option, he chose *Fargo*, because of the A(a)rt.[3]

We should be clear that Michael *is* concerned about his artistic life. Clearly, he wanted *Fargo*, but was willing to take *The Minutes* primarily because of the pay. We could say that Michael is making the decision based on pay, and some would suggest he is making a "commercial" art decision. Things get complicated when he accepts the revised *Fargo* offer. In Michael's mind, this was the more exciting opportunity artistically *and now it came with better pay*. So, did he then make the same "commercial" decision by accepting *Fargo*?

And who decides what a "commercial" decision is, anyway?

Parameters surrounding decisions are not always static; they can evolve or change drastically. Indeed, "things" changed for Michael: length of the opportunity and the pay. Taking *Fargo* met more parameters for Michael and pay was just a parameter shifting in his favor. Was it luck? Perhaps—but Michael had little control over the counter-offer.[4] He just needed to make another decision because the parameters around the decision changed.

We should note the results of these decisions. *The Minutes* closed because of COVID. Michael appeared in *Fargo* despite COVID. He appeared on Broadway in both *Skin of Our Teeth* and *The Minutes* after his final decision to take the ten episode run in *Fargo*. Did things work out for Michael? Yes. But many of these outcomes were unforeseeable when his decisions were made. COVID came as a complete surprise to the entire world and Michael had no idea about the counter-offer until it arrived. Thus, we should not say that Michael was necessarily "lucky," but that due to the *dynamic nature of circumstance*, his decision to ask for more and then take *Fargo* allowed him to capitalize on opportunities as they emerged. After all, if he stuck with *The Minutes*, he would not have had the opportunity to do *Skin of Our Teeth* or *Fargo*, and would likely be in a different position financially during this period.

Hindsight aside, Joshua Rothman opines that decisions "...flow from (one's) values" and are simply a "(subjective and ethical) value maximizing equation."[5] Michael's personal values (established in the previous two Cases) are driving much of his decision making in this Case. Indeed, throughout this Set, we see him making decisions that are in line with—and supporting—his personal values. Case 2C is an explicit example of an artist aware of himself and his values. As Rothman suggests, Michael is making decisions to *amplify* his values as they manifest in the life he's created. As the preceding paragraph outlines, a value-based and deliberately-driven life can generate results.

Decision Model

The pros and cons list in the Case narrative tells us explicitly how Michael is thinking about this decision. As discussed above, we know Michael's priorities and how he ranks (or weighs) these priorities. We also know why he continued to use the Expertise model in the previous two Cases. It makes sense, then, that once he reaches the sustainability phase of his career, his decision strategy would reflect this experience and leverage different decision-making models. Here, we argue that Michael is using the Analytical model, which demonstrates (when the counter-offer arrives) that when decision-making parameters or circumstances change, one can choose to either stay with previous decision-making strategies or use a different model; in this Case, the results speak for themselves.

Step 1 (Gather ALL information) is unmistakable as we see Michael engage the decision; there seems to be little he missed. Demonstrating his experience at this point in his career, Step 2 (Verify that you understand the data) is only lightly addressed in the Case narrative as he has a clear understanding of the Theatre Ecology (see below). Step 3 (Verify the impact of the data) emerges as the primary focus of Michael's decision making in the narrative. We see this when the counter-offer emerges: he returns to this Step and evaluates the offer's impact with what is important to his professional and non-professional life. Since Michael appears to have a decision that is (arguably) somewhat binary, we do not see him engaging in Step 4 (Eliminate data…) before he responds to the counter-offer, Step 5 (Objectively decide…).

Michael's decision-making model choices are clear in this Case Set and we should note an *evolution*. In Cases 2A and 2B, he uses the Expertise model and experiences the Theatre Ecology's dynamic elements. This is a reasonable choice since he 1) wants to be an "expert," 2) is learning about the profession and 3) becoming a working actor is his focus. However, in this Case, he switches to the Analytical model and stays with it throughout the narrative despite the counter-offer, which seems reasonable once an artist or arts venture reaches the sustainability phase. Therefore, in dynamic decision-making environments, *adjusting* one's decision-making strategy is a valid response.

Ecology Discussion

There is no doubt that at this point in Michael's career, he has deep understanding (and perhaps a comfortableness) with the Theatre Ecology—and as we learn, a TV and Film Industry Ecology as well. We see no struggle understanding an ecology's element or its impact. He is focused on a decision that is a *result* of both ecology's standard operation. Elements are known, their operations and relationships within the ecologies are both recognized and leveraged; the Case is about a decision occurring *as a result of—and previously acting on— this knowledge*. Michael is making decisions about his career at least partially based on the ecologies in which he finds himself. This is the perfect example of the *Entrepreneurial Ecology of the Arts* value in arts venture decision making.

Addendum: Is Michael an Entrepreneur?

Lastly, we return to a question posed in the discussion section of Case 2A: is Michael an entrepreneur? As one may surmise, the answer is not as clear as we would like.[6] Michael is not starting a business, he is not legally incorporated according to the Case narrative and not producing a *tangible* product per se, though some might argue he provides a "service." He appears not to be innovating the art of acting (or his roles) and is following a path of replication in his career trajectory. He is, however, engaging in a value exchange between the producers of the plays and their audiences. Additionally, he recognizes opportunities and takes risks.

Some would argue it doesn't matter if Michael is an entrepreneur or not. Others could read the paragraph above and note that according to many definitions, he is likely an entrepreneur though not traditionally defined. Both positions are valid. For those more on the business side of the argument, being incorporated is the legal definition of a business; Michael is not incorporated, so how could he be an entrepreneur? On the other hand, there is a clear value exchange, which puts him on the entrepreneurial on-ramp. Some could suggest that Michael lies in the middle of the argument: he's not a business, but he's acting entrepreneurially. The slight problem with this argument is that he also isn't innovating. Michael is following a well-worn path for most actors and the Case Set supports this argument. Others may not see the validity of the question at all.

However, the authors suggest that Michael *is* an entrepreneur. When attempting to answer this question, we suggest 1) consider the definitions above *in the context of the individual or their circumstance*, 2) accept that the answer may be context-based and 3) that "being an entrepreneur" or "being entrepreneurial" may be a matter of degree. For example, if a pastry artist with a middle-class background opens a bakery in an urban area, they are replicating a pre-existing model. If the bakery produces a notable or popular pastry, then it's simply a good pastry. If it's the best pastry in the state, are they considered entrepreneurs simply because they produce the best pastry in the state? No, they are judged only on the product—just like a professional athlete. However, if the artist experienced years of hardships during their formative years and overcame them, are they *more likely* to be considered "entrepreneurial" *in some way*? Or does the bakery just produce the best pastry in the state?

The example immediately above argues that context matters. When it comes to this Case and this question, we can form our opinion based on extrinsic definitions or we can form it based on Michael's context. It is hard to come to the conclusion that Michael is an entrepreneur since he is *mostly* replicating the model of professional actors before him. But if he *is* an entrepreneur of some degree, the proof likely resides *within* Michael. In Case 2A, we saw that he attended college as an English major, not a theatre major and assumed a financial risk to become an actor. Throughout the Case Set, we see Michael not only embracing these decisions, but moving through his career with passion, purpose and dignity—a set of admirable if not *entrepreneurial* acts for those among us lacking these attributes. He innovates (at least moderately) by choosing non-acting jobs to advance his knowledge of the Theatre Ecology. Michael recognizes and acts on opportunities supporting and honoring his sense of self, *through* his decision to be a professional actor.

Let us consider the following: being entrepreneurial doesn't require a business degree, legally registering a business or creating an innovative product. Instead, taking risks to act on opportunities that innovate, advance, feed and justify *self* when one's habitus is suspicious of this path, may be more entrepreneurial than all the definitions of the word combined—despite our own self-doubts. Being "entrepreneurial" then, might also mean being "entrepreneurial" *for* one's life *because* of one's goals, desires, circumstances, context or upbringing.

Notes

1 The show was still in Chicago in May of 2013 when Michael's son was born, allowing him to attend that important family event. Once the show went on the road, his wife and young son were able to travel with him.
2 He went back into the role in 2019 for six weeks on Broadway, to fill-in for an actor who went on medical leave.
3 We note that the financial stability of one's family is a vital concern held by most. Making decisions based on money is common in many arts disciplines when one reaches the sustainability (and especially family) phase of their career.
4 Some would suggest Michael had more control than one might think. For example, he "…told his agent to see if there was any way he could get more money for *Fargo*, by (for example) doing four episodes instead of three."
5 Joshua Rothman, "The Art of Decision Making," *The New Yorker*, Jan. 14, 2019. Available at: https://www.newyorker.com/magazine/2019/01/21/the-art-of-decision-making.
6 To remind the reader, our working "definition of an entrepreneur" from Chapter 1 is someone who 1) takes risks, 2) innovates and 3) recognizes opportunities. The extensions are starting a business and engaging in a value exchange.

Bibliography

Beckman, Gary D. *The New Arts Entrepreneur: Navigating the Arts Ecologies*. London: Routledge, 2022.

Bikart, Joseph. *The Art of Decision Making: How we Move from Indecision to Smart Choices*. London: Watkins Publishing, 2019.

Rothman, Joshua. "The Art of Decision Making." *The New Yorker*, Jan. 14, 2019. Available at: https://www.newyorker.com/magazine/2019/01/21/the-art-of-decision-making.

Trenton, Nick. *Think in Models: A Structured Approach to Clear Thinking and the Art of Decision-Making*. Self-published, Nick Trenton, 2019.

CASE SET 3

FROM MUSICIAN TO EXECUTIVE DIRECTOR

11
CASE 3A: TROMBONE OR NON-PROFIT?

The caller had the kind of news a young trombone player likes to hear: 23 gigs for Patrick's brass trio in the next 30 days. He knew several events were already scheduled for his larger brass quintet the same month. It was suddenly looking like a very busy January.

Patrick hung up the phone, then sat quietly for a few minutes, thinking, reflecting on his life as a freelance trombonist for the past six and a half years since he graduated from college. There had been some decent gigs—principal trombonist for two regional orchestras, a live broadcast on WFMT radio with the brass quintet he founded in college, two years as featured musicians every day of the holiday season on the main floor at the Carson Pirie Scott department store with another brass quintet, downtown guest performances with the Chicago Brass Quintet, six shows of Magic Flute with Opera Midwest. Good gigs, but no big breakthroughs to good paying work.

The 23 new gigs were good news. Still, Patrick sensed he was at a crossroads. He could keep doing freelancing. He also had other creative opportunities. Could he do it all? Did he want to?

Freelancing had been up and down over those nearly seven years. Initially, Patrick got some calls for gigs from his college trombone teacher. That teacher was very good to Patrick, helping him get started and become known around Chicago. Patrick was still a long way from "first-call" trombonist in town, so he might look forward to moving

 DOI: 10.4324/9781003414483-15

up that chain as he did more gigs and people got to know him. Still, it had been almost seven years. There were lots of gigs he had yet to crack—like playing extra with the Lyric Opera Orchestra, or maybe someday with the Chicago Symphony, the big dream. National dance companies came through Chicago and needed a pick-up orchestra, yet Patrick had not been in that orchestra. Lately, there were fewer calls for freelance gigs.

The two brass quintets Patrick played in were constantly hustling for gigs, which meant some paid work like weddings and events. There was also the occasional concert featuring only them, such as at Woodstock Opera House, where they were so well-received that the venue quickly booked another concert for the next year. Both quintets were in flux, as the college bonds keeping them together lessened and, of course, some were now married. The feeling was just not the same when the lead trumpeter in one quintet, Bob Murray, moved to Canada in August, 1986, for a real job in an orchestra there. That quintet found a new trumpeter and hoped that feeling would return over time. Playing in the quintets was the most musically-satisfying experience for Patrick, as they rehearsed regularly and played at a high level. Freelance gigs that were one rehearsal and a performance were more stressful for him and yielded an unsatisfying musical result.

A brass trio was an offshoot of the brass quintet that Bob Murray led. That trio played almost exclusively for school gigs, mostly booked by one source, the same one that was calling Patrick now for 23 gigs in the next month. For school performances, the three players had their schtick down and student audiences loved it; the musicians just showed up.

In 1983 Patrick started, with Bob and his wife Molly, a non-profit called The Performance Company (TPC). It was the best of times and the worst of times to start a non-profit. The jobs market was at a real low. Patrick's brother Scott was walking down the street in 1983 on his way to a job interview in Portland, Oregon and happened to see the front page of the daily newspaper at a newsstand: "Worst Unemployment Since 1940!" screamed the headlines. Thus, starting one's own thing to make some money was suddenly a decent option. Additionally, the stock market was soaring, which made it attractive for donors to give generously from their gains. Bob's father was having success as a stockbroker, and provided initial funding to get TPC started.

The Performance Company gave each of the founders a chance to explore performances that nobody was hiring them for: creative combinations of music, theater and dance. Using the first few years of donated funds, they produced shows each of them wanted to produce: a four performer version of *Carmen* (with Molly singing Carmen), a 12-performer version of *The Nutcracker*, featuring Bob's brass quintet arrangements and a full production of *The Soldier's Tale* for musicians, dancers and actors. Then, Bob and Molly stepped away, leaving it to Patrick to decide what to do next.

Luckily, a new kind of opportunity came along just as they had run out of funding and ideas: artists-in-residence in elementary schools. As a solo trombonist, Patrick was an artist-in- residence through the Illinois Arts Council. He enjoyed the combination of working with schools to help their brass students improve, meeting with local music teachers, and having solo performances in the community. There was also time to practice trombone. He was a celebrity wherever he went in these small towns and that was a surprising treat, too.

In March 1985, the company did its first residency as a team of six, in Danville, Illinois. The energy was super-charged when six artists walked into Liberty Elementary on day one of their four-week residency, and it built over time via classroom demonstrations of their music, drama and dance skills, plus weekly performances for the whole school, and nightly artist dinners at the house they were sharing. Patrick loved that experience, so he pursued more company residencies and found two more schools in Chicago that wanted them, and one in Springfield, IL. They just finished the Chicago project when he received the phone call for 23 brass trio gigs. His mind was on the coming residencies.

The trio and quintet work, plus the residencies for different combinations of musicians, actors and dancers, had kept Patrick busy all fall. Within the trio and quintets, he took on more of the management as original players left and new players arrived. For the in-school residencies, he managed all the administrative tasks before, during and after. All of this was working fine and he was handling it all quite well despite his busy schedule. However, the call to do 23 brass trio gigs in the next month, added to a few quintet events already on the calendar, was more than Patrick thought he could handle.

It's Not You, Trombone, It's Me

Patrick was reconsidering his commitment to freelancing for several years by that point. The personnel changes in the brass ensembles made them more of a hassle and less fun. It seemed like they were always training some new player. The two regional orchestras in which he was principal trombone had occasional high moments, but these gigs mainly involved too much rehearsal time—and the pay was lousy.

Friends were getting jobs in full-time orchestras. Patrick wasn't even signing up for auditions. Bob was now playing second trumpet in the Victoria Symphony in Canada. His letters told Patrick all about it, insisting he was as good a trombonist as any in Victoria and that Patrick could secure an orchestra job if 1) he really wanted one and 2) pursued a position.

Trombone was Patrick's "thing" since he was in high school in Oregon. It had given him purpose and meaning and pride for many years. On the other hand, this other thing, The Performance Company, let him be "creatively creative," as he described it to a friend in those years. As he wrote to his trombone teacher from high school, about TPC, "I'm not just one thing or another any longer. Not just a trombonist or a salesman or whatever. I'm an 'all-around-creative-kind-of-guy.'"

Patrick needed to decide: was he going to do all the trombone gigs in the next month, thereby needing to cut back on his The Performance Company activity and hope it didn't wreck the momentum that TPC had been building? Or was it time to cut back on the trombone, so he could give The Performance Company its best chance at success for the future?

Reflection Question

1. How would you approach reconciling both the facts of the Case and Patrick's feelings thus far?

Wanting to Have Your Cake and Eat it, Too

As Patrick saw it at that moment, the problem was this: Should he do the many trio gigs or hire someone to do them for him? Doing all the gigs would mean more money in his pocket, but it could also mean shortchanging preparation for the residencies that The Performance Company previously scheduled.

The criteria that formed in his head for considering a decision included these:

1. Which has more future potential, financially and as a stable career?
2. Which makes me happier, brings me energy?
3. Which provides the best opportunities to be "creatively creative?"
4. Which provides money right now, so I don't starve?
5. Which keeps my options open for the future beyond this next month's gigs?

For Patrick, the most important of these criteria was future potential, both financially and as a stable career. He married a year earlier in December of 1985 and his wife was an established professional photographer with a steady, though not huge, income. So, his priorities shifted somewhat to thinking about the future, not just where the next dollar was coming from.

A close second was thinking about what would provide him energy. Patrick's good friend Cindy Jackson offered a simple formula for thinking about romantic relationships, which he now found useful for thinking about work. "Are you *getting* more energy from it than you are *giving* to it?" Cindy said if the answer was "no," it might be time for a change. Being "creatively creative" gave him lots of energy, so that was the "how" for getting more.

Patrick wanted to have his cake and eat it, too. He was hoping there was a way to continue playing trombone so he wouldn't be walking away from the dream he had for many years, while cutting back so he could pursue this newer project. Yet, he worried it might be like being in serious relationships with two people at the same time—it doesn't work out very well in reality.

Organizationally, there were several very positive signs of future potential for The Performance Company. For one, they found customers who were willing to pay for the organization's product—residencies in schools by a small team of artists. Starting with several underwritten by the Illinois Arts Council, they branched out to ones paid for by the schools themselves in Chicago, through their Title One dollars.[1] Nearly every school in Chicago Public Schools had these dollars to spend, so the potential was significant. Secondly, they received their first foundation funding. Woods Charitable was their first funder, giving $5,000 to help underwrite their first Chicago residency. That grant was followed by smaller grants from the Chicago Community Trust and the Fel-Pro Mecklenburg Foundation. Like the schools, there were many foundations, so the potential seemed even greater.

The data assessing Patrick's future as a freelance trombonist was, at best, mixed. Gigs from contractors and his college trombone teacher were on the decline. Brass quintet gigs had also died off, as members moved on with their lives and nobody was actively pursuing gigs for them as a group. Doing brass trio gigs in schools for the rest of his life did not feel like a promising future.

Patrick was simply not pursuing an orchestra job: practicing orchestral excerpts, flying to other cities to take auditions, etc. A letter to his father from that time indicates he was, at best, ambivalent about playing in an orchestra full-time: "I left college all set to find an orchestra to play in. But I guess I was never really 'set' to do that. I just had reservations about sitting in an orchestra for extended periods of time."

As for getting more energy than he was giving, he thought the scales definitely tipped away from the trombone. For one, freelancing was getting old. "I quit all that stuff I was doing that was just noise…like playing BS orchestra gigs," Patrick told a friend. And this to another friend: "Playing in some BS orchestra or working some BS music job does little for society."

On the other hand, he was getting great energy from all he was putting into The Performance Company: "I'll starve doing this thing, but I'll get lots of kicks before that day comes. Kicks—that may be what life is about," he wrote. Patrick was feeling energized by the early success of his nonprofit, and feeling confident it would lead to good things over time. Writing to his father, he shared: "Never, not even with the brass ensembles have I felt so positive and sure of a positive outcome." Pretty heady stuff.

After considering all the data, the options available to Patrick were, basically, these:

1. Play all the gigs and stop doing TPC for a month.
2. Play some of the gigs and keep going half-speed at The Performance Company.
3. Play none of the gigs, by hiring a trombone player, and go full speed at TPC.

Patrick weighed the evidence and his feelings. On the one hand, he was not emotionally ready to abandon the trombone altogether. He invested years into being a great musician, which was the core of his identity and self-worth since high school. This was important to him, even if it was only an emotional habit. On the other hand, The Performance Company was pulling him away from the past and into a future of 1) more demand for what he could provide, 2) more variety in daily tasks and 3) more potential for growth. Patrick did not want to do anything to slow that progress in any way.

After giving himself a little talk about the significance of the choice before him, Patrick picked up the phone, called another trombone player and offered him all his gigs for the next month. If he hated being away from the trombone after a month, he could always go back to it, perhaps with new energy to offer.

Patrick saw the call as the beginning of the end of his trombone career. Once the trio had another trombonist for those 23 gigs, they could get along without him. The French horn player was nice enough to call Patrick after a month and see if he wanted to come back, but by then, he had changed. He was used to the idea that he wasn't playing trombone anymore and was okay with the decision. The thing is, he no longer cared, which was a big surprise to him. He was now something other than a trombone player, for the first time in many years. Patrick turned her down. That was really the end.

Does Patrick regret his decision? Not often nor in any big way. Overwhelmingly, he celebrates that decision, made by a younger and less-experienced "him." What Patrick received in return for that decision was more energy than the considerable energy he happily and eagerly put into music, for 38 years. Whether it was as clear and conscious as described above, his process was good enough to come to the right conclusion, the right decision for him.

Reflection Questions

1. Given the data presented, do you agree with Patrick's decision?
2. If you were in the same situation, which decision-making model would you use to solve this problem? Why?
3. If you believe Patrick made the wrong decision or used an ineffective decision-making model, how would the decision change if you were in charge?

Discussion: Case 3A—Trombone or Non-Profit?

Summary

The beginning of this Case Set outlines a "life decision." With the almost infinite rationale, processes or methodologies one could use with any decision, we must begin with the following: decisions of any kind are unique, contextual and most of all, idiomatic. Most readers would likely agree, but perhaps we can (thanks to our colleagues in the social sciences) articulate how this agreement operates.

Without getting into the sociology weeds more than we have to, there are two terms that might help us understand the decisions we make, and shed light on the collective "us:" *habitus* and *field*. To dramatically over-simplify this theory popularized by Pierre Bourdieu, one's habitus can be defined as: the sum of a person's total experiences when engaging in different fields (i.e.: social contexts). Thought of in this way, we could surmise that individuals confronted with the exact situation may either reach the same or different decision based on their habitus. For example, if Patrick had different parents (a household *field*), was interested in another art form (an artistic *field*) or attended a different high school (an educational *field*), his decision may have been different or the process he undertook may have changed (*or not*) his choice to pursue The Performance Company (TPC). According to Bourdieu then, the myriad of different fields an individual encounters plays a significant role in not only the decision someone makes, but the process they undertake to make that decision.

Leaving Bourdieu, we can begin to identify what Patrick encountered. Initially, there were two significant changes: fewer freelance jobs and an important member (Bob Murray) moved to Canada. This resulted in trying to find a new member and rehearse the ensemble to a level Patrick found acceptable—thereby establishing the initial dissatisfaction. Coupled with what emerged as a multitude of tensions (23 gigs versus established elementary school residencies) the pressure was building. The desire in this case was simply artistic satisfaction through music making, though the tension of administering and rehearsing the different ensembles—in addition to TPC—only added to the feeling of something needing to change. Indeed, trying to realize a life goal versus being overwhelmed trying to accomplish that goal emerges as the primary tension requiring a decision. Perhaps better put: Patrick's feeling of being overwhelmed yielded a sense of dissatisfaction, which is what his decision needed to solve.

As the decision emerges, it becomes clear that the top two priorities for Patrick are future potential (in all realms) and happiness; both are reasonable priorities. However, he is clear that the first priority (future potential) was important, yes, but his newlywed wife's ability to provide a somewhat steadier income helped to support the second priority (happiness). This, in addition to the assistance of a stockbroker relative who initially helped to fund The Performance Company, demonstrates that entrepreneurial ventures typically begin with many hands. As artists, we know that much of our work requires others and entrepreneurs are (despite the various pseudo-myths surrounding the phenomenon) no different; support of all kinds comes in many forms.

Somewhat predictably, the first decision was typical: can we solve both problems at the same time or at least mitigate them at some level to avoid the real decision? We see this in the three possible decision options, which amount to going down a road and being gently confronted with the conundrum Robert Frost's poem "The Road Less Traveled" eloquently describes. Here, Patrick sees three options to accomplish the two priorities mentioned above. We should also note that the process of determining priorities and crafting them into potential solutions 1) typically takes time while one struggles with sensations of being overwhelmed or dissatisfied and 2) requires an objective sorting through these feelings and refining them into a few, targeted actions.

As the freelance gigs were drying up and Patrick was watching "this music thing" slip away, a wonderful realization occurred: he really wasn't into this orchestra "thing" after all. This realization allowed a decision to emerge, resulting in a commitment to a new field that would change Patrick's habitus. To say that his life changed because of this decision is true and Bourdieu, we believe, would agree. Indeed, some decisions truly are life changing. Others, not so much. Note again that some options were available to Patrick because of the modest financial investment present in a relationship *field* (i.e.: the stockbroker relative). This generated more potential choice of actions to manifest the two priorities. Importantly, however, we note that sometimes, choice is a luxury. Entrepreneurs of all kinds encounter choice when faced with an opportunity or a matter of survival; yet at times, there really is only one choice. This is especially true when one is trying to negotiate matters of personal ethics, belief systems, desire or dignity, among others.

Factors Forcing the Decision

Obviously, a few matters were helping to create this decision. First, freelance music jobs were becoming harder and harder to secure. Second, administering the different ensembles became laborious, which led to a sense of being overwhelmed. This created a questioning of Patrick's life goal (or purpose) in becoming a full-time orchestra musician. What we see here is a tension—if not the central aspect of this case: was being overwhelmed with little artistic satisfaction the fulfillment of his life goal?

Previous experience, a clear articulation of goals and being alert to personal satisfaction (artistically or otherwise) combined to force the decision. This sense of fulfillment is as much a feeling as it is a reality. While we may need to endure situations where we do not feel fulfilled, Patrick was also sensing that being constantly overwhelmed and questioning his artistic dissatisfaction was simply not the life he wanted.

Lastly, we see something rather common in decisions like these: overwhelming data. With gigs drying up, key ensemble members leaving, increased administrative responsibilities, continued reflection upon one's life goals and this sense of dissatisfaction increasing, it is clear that facts and feelings were both pointing to something. If we consider the option of The Performance Company, we see more positive facts and feelings in terms of life and artistic satisfaction. While risky, Patrick chose TPC and became its Executive Director; this trajectory came with its own set of challenges.

Decision Model

The vast majority of case studies emerging from our business school colleagues focus on venture startup, sustainability or scaling; the ones that follow in this Set are no different. One could make the argument that this Case is the most important (or at least the most timely) for emerging arts entrepreneurs still in college classrooms and in the midst of their entrepreneurial training. Yet as mentioned in the introductory chapters, we make many decisions every day, but far fewer about our long-term lives. Partners, careers, jobs and life trajectories tend to be "the big ones" and the decisions we make immediately after our college career are probably the most important. Not because they're critical necessarily (there's typically time to move into new directions if a first set of decisions does not work out as planned), but because they provide a foundation…sometimes solid and sometimes not.

In Case 3A, Patrick is clearly aware of a number of ecological systems: self (emotional, physical, etc.) and the Broader Economic Ecology (to a lesser degree than a business major but arguably more than a typical, trained artist). However, his original goals (being a trombonist in a symphony and having enough money to survive) became subject to change. This malleability was based on his *habitus* and the *fields* in which he resided at the time and an openness to interrogating his goals and trusting his feelings. (Note that one's *habitus* and its engaged *fields* are dynamic, just like any ecological system.) Lastly, we can see (rather strongly) that Patrick is data driven—whether it be data pertaining to self or things more quantitative.

This penchant for data of all kinds and Patrick's subsequent analysis suggests that he would feel most comfortable using a decision-making model from the Linear grouping. As far as determining which one, we can check this hypothesis by testing the Step 4 (*Eliminate Data*) parameters and the "if-this-then-that" *feel* of the Analytical model. In part two of the Case, he articulates a number of options (Step 4 of the Rational model) and is **not** eliminating data (Step 4 of the Analytical model). Additionally, though there is some analysis for every option (Step 5 of the Rational model), the final decision is not objective (Step 5 of the Analytical model) and appears more goal-based (even though his goals appear to be changing during the decision-making process). Patrick's process, then, is not an "if-this-then-that," analytical exercise where a "logical" decision simply emerges from empirical data. Further, since his entire ecology of self (emotions, for example) and goals (happiness and life fulfillment) are clearly a part of the decision-making process, this points to a Rational model.

If we go one step further, steps two and three (Identify Decision Criteria and Allocate Weights) are helpful. For evidence of these steps, we see Patrick explicit in identifying five criteria (Step 2 Identify Decision Criteria) at the beginning of Part 3. Additionally, he speaks about weighting the criteria throughout the last paragraph.

Yet if we were to prove our theory beyond a reasonable doubt, Step 8 (Evaluate the Decision) would be the *coup de grace*. The penultimate paragraph of the case demonstrates the evaluative outcome when the Case states that "…he no longer cared (about being a trombonist), which was a big surprise to him," which emerges somewhat quickly after the decision is implemented (Step 7). While there were many decision-making processes (i.e.: steps) occurring both linearly and somewhat simultaneously in the Case as data was identified, what is also occurring is a radical change in identity: from a working artist to an executive director of an arts non-profit organization. Throughout Case 3A, we could view this decision-making process as simply a "big life decision"—and it certainly was—yet we could also view this process (in more meta terms) as a disentanglement of a previous identity, which was already in process perhaps before he realized. If viewed in this way, it is not surprising Patrick came to the evaluation he did so quickly. Clearly the entire Case is based on a sense of discontentment about the state of things, and with that, the frustration generated by this dissatisfaction. In some sense, this frustration likely created the criteria for Step 8 (Evaluate the Decision), hence why a quick and positive evaluation was reached so quickly. Additionally, the last paragraph of the Case is straightforward in its evaluation.

For emerging arts entrepreneurs, launching an arts venture will result in an identity (and *habitus*) change based on new circumstances and *fields*. Patrick would no longer be solely an artist, but an artist who is also a founder of an arts organization. As frequently advocated in *The New Arts Entrepreneur*, one should remain an artist first and an executive second. This is why both the formation of the four-person business team and crafting your position as one of decision maker is vital to one's life satisfaction, identity, venture sustainability and frankly, artistic integrity. In essence, when one approaches an arts business in this manner, it is far easier to insert one's innate creativity, artistic intuition and skills into the operation and decision making of the business. We see this when he states " ...I'm an 'all-around-creative-kind-of-guy.'" So yes, one becomes a different person when launching an A(a)rts venture, but one who can retain their artistic integrity in this new medium of "business."

Lastly, one point about the Linear grouping is the term "data." We could argue that "goals" and "feelings" are more qualitative than quantitative: 1) a goal is a desired outcome which could be tangible or intangible and 2) "feelings" can be both a goal and an intangible data point. Yes, both are subjective, but "data" nonetheless. A "feeling" then, can—and likely should—be weighted in the decision process. Its weight should be subjectively determined and could rank higher or lower than empirical data.

Ecology Discussion

In Case 3A, the ecologies encountered primarily focus on the Broader Economic and Non-Profit. For example, Patrick points to the Broader Economic Ecology when he mentions that "The jobs market was at a real low," (i.e.: the Unemployment Rate was extraordinarily high) and he is correct. In January of 1983 the Rate was 10.4% and declined to 8.3% at the end of the year—far higher than the roughly 5–6%, which indicates near full employment. (see Table 11.1).[2]

Table 11.1 US Unemployment Rate 1980–1989

	Jan	*Feb*	*Mar*	*Apr*	*May*	*Jun*	*Jul*	*Aug*	*Sep*	*Oct*	*Nov*	*Dec*
1980	6.3	6.3	6.3	6.9	7.5	7.6	7.8	7.7	7.5	7.5	7.5	7.2
1981	7.5	7.4	7.4	7.2	7.5	7.5	7.2	7.4	7.6	7.9	8.3	8.5
1982	8.6	8.9	9.0	9.3	9.4	9.6	9.8	9.8	10.1	10.4	10.8	10.8
1983	10.4	10.4	10.3	10.2	10.1	10.1	9.4	9.5	9.2	8.8	8.5	8.3
1984	8.0	7.8	7.8	7.7	7.4	7.2	7.5	7.5	7.3	7.4	7.2	7.3
1985	7.3	7.2	7.2	7.3	7.2	7.4	7.4	7.1	7.1	7.1	7.0	7.0
1986	6.7	7.2	7.2	7.1	7.2	7.2	7.0	6.9	7.0	7.0	6.9	6.6
1987	6.6	6.6	6.6	6.3	6.3	6.2	6.1	6.0	5.9	6.0	5.8	5.7
1988	5.7	5.7	5.7	5.4	5.6	5.4	5.4	5.6	5.4	5.4	5.3	5.3
1989	5.4	5.2	5.0	5.2	5.2	5.3	5.2	5.2	5.3	5.3	5.4	5.4

Table 11.2 US GDP 1979–1987

Year	Q1	Q2	Q3	Q4
1979	0.7	0.4	3.0	1.0
1980	1.3	–8.0	–0.5	7.7
1981	8.1	–2.9	4.9	–4.3
1982	–6.1	1.8	–1.5	0.2
1983	5.4	9.4	8.2	8.6
1984	8.1	7.1	3.9	3.3
1985	3.9	3.6	6.2	3.0
1986	3.8	1.8	3.9	2.2
1987	3.0	4.4	3.5	7.0
1988	2.1	5.4	2.4	5.4

The reason the Rate was so high was because two recessions occurred almost back-to-back: one beginning in the second quarter of 1980 and ending in the first quarter of 1981; another began in the first quarter of 1982 and ending in the first quarter of 1983.[3] (See Table 11.2). What made the early 1980s more difficult economically for the country was a prolonged period of unemployment above 5%. In fact, the country didn't experience full employment until the next decade.

Lastly, the case points out that the stock market was "soaring" in early 1983. We would typically think that during a recession and period of high unemployment, the stock market would reflect these more depressing numbers. Indeed, that is the case—but only for a time. If we look at the DOW in Figure 11.1, we see the stock market helping to pull the country out of the 1982 Q3 slump. In this case, the DOW was a leading indicator of things to come.[4] Early 1983, then, was a good time economically for Patrick to make the decision to launch (or commit to) a new venture.

As with the Broader Economic Ecology decision, Patrick also has a good understanding of the Non-Profit Ecology. Specifically, knowing that many foundations partially invest their endowments in the stock markets was another positive indicator. This meant that soon, foundations were going to see a larger ROI (Return on Investment) in the

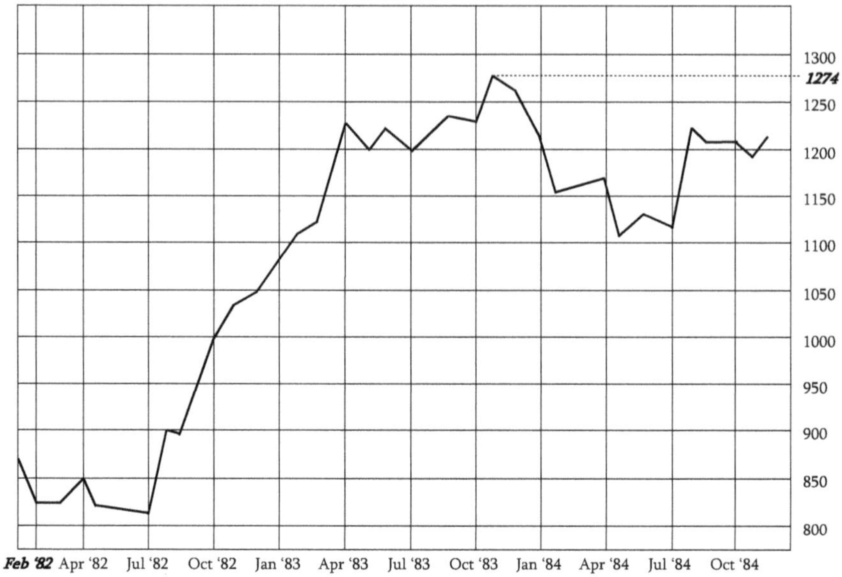

Figure 11.1 Dow Jones Industrial Average 1982–1984.

coming quarters, which they would have to grant to non-profit organizations. Having a portfolio of new funders (Woods Charitable, Chicago Community Trust and the Fel-Pro Mecklenburg Foundation), pursuing The Performance Company as Patrick's full-time effort was beginning to seem like a good start, especially with the momentum these new grants fostered. Additionally, with Title 1 dollars from the US government that needed to be spent by schools—not to mention potential city dollars—TPC had another revenue stream besides foundations and private philanthropy.

Many important Broader Economic Ecology indicators were pointing to the author committing to The Performance Company as a solid decision. This, coupled with Patrick's feelings about his musical goal, gigs dropping off and TPC appearing as a good way to achieve his two priorities, meant "the potential was significant" and, as we'll see in the following cases, it certainly was a tremendous opportunity.

Notes

1 Title One was a part of President Johnson's "War on Poverty." It was authorized by Congress in 1965 with the intent to provide federal financial support to public schools. The law was modernized in 2001 and renamed the "No Child Left Behind Act."
2 Bureau of Labor Statistics, "Databases, Calculators and Tables by Subject." Available at: https://data.bls.gov/data.
3 The US economy *typically* enters a recession after two successive quarters of **negative** GDP growth. Contrastingly, the economy emerges from a recession after two successive quarters of **positive** GDP growth. *Bureau for Economic Analysis* data for Table 11.2 is based on the Federal Reserve Bank of St. Louis (FRED), "Table 1.1.5. Gross Domestic Product: Quarterly." Available at: https://fred.stlouisfed.org/release/tables?rid=53&eid=12998&od=2023-04-01#.
4 Data for Figure 11.1 from Barchart.com, "Dow Industrial Average." Accessed December 21, 2023. Available at: https://www.barchart.com/stocks/quotes/$DOWI/interactive-chart.

Bibliography

Barchart.com. "Dow Industrial Average." Accessed Dec. 21, 2023. Available at: https://www.barchart.com/stocks/quotes/$DOWI/interactive-chart.

Beckman, Gary D. *The New Arts Entrepreneur: Navigating the Arts Ecologies*. London: Routledge, 2022.

Bureau of Labor Statistics. "Databases, Calculators and Tables by Subject." Available at: https://data.bls.gov/data.

Federal Reserve Bank of St. Louis. "Table 1.1.5. Gross Domestic Product Quarterly." Available at: https://fred.stlouisfed.org/release/tables?rid=53&eid=12998&od=2023-04-01#.

12
Case 3B: Mayor Daley Takes Over

In 1989, Richard M. Daley became Mayor of Chicago. He kept the role until 2011, becoming the longest-serving Mayor in Chicago history. In June of 1995, the Illinois State Legislature handed him control of the Chicago Public Schools (CPS), which a few years before was called "worst in the nation." After gaining control, he named a key lieutenant as the schools' chief executive officer and another as chair of the mayoral-appointed school board.

Mayor Daley waited 15 months, until October of 1996, then placed 109 of the city's 557 schools on "probation." Under probation, the principal and all teachers at a school were threatened with replacement if the school's reading scores did not improve. The bar for staying off probation was very low: just 15% of your school's students needed to be reading at grade level. Still, 109 schools couldn't meet that bar.

Another policy change of Daley's in 1996 was his ending of "social promotion," the practice of sending students to the next grade each year, even if they had not mastered the skills of their current grade. While controversial, these two new policies sent a message: things were going to be very different at the Chicago Public Schools.

If the changes in policy and the public pronouncements from the mayor himself were not enough, his lieutenants were on-message, as well. The chair of the school board one day said this to a reporter from

DOI: 10.4324/9781003414483-16

the major daily newspaper: "A lot of people are going to complain that this doesn't include dancing. I'm not saying it can't include that—I don't care if people stress pizza-making, as long as our students learn to read." Suddenly, the head of the school board was equating, at least to arts education organizations' ears, dance-based lessons with something that sounded nonsensical—pizza making. Organizations heard this as a threat to their ability to work in Chicago schools.

There were many arts education nonprofits in Chicago at the time, including organizations dedicated exclusively to arts education in schools, as well as arts-producing organizations with special programs introducing their discipline to students via field trips and workshops. Organizations and programs had grown or launched in response to the arts being cut from the Chicago Public Schools' budget in 1979 during a CPS financial crisis. Some schools had, in the early 1980's, found creative ways to keep teaching the arts to their students, if at a reduced level from pre-1979. Then school reform came to Chicago in 1988, giving each local school control over much of their budget. Many schools prioritized the arts again then, and non-profits doing arts in schools saw their revenues from CPS soar.

In response to the Mayor getting control of the schools and making reading his priority, a group of the specialized arts education organizations began meeting to identify and solve common issues. They sent out a survey to the group's members asking what each organization's revenue from CPS had been in each of the past four years. The responses showed a precipitous drop in revenue of 40% across six organizations, from $3.9 million of revenue to $2.35 million. The schools were responding, it seemed, to Mayor Daley's focus on reading scores, by reducing the funds (and classroom time, the organizations said) available for arts programs.

While The Performance Company (TPC) was increasingly performing programs with literacy components, the organization was still essentially in the arts-for-arts'-sake business, not the arts-for-reading-scores business, when the Mayor started getting tough with schools in 1996. Patrick (their founder and Executive Director) remembers walking into new schools in those years to try to meet with the principal to sell them TPC's services and encountering the office clerk. "I'd like to talk to the principal." What's this about? "I'm from The Performance Company.

We use music and drama and dance to teach students." The clerk would then direct Patrick not to the principal, who had all the purchasing power, but to the music teacher.

Earned revenue from schools buying The Performance Company's services was about 25% of the organization's annual revenue and had totaled as much as $367,000 per year. That amount went down 38% over the four years on the survey, which left a $140,000 hole in their annual budget by the fourth year. Equally important, if less schools were saying yes, the organization was not meeting its mission to serve more students. That could mean individual donors and foundations would be less willing to provide funding. At this point, there were options: The Performance Company could sit and wait for Mayor Daley to change his mind or for the schools to stop listening to him. Or TPC could change how they did things.

If the organization made changes, there were risks. Donors who liked the art-for-art's-sake work that TPC had been doing might not be eager to fund something different. Staff who came there to do arts in schools might be unhappy and leave if the organization changed its programs. Board members who gave their time and money for the sake of children engaging with something the board members loved—the arts—might rebel and leave. Worse yet, they might stay and be a thorn in the organization's side.

Reflection Questions

1. How should The Performance Company respond to the new policies and politics at Chicago Public Schools?
2. What would you recommend as TPC's two or three top options? Why those?

All or Nothing

In the Spring of 1996, The Performance Company decided to act. Every school principal and philanthropic foundation in Chicago was sent the TPC newsletter, the front page of which declared the organization was changing its mission and was now in the reading improvement business.

TPC would still be using the arts, but the end goal was an improvement in students' reading skills. To show they were serious about this, The Performance Company announced a study they were launching with an outside program evaluation company to see what the measurable effect of their program was on students' reading scores on the mayor's preferred assessment, the Iowa Test of Basic Skills (ITBS). These were high stakes, as The Performance Company was betting its survival on the hoped-for ability to make a measurable difference in students' reading skills and scores. If the study showed no difference between their students and the control group, TPC would be out of business.

The process leading to this bold decision and declaration centered around a task force of important board and staff members, who met over a period of six months and debated how far they were willing to go. Couldn't they just modify existing programs enough to say they were addressing the Mayor's priorities? Why go all-in on reading? Why not keep what's working and add to it, maintaining the past while looking to the future? Did they really need to change the entire mission? TPC started as artists, so how could they still feel like the arts were at the organization's core, if the mission was changing?

Even though The Performance Company created this task force, the decision was still largely the executive director's to approve. Patrick was the founder, the longest employee and the leader of the organization. He knew it must be a group process in order to have other stakeholders embrace whatever new direction was chosen and, thus, to have any chance at success. Additionally, he knew the group's input and insights would make any decision smarter than his ideas alone but the task force knew they needed the executive director to be fully behind any decision, too. He remembers the meeting where the whole group finally said out loud what had been building for several meetings, with the support of data and emotional discussions: TPC should be in the reading business and should go there with its fullest commitment, no halfway measures. A board member said it, looked at the executive director expectantly, paused, until he said, "Yes, that's it." Smiles began, with looks all around the table, as if to ask, "Are we really going to do this?" Followed by "Yes, that's it!" from everyone. Then energetic planning flooded forth: write a new mission statement, create all new programs, train all the staff to do the new programs, do a big study and announce the results publicly.

Teaching arts skills to students K-8 was the old mission. The Performance Company's staff of teaching artists previously went into classrooms to use the arts to teach whatever they wanted. Relying on the artists' creativity to develop engaging and useful arts-based lessons was TPC's strategy. Students sang songs, beat out rhythms on percussion instruments, wrote short scenes to act out, pushed back desks and danced across the open space.

Kindergarten to 6th grade students learning to read through the arts was the clear focus of the new mission. TPC would need to use its teaching artists' years of classroom arts experience to now create a whole new curriculum addressing students' reading skills. Further, the organization promised on the front page of its own newsletter to participate in a study of this effort and report it publicly in nine months.

The study would use a rigorous design consisting of a pre- and post-test, and the scores of control and experimental groups. It would look at fourth graders who were taught by The Performance Company from January through May of 1997, and compare them to non-TPC students in the same schools. Classrooms would be chosen randomly by their teachers drawing names out of a hat to see whose classroom would be participating and whose would be the control groups. All students had third grade ITBS scores from the prior year, to serve as the pre-test. These previous scores would also enable the researchers from the outside program evaluation company to check to see if the groups were comparable at the start (which they were). Then all would be tested again on the ITBS for fourth grade in late May of 1997 and scores would be compared to see how much each student improved.

From January to May, students would experience The Performance Company's new arts-based reading curriculum in their daily classroom. TPC chose to focus on reading comprehension, which is the skill ITBS tested. They found research about a key comprehension skill being visualizing as one reads, which resonated with their theater artists. As one of them said:

> That's what I do as an actor as I read a new script to prepare to perform it. I get a picture in my head of what is supposed to happen on stage, in what sequence, then go deeper to think about

why it is happening, what my character is thinking and was doing before each scene.

As a result, the team created a curriculum where students were reading drama scenes, drawing pictures of them and making small paper versions of the physical setting, like a set designer would for a play. Then they were acting out scenes. All of this was based on the idea of making the written word visual for all to see.

The Envelope, Please

The results were ready in October, 1997, after the researchers spent the summer analyzing the test scores. Students whom TPC taught made 33% more improvement than the control group who received the standard curriculum. The Performance Company students averaged 12.1 months of improvement in their reading skills, as compared to just 9.1 months of improvement for the control group.

Such clear results caused quite a stir, which continued for a full and exciting year. The organization hosted a press conference immediately to announce the results. Chicago Public Schools' Chief Education Officer was a featured speaker at that press conference, endorsing arts-based methods, and praising the results and the rigor of the study. The city's widely-read weekly business magazine covered the announcement and study results as a business story on the day of the press conference. Coverage followed quickly by the two major daily newspapers, the major radio station for news, the local National Public Radio (NPR) radio station and beyond.

As hoped for, the Chicago schools responded. Contracts went up the following year (1998–1999), as TPC used the study results, the Chief Education Officer's endorsement and copies of press coverage to market its new and successful reading programs. The organization's overall budget grew from $599,812 in 1997 when the study began to $687,000 in 1998 after the study's release, then jumping to $933,000 in 1999, and $1.1 million in 2000. This was a revenue increase of 83% in just three years, as schools and funders responded positively to the study's results.

Becoming a reading organization based on arts methods separated The Performance Company from the major for-profit publishers of reading curricula, and from arts non-profits. Having an outside study demonstrating that arts-based methods produced measurable reading results separated TPC from every competitor. Measurable reading results, it turned out, was a need, a "hole in the market."

Not everything changed right away for The Performance Company. For example, it took some time to change the organization's name to reflect its new mission. The TPC name communicated nothing about reading education. In 2003, the organization changed its name to Read, Believe, Achieve (RBA).

There were results at other arts education non-profits in the following years, as well. One organization that had been operating for 119 years merged with another arts education non-profit, citing "a combination of recession, public policy challenges, and limited philanthropic support." Another organization, once the dominant provider of artist residencies and performances for Chicago schools, saw its revenues shrink by half, then recovered somewhat by merging with several other arts education non-profits. None of these previously successful organizations made the choice to change their programs nor their missions in response to changes in educational policy.

Reflection Questions

1. Did The Performance Company make the correct decision? Why?
2. At that point in his career and experience, would you have advised Patrick to just set the problem aside and wait for the solution to appear, if you had been his consultant or friend? Why or why not?
3. What other decision-making models might have been appropriate for Patrick, at that point in his career as an executive director? Which decision models should Patrick not use in this Case? Why not?

Discussion: Case 3B — Mayor Daley Takes Over

Summary

Many arts non-profits encounter a change in an Ecology at one time or another; in this Case, Educational—not Arts—Policy. While some non-profits respond to a Policy change due to new research or thinking (typically formally reported), The Performance Company (TPC) responded to a *local* educational Policy shift, which focused on reading scores in public schools. While TPC's actions were due to decreased revenue in the Chicago non-profit community, it responded in a way that was both entrepreneurial and directly embraced this new Policy.

For The Performance Company, it was clear they could not continue with their original mission at a decreased earned income level. The potential directions they could pursue, however, were on a continuum: they could gently move to a new Educational Policy direction, or significantly embrace a complete change in their mission. In the end, TPC took a risk—a big risk. This risk was in shifting the organization's original arts education mission, to art being a pedagogical (i.e.: educational) technique empowering a new mission. In essence, though the mission shifted from arts to reading, the arts were still used in classrooms, just in a different manner. Case 3B is truly exemplary in that though the mission changed, a wholesale change in the *core* mission did not follow. The critical nature of the arts remained, as it became a tool (or method) for a new mission.

What the organization did then, was to leverage not just their original mission (arts education) but literally act as an entrepreneurial organization. As mentioned frequently by this point, risk is one litmus test to determine if someone (or some organization) is being entrepreneurial. While some might debate what The Performance Company did as entrepreneurial, in the context of "risk" it seems as if they were. However, when we critique arts non-profits in this way, we must also remember that their served community before the shift was at risk of not receiving arts education. Therefore, we could consider this Case as a calculated risk to TPC's mission in an effort to mediate a community risk *and* respond to new Educational Policy.

Factors Forcing the Decision

Local Educational Policy is forcing The Performance Company's decision to change their mission. In part one of this Case, the author describes the Policy's impact on the bottom line of the organization. With a 40% drop in earned income from the schools across the six local arts organizations surveyed and the 38% decrease TPC already absorbed over four years, the issue was not simply funding, it was the organization's survival. Diving deeper into the impact of the funding decrease, the Case states the following:

> Equally important, if less schools were saying yes, the organization was not meeting its mission to serve more students. That could mean individual donors and foundations would be less-willing to provide funding.

If we take the quote above sentence by sentence, there are actually significant threats to the organization besides financial. The most important threat is in the first sentence—not meeting its mission. In the US, if a non-profit organization is not meeting its *mission* as stated in its incorporation documents, a Secretary of State or the IRS could revoke its status as a 501(c)3 organization.[1] Revocation is severe. This means the organization can no longer operate (rendering employees without jobs), board members are left with the task of settling the organization's debts, assets and final distributions, and the organization cannot seek future funding. (Though there are other consequences, these three outline the most critical). Yet the most important is that a community is no longer served. This demonstrates what most would argue as the critical nature of non-profits: as they execute their stated, legally enforceable mission, communities are bettered. When the organizations go away, communities suffer.

Now that we've discussed the critical importance of Policy in the Non-Profit Ecology, it's time to address the financial aspect. Foundation support and Private Philanthropy are the lifeblood of many arts non-profits. While each of these two elements require their own skills to secure, the mission of the organization is critical to these funder's continued support.

Patrick is clear that if they changed the mission, Private Philanthropy *could reasonably* make the case that they no longer wished to support the organization. Further, arts non-profits typically select Foundations with compatible granting priorities as targets for grant proposals. If TPC made this change, their entire Foundation portfolio (and the work it took to build those relationships) *could* need a complete overhaul. A portfolio change would take time and money at the very least.

To summarize this subsection, the factor forcing the decision was singular: local Educational Policy change. However, this does not tell the whole story. Policy of any kind is *designed* to have impact and the potential impact of this new Policy was absolutely real. If The Performance Company went ahead with their mission change and failed, they would have a difficult time trying to re-define themselves as an organization and could face abandoning the community they served for over a decade. Yet, if they succeeded, they could continue to impact the same community in new ways, while still retaining their integrity as an *arts* organization. However, if they did nothing, it was clear that the financial impact (decreased earned income funding) would leave a larger hole in subsequent yearly budgets.

Decision Model

As mentioned in the paragraph above, it's clear what The Performance Company is facing: change or face an ever increasing budget shortfall each year. The more interesting aspect of this Case is its rather simple binary nature: change to meet change or not. Any direction TPC decided to pursue, however, would be risky, and a middle ground that met the new Policy's challenge to the non-profit education community simply didn't emerge. Yet if we reframe the decision as more about risky action versus risky inaction, it's not surprising that a precious middle ground was elusive—*kinda* going to the gym is not *going* to the gym.

Since The Performance Company had been operating for some time, it's not surprising the organization leveraged its Steady State Model; clearly Patrick recognized a critical change in a very active (local) Non-Profit Ecology. This Steady State Model knowledge helps to identify the decision model grouping. In this Case, TPC's understanding of their ecologies demonstrates a command of their operational domains. It makes sense, then, that thinking about the Domain grouping first might help to identify the model(s) Patrick used to make this decision.

Given that 1) The Performance Company was 13 years old at this point and 2) a number of aspects to potentially leverage for a new mission suddenly appearing, the most likely model used in this Case is the Expertise model as opposed to the Intuitive model. Step 1 (Observe the Problem) and Step 3 (Identify Patterns) are the best arguments for the Expertise model. We see Step 1 when Patrick resists the urge to look at the Broader Economic Ecology for clues to when TPC's increasing financial shortfall might end. This demonstrates that identifying the correct domain (or Ecology) when an Ecology element shifts both focuses the decision and saves time. Further, Patrick is clear that the Policy shift was impacting the organization, but also clear that it would create a negative pattern in their yearly budgets, as it was with similar organizations—Step 3.

We see Step 2 (Assess Aspects) before the decision is made, certainly, but also later where The Performance Company develops and implements the new curriculum. Step 4 (Determine Potential Courses of Action) appears in both the early and later parts of the Case, as it clearly describes the negotiation of a new mission / curriculum versus an old mission / curriculum. Note that once we leave the Linear models grouping, the steps comprising the individual models may not be linear, as we saw in Case 3A. In the early stage of the Case, Steps 2 and 4 help to create a "soft decision" or "working trajectory" of sorts. Later, these same steps are used to develop Step 5 (Determine a Single Course of Action), which occurs when the Case states: "A board member said it, looked at the executive director expectantly, paused, until he said, "Yes, that's it."" This suggests that 1) real-life decisions are not as formulaic as we might like and 2) we should expect and embrace a more fluid process in decision making once we leave the Linear model groups.

A strong argument could be made that the Expertise Model is used in Case 3B, and what helps to secure this argument is the use of strategies. For example, we see a proof-of-concept strategy with the nine-month study and a launch strategy: "…write a new mission statement, create all new programs, train all the staff to do the new programs, do a big study and announce the results publicly." Of course there are other strategies embedded within the Case, but the larger take-away is that when experience begins to drive decision making, strategies (both micro and macro) organically emerge. Typically, we notice them when one inserts a strategy (from our own or other's experience) into (or occasionally substituting for) an implementation plan. Of course, these strategies could be completely unique, contextual and creative as well.

Ecology Discussion

One of the best ways to describe The Performance Company's movement through the Entrepreneurial Ecology of the Arts (EEA) is that it is a good example of contextually modifying an Ecology to leverage the basic model. While some arts organizations would require a wholesale reconsideration of its Steady State Model (SSM) with a risky mission change, TPC does not (Figure 12.1).

Perhaps the most obvious ecology needing slight modification is the Non-Profit Ecology. At the top of this ecology is Arts Policy and since the ecology itself emerges from this element, it should not change. However, if we add Educational Policy to the Ecology's Intellectual Inputs subgroup, we account for the impact of local Educational Policy in creating the decision opportunity. Additionally, a strong case could be made that this element would be a better fit in the Geography Ecology. After all, the center of this ecology is the market (in a for-profit sense) but with a non-profit organization, it is best conceived as the "community served." Yet, out of the three main subsystems of this ecology, there isn't an obvious fit. However, since TPC is responding to a local Policy issue, the authors would suggest the element's best placement is in the Geography Ecology.

Importantly, we should note that in the 1990s, the Clinton administration made it a *national* educational priority to improve reading scores, led in part by then Vice President Gore. Though The Performance Company experienced a policy change locally in Chicago, it *was* a national effort. If Educational Policy was placed in the Non-Profit Ecology (a more broad-based system) then TPC could use this element somewhat in the way they would Arts Policy. Specifically, they could then account for national educational policy initiatives and use them as a basis to newly design or improve existing projects. Additionally, TPC could become more

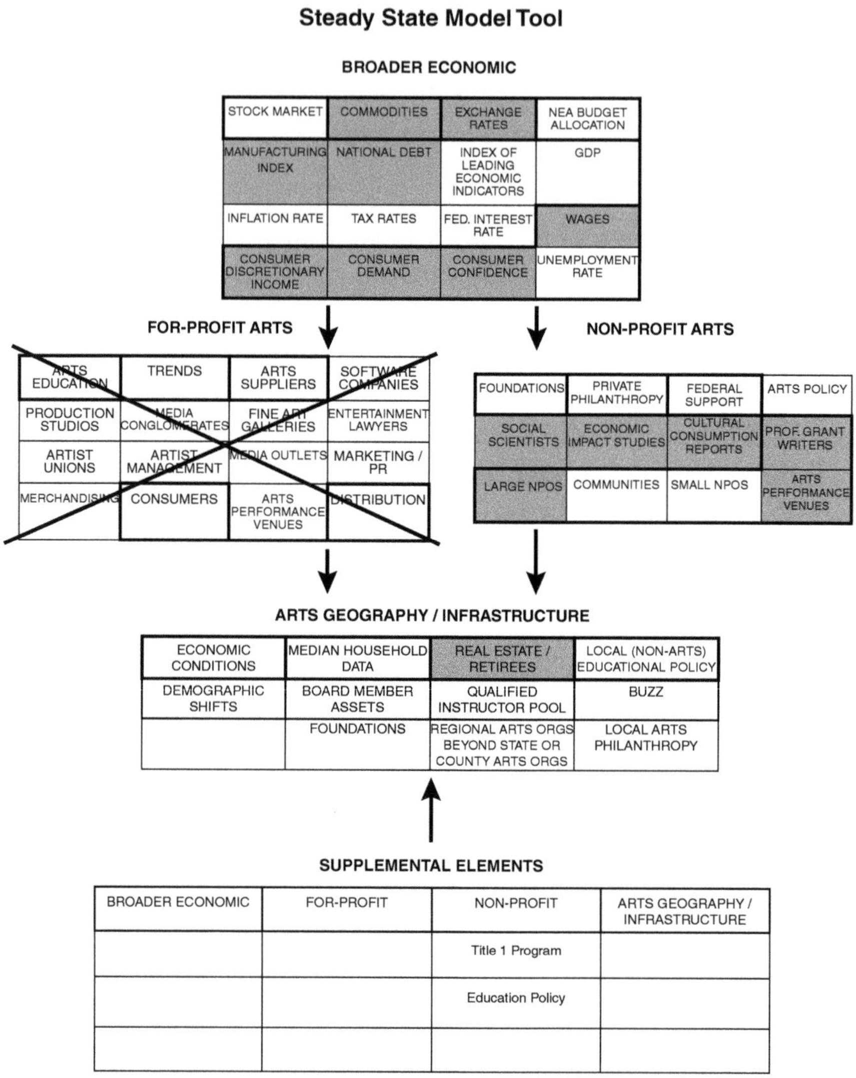

Figure 12.1 Steady State Model for The Performance Company.

familiar with that policy literature and perhaps, add an additional element—Educational Impact Studies. This would assist them in learning about new educational techniques they could leverage for grantors making funding decisions based on the "cutting edge" research. However, since education policy is the element forcing this reconsideration—not a direct change in the Non-Profit Ecology—it is recommended that Educational Policy be put in the Non-Profit Supplemental Elements box in The Performance Company's SSM.

One of the most basic uses of the EEA is venture development and sustainability. Since the 1990s lacked a recession (hence the phrase, "The Go-Go 90s"), the Broader Economic Ecology was expanding due mostly to personal technology becoming mainstreamed. With many enjoying new-found wealth and general good will, it's not surprising the media's focus went from the gloom and doom of Wall Street and Washington DC intrigue to more local matters. This, in part, suggests why The Performance Company (and later as *Read, Believe, Achieve*) was so successful. It was not only a good venture design for the geographic demographics, there was simply more tax base and private investment monies to support arts education non-profits. While it may be a trope to say that TPC was in the right place at the right time (and clearly made a good initial decision), they also leveraged a growing economy and an emerging focus on the quality of education both nationally and locally.

If we look closer at The Performance Company's success, we see local Private Philanthropy sustaining their initial effort. It would not have been there if (in part) the Broader Economic Ecology wasn't as vibrant as it was in the early 1990s. Since the Stock Market was in good form throughout much of the decade, it fueled more philanthropic giving nationally and strengthened the Non-Profit Ecology. However, the Chicago area is nothing if replete with significant wealth, poverty, need and decades of political corruption, which lead partly to the need TPC originally identified. What we have then, is a textbook (and obviously successful) organizational *response* to the Broader Economic and Economic Conditions of their Geography Ecology.

Note: Figure 12.2 shows the Hybrid Ecology active for TPC at the end of Case 3B.

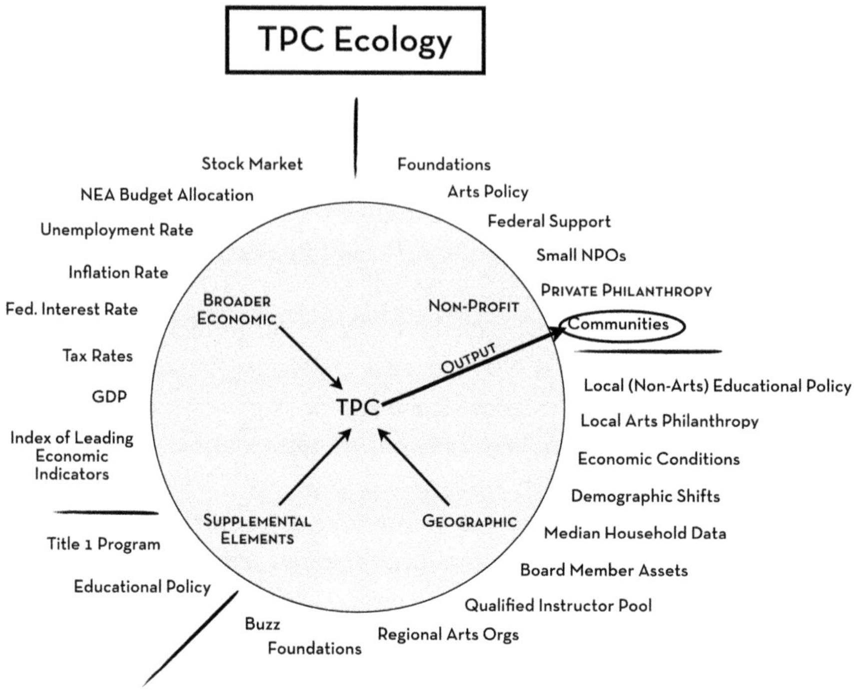

Figure 12.2 Hybrid Ecology for The Performance Company.

Note

1 Most states allow the Secretary of State to oversee the dissolution of a 501(c)3.

Bibliography

Beckman, Gary D. *The New Arts Entrepreneur: Navigating the Arts Ecologies*. London: Routledge, 2022.

13

Case 3C: Hire Artists or Teachers?

Once The Performance Company (TPC) changed its name to Read, Believe, Achieve (RBA), a number of additional decisions were required. One of these was who should deliver the new programs underlying the new name. Most of the existing staff were excited about the new mission, stayed to make it happen and were re-trained. A few staff left within the year, so new people were needed to replace them.

The nature of the work at RBA changed. Program staff had been teaching students directly. Now they were training teachers in the summer, and coaching them all year as the teachers delivered the new reading curriculum. This move from working with students to working with adults was, RBA was discovering, a bigger change than they had expected.

During the first year after the name and program changes, Read, Believe, Achieve's Executive Director, Patrick, began hearing staff suggest the organization hire some former teachers, rather than artists, to be the organization's trainers and coaches. Veteran TPC teaching artist, Big Jack Thompson said:

> I can feel some teachers thinking, "Why am I listening to these artists tell me how to teach reading? What do they know about my job?" They don't usually come right out and say that, but I'm feeling it in their questions, their body language.

 DOI: 10.4324/9781003414483-17

His background was typical of who the organization hired in the past. Trained as a theater artist, he had solid experience as a professional actor, director and drama educator for teens in Chicago. Big Jack had worked for The Performance Company for over ten years at the point when the organization's focus shifted from students to teachers. He was a wonderful mix of charm and persistence, convincing teachers, with his experience and loving demeanor, to follow the curriculum. Big Jack's opinion carried weight with Patrick and with other staff.

Big Jack wasn't the only one saying Read, Believe, Achieve should consider hiring teachers instead of artists, now that the mission and programs had changed. Teachers themselves were saying this in surveys at the conclusion of their training sessions. Even those on RBA's staff whose task it was to convince new schools to partner with Read, Believe, Achieve, were reporting that some principals now wanted to know the backgrounds and qualifications of RBA's coaching staff. Did the coaches have teaching degrees? Did they have advanced degrees? These RBA staff wanted an answer that was better than, "They're artists."

The Hiring and Training Process

The hiring process developed steadily from the early days of The Performance Company. In those early years, there were a string of great hires, who were all artists and still with the organization years later. But mixed in with those great hires were some real clunkers—employees who lasted a few months or even a full year, and caused all kinds of pain and disruption. As a result of the bad hires, TPC sought help from a skilled HR consultant. Over the period of several years, the consultant taught the company's leadership staff a systematic way to hire. This began with identifying a new hire's *capacity*, *willingness* and *fit* for the position. In the early days of The Performance Company, teaching artists needed to teach arts skills to children grades K–8, have deep skills as an artist, be willing to take direction from others, and "fit" with the mission of serving students in low income neighborhoods. When that mission changed from arts to reading, even the title for those staff changed, from teaching artists to teacher coaches. Hires now needed to teach reading skills, be willing to train and coach adults, and fit with the mission of literacy rather than arts.

The Performance Company's HR consultant also helped put in place "behavioral interviewing." This meant interviewers asking questions that often started with: "Tell me a time when you...." Questions of this type revealed what a candidate did in the past, which could predict what they would do in the future. Would they show up every day, driven by a burning desire to excite students' arts talents? Or did they just want any job, not specifically this one? If so, they might quickly decide the work was too hard or opt to try shortcuts. The organization's leaders were serious about uncovering everything they needed to know about each possible new hire. Additionally, they saw the negative results when their hiring process was less exacting.

Steps in TPC's hiring process included:

A. Teach final candidates for the program team an arts-based activity.
B. Observe them teach in the field.
C. Observe their response to direction (one of TPC's criteria) by asking each finalist to change one thing about their activity presentation and teach it again.

Once hired, new program staff went through a robust orientation and training process which included learning the organization's entire curriculum, one section at a time, and teaching it to a "practice classroom" during summer school. During their first school year with TPC, new hires shadowed a veteran program staff member one day per week to watch the veteran deliver the content to children. Then, one of the veteran program staff observed and coached them one other day per week while they worked in classrooms. After a year of this, they were ready to teach alone. Even then, the program team met once per week on their prep day to compare notes and learn from each other, newbies and longtime veterans sharing best practices. TPC valued employees who believed there was always something more to learn.

Artists versus Teachers

There were pros and cons to hiring either artists or teachers. The pros of hiring artists had always been their deep understanding of—and commitment to—the arts mission and a strong belief in its power to transform a young life through creativity and discipline. TPC had always looked for musicians, actors, and dancers who had learned their artform as a discipline and experienced teaching it that way, too, preferably to the same age as the students TPC was serving. The organization wanted team members who saw the potential in each young person and knew the arts were a way to unlock it, by helping each student experience their own uniqueness and value in the world. Teaching artists who stayed were solidly behind using the arts with students to accomplish the new mission of literacy.

On the other hand, the cons of artists—in educators' minds—included a lack of understanding of "what teachers go through in the classroom." For some teachers, there seemed to be a fear that RBA's staff would be asking them to do things that made no sense in classrooms, despite the fact that the organization's team had years of experience going into classrooms just like theirs to partner with teachers and teach the arts. One Read, Believe, Achieve coach had even taught the exact curriculum to students as RBA piloted. He generated great results with students. Though he had never been a full-time teacher, he knew what teachers go through. For Patrick, an artist's perspective on teaching was a plus, a fresh look.

A benefit of hiring former teachers as coaches for other teachers was their instant credibility with those they coached. Read, Believe, Achieve wanted former teachers who taught the grades they'd be coaching, K–1st, and were experienced with literacy education at those grade levels. All they had to do was learn RBA's arts-based methods for teaching reading, then practice teaching those activities in classrooms the organization provided. Then they could tell teachers, "When I did this with students, here's what I did and how it worked."

Former teachers' lack of deep knowledge of—and dedication to—the arts was the main con of hiring them to be Read, Believe, Achieve's new coaches of other teachers. Could those who did not have an arts degree bring the same (or enough) passion to the classroom as an artist? Students, it has often been said, can spot a phony a mile away. If you're not totally committed to what you're teaching in their classroom, they'll refuse to learn from you. The same thing might be true with teachers. If RBA hired former teachers as coaches, and those they were coaching sensed their coach didn't fully know the arts content or fully believe in the mission, the coach could be ineffective. Read, Believe, Achieve knew they needed to train new coaches on a variety of skills, in addition to instilling the organization's mission.

Another issue RBA considered was whether former teachers would change the culture of the programs team. The current team started their adult lives as artists of one sort or another, and they carried those sensibilities and mutual respect into their team's work at RBA. Individually, they performed on the weekends, produced live theater, and composed music. When they met as a group weekly, they often started with physical warmups and stretches, incorporated singing into the sessions, and drew elaborate visual depictions of ideas they were discussing. Planning of teacher training sessions prioritized exploration and discovery, creativity and "aha moments." Even though Read, Believe, Achieve's artists created brilliant methods that were fun and showed measurably better student results, would former teachers embrace this dynamic? Would they make the artists feel suddenly insecure about the literacy components? Or would former teachers bring new and positive discipline to the team?

While the next school year approached, the question was this: Does Read, Believe, Achieve hire former teachers to be coaches of teachers? Or do they stick with only hiring actors, musicians and dancers?

Reflection Questions

1. Should RBA hire former teachers to be its coaches? Explain your reasoning.
2. If yes, what criteria should Read, Believe, Achieve use to be sure they are hiring the *right* teachers? Feel free to put your criteria into RBA's categories of able to do, willing to do, and fit factors.
3. What "Can Do, Will Do, and Fit Factors" criteria might you use when selecting other staff and partners for Read, Believe, Achieve, such as marketing help, business consultants, lawyers and accountants, given RBA's literacy mission and arts-based organizational culture?

Sliding Down a Slippery Slope

After several years of implementing its new mission and literacy focus, RBA started hiring former teachers. Several of the teaching artists who stayed to become coaches decided to move on, so there were openings to fill. Why not deal with the pressure from educators by hiring some former teachers as coaches? It was about as simple as that: no big process for figuring out if this was a good idea or not, just try it. If the experiment didn't work, just go back to hiring artists. Doing this gave Read, Believe, Achieve's staff an answer when principals and teachers asked them about coaches' credentials and teaching backgrounds. That first summer after their initial hire, a teacher raised her hand during training and asked, "Have any of you even been a teacher before?" The answer was: "Yes. Kelly was until last year, and she taught Read, Believe, Achieve in her classroom." Simple, and that eliminated one concern.

Fitting RBA's new literacy mission was important for staff who directly delivered the organization's new mission to teachers and students. But it was also important for other staff and even the organization's outside partners and board members. As Executive Director, Patrick had read a job ad for an accounting job at Starbucks years before, which said that candidates should be "a lover of all things coffee." Now he was beginning to understand that idea for his much smaller organization. Patrick wanted everyone in the organization and all outside partners to love using the arts to bring literacy skills to under-resourced students.

Being around many teachers over the years, Patrick saw some who were comfortable teaching and guiding children but froze when asked to present to fellow teachers at a workshop. That made Read, Believe, Achieve aware that just because someone is great with young students does not guarantee they'll be great with teachers. To find and hire new coaches for RBA's literacy mission, the team added several criteria:

1. Able to coach other adults.
2. Willing to confront other adults and ask them to change.
3. Strong literacy knowledge.

Read, Believe, Achieve's team knew they needed people with a strong arts background. Coaches would be helping teachers—many of whom possessed limited or non-existent arts skills or experience—to implement its arts-based curriculum. This included singing songs and acting out two-person dramas in front of the classroom. Uncomfortable singing in public? You won't be good in an RBA classroom. The coaches mainly "guide from the side" in teachers' classrooms, but teachers occasionally want them to demonstrate how to lead a song or other arts-based activity with students. A failure here resulted in the teacher losing confidence in the coach; an unwillingness to perform the activity soon followed.

When RBA began hiring them, teachers were outnumbered by the existing staff of artists. However, former teachers gradually became the majority of the coaching team. Patrick hired several in whose classrooms they worked previously, which guaranteed they could deliver the curriculum and talk about their experiences.

Training teachers as coaches was, initially, the same as training an artist to be a coach. However, over several years, schools were telling the organization's staff later and later in the summer they wanted to partner. This resulted in RBA not knowing how many coaches they needed until late August. Read, Believe, Achieve was forced to hire new coaches at the last minute, give them a quick training in the organization's philosophies and activities, then throw them into teacher training in late August as leaders of a few activities.

After several years, Read, Believe, Achieve began to let new coaches who were former RBA teachers skip their first year "practice" of one day per week of teaching the curriculum in a classroom. They'd already done those things. In this way, the organization could book them another day per week as a coach. These were not immediate, deliberate decisions, so much as gradual random changes.

One more gradual change was the amount of training coaches gave to classroom teachers in the summer. At one point, this was five full days, with time for learning to sing RBA's songs, lead its drama activities and discuss the role of the arts in the organization's work. Even five days seemed short, initially, compared to the three-week summer sessions RBA managed previously. Big Jack remembered years later that teacher training shrunk to just two days, as former educators became program team leaders. They felt the organization was asking too much of teachers during the summer. Given less time for training, teaching teachers to think like artists was something receiving less and less attention.

Reflection Questions

1. What are RBA's implementation issues, at this point, from hiring former teachers?
2. How is RBA doing, in your opinion, at learning from and responding to implementation issues? Why?

A Culture Change or a Blindspot?

As time passed, slowly but surely, discussion by discussion, Read, Believe, Achieve's culture changed. It was subtle, like the story of the frog in a pot of water that is slowly being heated to a boil. A frog will not notice the heat, until it is too late.

Patrick knew they were in trouble when, after several years of hiring former teachers as coaches, he went on a school visit one day to show a potential large donor RBA's work. The coach for the school was a former teacher, hired the previous year, whom Patrick had not seen in a classroom yet. She had a year of coaching under her belt and the executive director was looking forward to seeing her at work. The director of programs—her boss and another former teacher—gave her glowing reviews.

As the donor and he watched in classroom one, Patrick noticed that some students were leaving to visit the Extra Dosage Instructor (EDI) during class. Patrick made note of this because the whole concept of EDIs is to give *extra* doses, not the same number of doses but in a different room with a different adult. Doing it in a different room (meaning students missed the teacher's regular reading lesson) was subverting these goals. He wanted to discuss this with the coach later.[1]

In classroom two, Patrick did not see the teacher doing any of the drama activities he was expecting to see at that point in the school year. He told the potential donor ahead of time that the program was arts-based, something the donor was excited to see in action. Thirty minutes into the 40 minute class time, Patrick took the coach aside and quietly asked her why they were not seeing the teacher do any of RBA's drama activities. "Some teachers are not comfortable doing drama activities with their students. I'm not that comfortable doing drama activities myself, either, so I let them do something else for those skills, instead," the coach told him. Patrick was flabbergasted but couldn't show it with the prospective donor still in the classroom. "Can we at least see you meet with the teacher to do your coaching conversation with them, to discuss what you saw them doing today?" he quietly asked the coach. "I have to go to another school right after this class," the coach nonchalantly replied, "to get them ready to do something for RBA's development staff next week, a favor. So, I won't be meeting with the teacher here today."

When Patrick got to the office the next day and told the director of programs what he saw (and did not see), she seemed nonplussed by it all. Mostly she seemed to want to defend and protect the coach. She could tell the executive director was not happy, but she did not seem at all surprised nor concerned enough to want to fix anything.

Patrick used to attend most of the program team's weekly meetings. He loved the stories he'd hear there about the actual work in classrooms and what was working, not working, funny, sad, real. But he stopped attending any, unless invited to present something, which happened only rarely now. Thus, school visits were his main contact with RBA's work and its mission.

Suddenly, Patrick was feeling very out of touch and was fuming, both about what he witnessed and his program director's response. Apparently, former teachers they hired believed their experience and teaching credentials gave them permission to adapt—or abort—the very techniques that made RBA's curriculum effective. Arts-based work set the organization apart. Former teachers were leaving it behind.

When Patrick called a longtime advisor to tell him this story a few days later, the advisor responded:

> You're a drama-based program. Skipping the drama activities means she's not doing your program. Your other secret-sauce ingredient is your coaching, which your coach is ignoring, at least one day and with her boss's boss and a potential donor watching. Imagine what she's doing while you're not there.

A long discussion ensued about how things came to this point, where RBA's head of programs and one of her program delivery staff could ignore the curricular design, content and results. The advisor summed it up to the "eternal optimism of teachers." "That sounds like a good thing for teachers to have" the executive director said. "It could be a good thing…" said the advisor, "…but not when you want student results." He said that teachers with eternal optimism say to themselves, "This student did not learn to read this year. But that's okay, as they'll learn it next year."

One other person Patrick asked to weigh-in on this was RBA's former director of programs—the author of the curriculum. As a visual artist and dancer, she said artists tend to be persistent about finding creative solutions or compromises that get close to the desired outcomes for whatever problem they encounter. However, in her experience with hundreds of teachers Read, Believe, Achieve trained in the methods she created, teachers were:

> ... indoctrinated into a world of 'no.' From their first year as a teacher they are told no: there is no money to buy necessary supplies, no time for doing more, no permission for doing things differently, no extra staff to support them. They tend to accept the status quo and become uncomfortable fighting for anything more or different. Also, they are reluctant to push other teachers to do anything differently.

Patrick had read enough studies and books to know this did not have to occur. Read, Believe, Achieve hosted a speaker at its summit several years before who was a longtime school board member in Kennewick, Washington. Kennewick's school district set a goal of 90% of their 3rd graders reading at grade level. That was a monumental but important improvement from the 57% at level when the district's efforts started in Fall of 1995. He told the summit crowd that he and the board thought it would take three years to reach their 90% goal. It took twelve years. They wrote three books about what they'd done. One key: they stopped accepting eternal optimism from teachers. "No exceptions, no excuses," became one of their mantras. If a student is two years behind in reading, the teacher's job in Kennewick now is to make sure that student makes the usual one year's worth of progress, plus an extra half year more progress, to begin to catch-up. Then, the next teacher does that again next year, and so on, until the child is caught up and reading at grade level.

It took the school board's commitment to this goal, then pressuring principals and teachers to not accept the status quo. Overcoming teachers' "eternal optimism," required effort, but their experience said it could be done.

Another piece of important information, which came out later, in October of 2018, was the first of several reports by Emily Hanford, a journalist at APM Reports. In it, she talked about the fact that most teachers were not taught in college about the research on how to teach reading (i.e.: the "science of reading"). So, they do whatever they've learned from experience along the way. But experience can be deceiving when it comes to teaching. Schools nationwide, she reported, get truly mediocre reading results because of these circumstances.

Hiring more former teachers, which seemed like such a good idea, resulted in changes to RBA's culture. The organization started with artists intent on arts experiences. Now Patrick's staff was a mix of artists and teachers. Once single-mindedly focused on getting measurable results, some staff were now comfortable "waiting till next year." RBA's staff had been a solid unit. Now that staff was an unstable mix of differing viewpoints and—seemingly—purposes.

In the end, they were those frogs in the pot. The temperature slowly rose and they did not notice. Were they now cooked?

Reflection Questions

1. Did Read, Believe, Achieve make a mistake in deciding to hire former teachers as coaches? Or did RBA just do a poor job at implementing that decision over time? Explain your answer.
2. What modifications to the hiring process are helpful in maintaining the results-driven, creative culture of Read, Believe, Achieve's programs team?
3. When something goes wrong, what can an organization do and what tools can it use, to determine if the problem was in deciding on a certain solution or in the implementation of that decision?

Discussion: Case 3C—Hire Artists or Teachers?

Summary

As Read, Believe, Achieve (RBA) pivots to a new mission, Patrick finds the organization's ethos at risk. As with non-arts ventures, the sustainability phase is both predictable and challenging simultaneously. While predictability can be comforting and make recurring planning easier, one's attention tends to focus elsewhere because of the comfort and stability it generates. The sustainability phase of most arts ventures is the most difficult because during the startup phase, one's energy tends to be hyper-focused on the different aspects of the phase: product development, marketing campaigns, etc. After all, it's exciting to start something new, especially when there are creative elements involved. But as actors and touring musicians during a long run know, performing the same role (or song) over and over again not only has challenges, the sheer repetition becomes—frankly—tedious. And when A(a)rt becomes tedious, an artist's nature logically turns towards either making it a bit more fun or moving on to different things.

Read, Believe, Achieve experienced a few challenges in shifting to their new mission as Case 3B described. However, if we consider Case 3B as the "startup" and Case 3C as the "sustainability" phase of the mission change, we might better understand how the move to former teachers changed RBA's culture. In Case 3B, Patrick methodically addressed a change in mission despite the risk environment; this focused the leadership and they made clear—if not measured—decisions.

Yet after a year of executing the mission change, demands from (again) school administrators, and now the artists themselves, emerged. When an executive director hears the same concerns from multiple segments of their community, they tend to act. RBA's efforts were directed both at this need and previous issues with a less rigorous hiring process. Again, this seems like a perfect response to the mission change. But what went wrong?

From a management perspective, the organization seems well prepared for the shift. There were clear goals, oversight and training for the staff, in addition to a significant effort to make sure the hiring process for the new teachers eliminated past problems. In part, we see the beginnings of something amiss when we read:

> Why not deal with the pressure from educators by hiring some former teachers as coaches? It was about as simple as that: no big process for figuring out if this was a good idea or not, just try it. If the experiment didn't work, just go back to hiring artists.

There are a number of key issues in the above quote: 1) Read, Believe, Achieve could address pressure from the schools by hiring teachers, 2) the phrase "no big process for figuring out if this was a good idea or not..." and 3) "If the experiment didn't work, just go back to hiring artists." First, pressure from both inside and outside the organization forced this decision and the consequences were significant in the *long* term—not the short term as in Case 3B. Second, there seems to have been a lack of understanding about the *cultural* impact of teachers to both the new mission and the organization. And third, the safety valve for the decision (going back to hiring artists) simply wasn't as robust as it could have been, especially given the previous sentence.

While it would be easy to say incorrect decisions were made because of the three issues mentioned above, determining where things went wrong in some sort of order may help us understand the complexities of the Case. For example, RBA lacking understanding of the broader cultural context or experiences of non-arts educators would be at the center. Yet despite all the human resource (HR) efforts in making sure Read, Believe, Achieve hired the right people, they were unsuccessful. We should note that the HR efforts described were focused more on the potential employee's *past* behaviors, as we see with the focus on "behavioral interviewing." Indeed, this seemed like the right thing to do and solved some past problems as well. However, the real issue is simply about culture. If a "teacher culture" existed, why didn't they know about it?[2] Perhaps the answer is really a question: Should a group of trained artists know about the culture of a non-arts discipline? And second, if they did know about it, even subconsciously, why did they then *decrease* the amount of time spent training and orienting new coaches?

This combination proved damaging to RBA's organizational culture and their mission outcomes.

It is a fact that any entrepreneurial organization—despite the efforts to make the best decisions possible—will make mistakes. While the impact of this decision was significant, there is a clear and engaged decision-making process with an accompanying execution strategy. RBA didn't go into this *exactly* on a whim as the decision process is similar to Cases 3A and 3B. But again, should Read, Believe, Achieve be aware of a different discipline's cultural predilections? Some would say yes: RBA had been in the educational arena for over a decade by this point and had access to non-arts reading teachers five days a week; they could have asked. But some may say no, RBA should not have known about the cultural predilections of former teachers because they were artists—there was no way they could have known, nor should they be responsible for being aware of disciplinary idiosyncrasies. Perhaps this Case teaches us that if you don't know the right question to ask (or if there *is* a question), you can't ask the question. Whichever way one falls on this Case, it is clear that cultural differences in the new hires existed, which (again) threatened their mission as an organization.

Factors Forcing the Decision

The Case is clear that both RBA staff and (again) client schools are forcing the specific decision to hire teachers. We should note, however, that Read, Believe, Achieve is at this point because of Case 3B; if they chose to ignore Mayor Daley's educational policy, Case 3C would not exist. Instead, they'd likely be in a position where their earned income stream was forcing them to make other, more uncomfortable decisions.

It is this aspect that provides a critical lesson about any kind of decision making. Simply put, decisions are like dominos. Once a decision is made and acted upon, others emerge; frequently these new decisions uncover aspects of the initial decision that pull us out of our comfort zone. For example, the decision to choose a college sends us on a certain path of decision making. Choosing another college forces us to travel down a different path. This is not new information to many but the point is that in any arts business, any decision will have not only consequences (good or bad) but will inevitably set us down a path to experience the impact of that decision.

Another interesting "factors" aspect of this Case is how Patrick balanced the input he received. It is clear that the schools with whom they were—or were soon to be—contractually obligated were reasonably demanding a certain level of expertise and training in the RBA staff as a result of the mission shift. This, coupled with the opinions and expertise of trusted employees, gave him a reasonable amount of confidence in moving forward with the final decision to hire former teachers. Clearly, from the executive director's point of view, the new employees were meeting the client school's demand that RBA broaden their employees' professional qualifications. Additionally, it provided an opportunity to execute some needed changes to their hiring process. On the surface, all of this seems reasonable.

Unfortunately, the "reasonable-ness" of this decision was simply that: reasonable. It makes sense to reevaluate the hiring process for non-artists when artists only have experience hiring other artists. This Case demonstrates that despite our best efforts to make the *best and most reasonable* decision possible, both aspects and consequences of a decision may be hidden—knowingly, unknowingly, covertly or in plain sight. In some respects, a decision is similar to a performance: we can plan a performance to the best of our abilities but inevitably, we can never control the *entire* performance from beginning to end. While we may get close to our view of "reasonable" perfection—and sometimes achieve it—the reality is that in the end, we seldom have the *control* we'd like.

Lastly, for arts education majors reading this Case, you are likely thinking that periodic observations of the new coaches would have alerted Patrick to how the classrooms were changing. This is true and if we were to identify a principal factor forcing the decision RBA *had control over*, this would be the primary one. As the Case states:

> But he stopped attending any, unless invited to present something, which happened only rarely now. Thus, school visits were his main contact with RBA's work and its mission.

Additionally, we see a secondary factor:

> One more gradual change was in the amount of training given to classroom teachers in the summer. At one point, this had been five full days.... Even five days seemed short, initially, compared to the three week summer sessions RBA managed previously. Big Jack remembered years later that teacher training shrunk to just two days, as former educators became program team leaders. They felt the organization was asking too much of teachers during the summer. Given less time for training, teaching teachers to think like artists was something receiving less and less attention.

Here, we see a gradual deterioration of teacher training in Read, Believe, Achieve's core mission. While one could easily fault them for this reduced training over time, it appears the organization was responding to teacher demands concerning their summer availability; RBA had control over this decision and accommodated.

Decision Model

If we approach the decision made by RBA as *two distinct* decisions about *two distinct issues* appearing as *one decision*, understanding the model(s) used may be easier. Let's consider the rationale *and decision* for hiring teachers as coaches as the *first issue*, as laid out in this previous quote:

> Why not deal with the pressure from educators by hiring some former teachers as coaches? It was about as simple as that: no big process for figuring out if this was a good idea or not, just try it. If the experiment didn't work, just go back to hiring artists.

The rationale is exposed in the first sentence—"pressure from educators." (This was outlined in the *Factors* section above.) Response to the pressure (i.e.: the decision) consisted of "...no big process for figuring out if this was a good idea or not..." As we've seen in Cases 3A and 3B, this is a departure from Read, Believe, Achieve's previous decision-making model history. This departure, in and of itself, is not unusual for arts or other organizations; not every decision can (or likely should) be made similarly as context can change how a decision is made and its outcome. However, this is a clear, Heuristic-based decision. RBA Observed the Situation (Step 1) and saw that the schools were putting pressure on the organization. Next, they Identified Critical Data (Step 2): they were in danger of losing client schools if they didn't hire staff with credentials the schools required. The decision they made was Simple and Proven (Step 3): Execute the Decision (Step 4), hire former teachers and if it didn't work "go back to hiring artists."

Obviously, this situation has near- and long-term *financial* consequences for RBA; they were going to lose contracts if their educator credentials didn't meet expectations. Oddly, when faced with similar consequences in Case 3B, they used the Expertise model, which is quite a departure from the Heuristic model used in this aspect of Case 3C. The differing outcomes of the decisions between the two Cases suggests that emerging arts entrepreneurs be consistent in using highly-related decision models when decisions have similar (or dependent) *consequences/impacts.*

The *second issue* concerns the new hiring procedures. Here, RBA took a different tact. Clearly, they recognized that previous hiring results were 1) not as consistent as they liked and 2) the new hires were going to play a critical part in the organization's mission. Patrick realized the hiring process not only required updating, but also that if they embarked on a new hiring process to fill the new positions, an improved process would generate the new candidates they wanted. This makes sense: if the process was generating flaws, fix the process to ensure success.

Read, Believe, Achieve used the Expertise model to solve this issue. They observed the problem and understood not only positive and negative outcomes in previous hires, but also that their process may have been flawed (Steps 1, 2 and 3). However, RBA excelled at Step 4 (Determine Potential Courses of Action), where they determined that an in-house solution to the hiring process was not going to solve the issue. Instead, they hired an HR consultant (Step 5—Determine a Single Course of Action) to educate staff over a period of time in an effort to solidify a more effective hiring process throughout the organization.

When looking at the two decisions required in the Case and the models used, it may be an oversimplification to say that the Heuristic model is not an effective decision-making model. Just as a thought exercise, however, if we switch the models used, what might Read, Believe, Achieve experience? Likely, that the "teacher culture" issue would have been uncovered and addressed through an Expertise model and the former teachers may have put RBA's mission at more immediate risk through a Heuristic model....or not. As mentioned in previous chapters, the power of the Heuristic model is that it embraces human intuition—and artists are nothing if not intuitive (well, most of us, anyway). While there is no way to tell if a Heuristic approach would have made the new employee selection better or worse, the fact is that despite the efforts to improve their existing hiring process through the Expertise Model, it produced a threat to RBA's mission.

Ecology Discussion

Since this Case reflects the decision encountered in Case 3B, there is no significant change to the Steady State Model. This said, if we agree the central issue concerns a lack of awareness of "teacher culture," (or an under appreciation of what it might take to change it to Read, Believe, Achieve's "artist culture") then it should appear somewhere in the Steady State Model. The easiest way to account for this addition—while retaining the integrity of the SSM and ecology appearing at the end of Case 3B—would be to modify the SSM's Supplemental Elements box as Table 13.1 illustrates.

Table 13.1 EEA Supplemental Elements

Supplemental Elements			
Broader Economic	For-Profit	Non-Profit	Arts Geography/Infrastructure
		Title 1 Program	
		Education Policy	
		"Teacher Culture"	

Notes

1 RBA believed the "dosage" of instruction is important to young students learning to read, much like the right dosage of medicine is important to someone trying to overcome an illness. RBA considered 20 minutes of instruction in a small group of

three students to be one "dose" of instruction, and five doses per week to be sufficient to overcome most reading difficulties.

2 The authors are aware the term "teacher culture" may appear harsh to some readers at first glance. However, the existence of a "teacher culture" is a known phenomenon. For example, Brousseau, Book and Byers identify the phenomenon as a set of teacher "opinions and beliefs" based on the number of years in the classroom. See Bruce A. Brousseau, Cassandra Book and Joe L. Byers, "Teacher Beliefs and the Cultures of Teaching," *Journal of Teacher Education* 39, no. 6 (1988): 33. Additionally, Feiman-Nemser and Floden acknowledged a "teacher culture" not only existing, but identified a debate about micro-cultures within a broader teacher culture. See Sharon Feiman-Nemser and Robert E. Floden, "The Cultures of Teaching," in *Handbook of Research on Teaching*, (New York: MacMillan, 1986), 505–526. Skaalvik and Skaalvik, however, use the term to describe "…positive social relations, supportive environment, collective teacher efficacy, and common goals and values…" critical to the development of an effective teacher group. See Einer M. Skaalvik and Sidsel Skaalvik, "Collective Teacher Culture: Exploring an Elusive Construct and its Relations with Teacher Autonomy, Belonging, and Job Satisfaction," *Social Psychology of Education: An International Journal* 24, no. 6 (2021): 1389–1406. Our use of the term is meant to describe the relationship between the existing Read, Believe, Achieve coaches and administrators, and the former teachers RBA was hiring as new coaches, which—in the authors' opinion—fall in line with the Skaalvik and Skaalvik definition. Our view, then, suggests that without the former teachers sharing the "common goals and values" of RBA educators concerning the importance of an arts-based pedagogy in elementary school reading curricula, there was a disintegration of "teacher culture" within RBA. Likewise, RBA did not identify that a "teacher culture" existed within their own organization, yet was trying to sustain it by changing their hiring process. In part, we learn from this issue that the simple act of attaching a word or phrase to a goal or a problem may actually help in venture decision making.

Bibliography

Brousseau, Bruce A., Cassandra Book and Joe L. Byers. "Teacher Beliefs and the Cultures of Teaching," *Journal of Teacher Education* 39, no. 6 (1988): 33–39.

Beckman, Gary D. *The New Arts Entrepreneur: Navigating the Arts Ecologies*. London: Routledge, 2022.

Feiman-Nemser, Sharon and Robert E. Floden. "The Cultures of Teaching." In *Handbook of Research on Teaching*, New York: MacMillan, 1986: 505–526.

Skaalvik, Einer M. and Sidsel Skaalvik. "Collective Teacher Culture: Exploring an Elusive Construct and its Relations with Teacher Autonomy, Belonging, and Job Satisfaction." *Social Psychology of Education: An International Journal* 24, no. 6 (2021): 1389–1406.

14
Case 3D: Spanish Version or Not?

From 1980 to 2000, the Hispanic population in the United States increased from 6.4% to 12.6% of the total population.[1] In real numbers, Hispanics in the US more than doubled in those 20 years, growing from 14.6 million people to 35 million people.[2] Most of this increase was showing up in large cities, including Chicago. Los Angeles, California and Houston, Texas in 2000 were the first large American cities to approach becoming majority-Hispanic.[3]

By 2003, Read, Believe, Achieve (RBA) was feeling this shift in demographics at the school level in Chicago. The city had long been extremely segregated, with whites, blacks and Hispanics all living in sharply separate neighborhoods. Thus, the neighborhood schools were usually either 100% black or 100% Hispanic. (The few white students in the Chicago Public Schools (CPS) mostly went to magnet schools or lived in predominantly white neighborhoods and went to majority-white schools). By 2003, school demographics were turning from black to Hispanic, as Hispanics moved into formerly black neighborhoods and black families moved out. Increasing numbers of students in RBA schools recently arrived in the United States from Mexico or Puerto Rico and spoke very little English, so their needs were different from what the organization previously experienced.

DOI: 10.4324/9781003414483-18

Previously, when teachers asked Read, Believe, Achieve what it did for Spanish-speaking students, its programs staff would say they stopped periodically in classroom teaching and let students who spoke both English and Spanish be the translators for those who only spoke Spanish. For the first 20 years or so, this was good enough to keep teachers from objecting. After all, many of them were doing the same thing, owing to their own lack of Spanish language skills. Teachers who spoke two languages were hard to come by, so most schools went without. Also, many classrooms had just one or two students who only spoke Spanish, so it was easier to rationalize this kind of approach.

A National Public Radio study found that no matter where they are going to school, most English Language Learners (ELLs) struggle because they have little or no access to quality instruction tailored to their needs.[4] Although 90 percent of these students are enrolled in designated ELL programs, at least one study argues that the quality of these programs is suspect.[5]

Things were changing for Read, Believe, Achieve. The organization decided to concentrate on K–3rd as of 2003. As it so happened, these grades had the highest percentage of Hispanic students who only spoke Spanish. Also, RBA changed its mission that year to focus on getting all its younger students to grade level in reading—a higher standard than just making more progress in reading.

Principal Pushback

Principals were pushing back when RBA offered them a program that was only in English, with RBA's standard explanation of "the students who speak English and Spanish will translate." Or, when Read, Believe, Achieve said, "We'll just work in your English classrooms," that plan was not okay with principals anymore, so more schools were saying no to RBA's program for their students.

One of Read, Believe, Achieve's longtime partner school principals explained it like this:

> We want to use the same reading program for our Spanish-speaking classrooms as for our English-speaking rooms. That way, when a student is ready to transition from the Spanish to the

> English classroom, they will have seen the same lessons as the students they are joining and be more familiar with the content.

That principal also made clear that she did not like it when publishers took their English-only reading programs and simply translated them, word for word, from English into Spanish. "It's like they have a computer do it or something. So, you get some lessons that don't work at all." She went on to explain that a Kindergarten or first grade lesson that is about sounding out single syllable words in English, might have flashcards with "cat," "rat," "hat" and "bat" on them. Those are one syllable words in English. But in Spanish they are two, three and four syllable words, spoiling a lesson's intent if simply translated from English to Spanish by that possible computer.

One of the most pervasive and long-standing complaints from teachers of English-language learners was the dearth of high-quality instructional materials for addressing student's language and academic needs. It's no wonder, as a 2006 report by the Congressionally-appointed National Literacy Panel on Language-Minority Children and Youth found that the number of studies of Spanish-speaking students' learning was about one fourth of the number of studies that a similar panel found for English speaking students.[6] Basically, the field just didn't know as much about what works for non-English learners as it did for English speakers. Thus, it was harder to create instructional materials and methods effective for this population.

Another finding that stood out was that English Language Learners (ELLs) should learn to read for the first time in whichever language they are most familiar with or speak best. If that's Spanish, it is best to teach them to decode printed letters and whole words in Spanish, then transfer that skill later to English, once they've learned enough English to know what the decoded words mean. In other words, teach them decoding attached to meaning, so it won't all be, well, meaningless.

Read, Believe, Achieve had to decide what to do. Should they create a way to continue serving schools with increased percentages of Spanish-speaking students? Or leave those schools and focus on expanding in African American schools where English was still the language of instruction in the early grades?

Maybe Forget about Spanish?

Fact was, there were still many schools in Chicago where Spanish was not the language of instruction. The Chicago Public Schools has over 500 elementary schools, and Read, Believe, Achieve was working with less than 50 of the total schools. For argument's sake, even if half the 500 schools had mostly Spanish-speaking students (which is surely an overly generous estimate), that left 200 schools for RBA to pursue for partnerships. If ten client schools stopped using them each year, there were 200 other potential schools. Plus, working only in English kept RBA's team highly specialized and more-likely to generate higher results due to that specialization—if in a smaller pool of schools.

But there were risks to a decision to do only English. Some of Read, Believe, Achieve's favorite schools and their principals could decide to not renew with RBA. Those schools and principals were some of the organization's biggest fans, and largest source of referrals. The coaches loved working with them and received great satisfaction from that work.

Risks: Adding Spanish

There were also risks to RBA if they pursued Spanish-speaking schools. One significant risk was creating an ineffective curriculum, which would damage the organization's reputation, and waste young reader's main opportunity to learn to read in any language. Contributing to this possibility and risk was the stark fact that nobody on Read, Believe, Achieve's staff spoke Spanish.

In addition, there was a great risk of teachers and principals, or even the larger Hispanic community in Chicago, calling foul. Who was RBA to be creating anything in Spanish and teaching in Spanish? As was just said, none of Read, Believe, Achieve's staff were Spanish-speakers. Also, none of the staff were Hispanic. In fact, no one on RBA's board of directors was Hispanic or a Spanish speaker. Critics could easily make a case for Read, Believe, Achieve being the wrong organization to lead the way to better materials in Spanish.

On the positive side for deciding to create something for Spanish-speaking classrooms, apparently no one else had taken that lead, including large publishers of reading programs for K–1st. Years of official educational policy from the Federal government was one reason for the shortage of high-quality materials for these students. It was national policy that Spanish-speaking students be instructed only in English. Thus, schools could not spend Federal dollars on Spanish materials. This reduced the market greatly. Word on the street was that major publishers needed to think they could sell at least $1 million of a new curriculum in the first year, in order to make it a worthwhile investment. Large K–12 publishers saw the Spanish market as too small to be worth the effort, and stayed on the sidelines.

Reflection Questions

1. What would you decide to do in this situation? Why?
2. If you decide Read, Believe, Achieve must have a Spanish program, do they create it from scratch or somehow turn RBA's English program into a Spanish version? Why?
3. If Read, Believe, Achieve decides not to develop a Spanish-speaking program, how does the organization maintain and grow their earned revenue streams as a Non-Profit organization?
4. Who would you employ to develop a Spanish program and what skills should they have?

Go for It!

They decided to go for it and create a Spanish version of Read, Believe, Achieve. Their reasons included the clear demographic trend toward greater and greater numbers of Hispanic people in the population, as well as the growth of Spanish-speaking Hispanic students. If RBA ignored this data, they feared they would find their market shrinking more and more in the years to come. Reasons also included principals' increasing sophistication regarding how to teach ELLs, and their increasing resistance to using Read, Believe, Achieve for their students, for lack of a Spanish curriculum. Policy at the Federal level had been anti-Spanish teaching in schools from 2001 to 2008, but the organization's leaders were hopeful that would change with whatever new administration came into the White House in 2009. Finally, as the organization came to better understand what ELLs needed, RBA realized that creating a Spanish version of their reading program was simply acting responsibly. There was a paucity of effective Spanish curricula in the market and this one could make a difference, if they did it right. Besides, unlike the large educational publishers, RBA only needed ten or more schools in Chicago to initially say yes to using their services to make it worthwhile to develop something new.

Could Read, Believe, Achieve do it right? Their goals for this new program included an adaptation, not just a direct translation. This meant they needed to find someone who understood how effective curriculum is created, who believed in the power of the arts to teach and engage young children more effectively, someone who understood how the arts worked, and who believed in getting measurable results when teaching children.

Patrick hired a small consulting firm consisting of two progressive teachers with deep credentials in Spanish curriculum and instruction, particularly at the K–2nd grade levels. Both consultants had backgrounds in the arts, as well, which gave Read, Believe, Achieve greater confidence that they understood RBA's mission and approach of using the arts to teach reading. The small consulting firm set out to learn how Read, Believe, Achieve constructed their English program, and to make suggestions for which parts just needed translating and which needed adaptation. Mostly they suggested relatively straight forward changes. For example, choosing different words to decode, which solved the syllables problem mentioned earlier. They loved all the songs Read, Believe, Achieve created for the English curriculum, and had fun coming up with new lyrics—needed for rhyming in Spanish or for syllable counts. (RBA also found a native-Spanish-speaking freelance vocalist to sing and record all the songs. This had the added benefit of teachers choosing to use the recordings as "sing along" versions, if needed).

As the consultants were almost finished adapting the curriculum, Read, Believe, Achieve hired a new coach who was fluent in Spanish, had her bachelor's degree in theater, and who had been teaching Spanish to students in Chicago private schools. Her job was to learn RBA's curriculum, train the teachers and coach them during their first teaching year. Patrick's team interviewed her and asked her to engage in several mock-teaching activities; this tested her teaching and ability to think on her feet. Then the consultants interviewed her in Spanish, testing the depth of her Spanish vocabulary and accent. Both would be important for native Spanish speaking teachers and principals to accept her as their partner.

The Spanish version launched in 2008 and client school sales numbers increased as a result. Schools reluctant to use Read, Believe, Achieve's services could now say yes because it provided something for all their K–1st classrooms and students. In the end, RBA kept their existing client schools and added more.

While it was never clear that any principal or community member objected to Read, Believe, Achieve creating and delivering a Spanish-based program, it is also the case that the Hispanic community of educators never went out of their way to endorse RBA's work, either. Read, Believe, Achieve were outsiders to that community and remained so, even after RBA hired staff who were Spanish speakers. The organization's leadership, staff and board, was non-Hispanic; it was a tough barrier they were unsuccessful at crossing. It did not overtly hurt the organization—but it also did not explicitly help. They were able to get sales in Spanish-speaking schools, yes, but at great effort.

In terms of reading results, assessment data for Spanish-speaking students was regularly ten to twenty percentage points higher than RBA's K–1 English-speaking students. Spanish results improved Read, Believe, Achieve's overall average of students reading at grade level—a key measure funders looked at each year.

Reflection Questions

1. Did Read, Believe, Achieve make the right decision by creating a Spanish version of its program? What in the case makes you think that?
2. Did they implement the decision well? Explain your answer.
3. What could RBA do better, to improve upon its Spanish decision?

Discussion: Case 3D—Spanish Version or Not?

Summary

In this Case, we see 1) how an entrepreneurial decision can better meet the needs of an emerging market/community, 2) how to act on an opportunity using the ecologies and 3) a sustainability strategy. In Part 1 of the Case, we learn that the increase in Chicago's Hispanic population (and population of school-aged children from Hispanic homes) was accelerating. Decision makers in Read, Believe, Achieve's (RBA) community (school principals) also recognized these trends and pressed RBA to develop a Spanish-based curriculum.

While it is commendable that RBA recognized the demographic shift, it is a completely different discussion about what to do about the data. It is easy for an entrepreneur to fix product delivery problems or market shifts around the edges—much like RBA did in the classroom by having translators early on in the shift. However, the elementary schools saw this issue more vividly than Read, Believe, Achieve, at least initially. Obviously, having a good relationship with decision-makers, collaborators and funders is crucial for any arts-based organization, but Patrick makes an important, yet simple decision that goes beyond "a good relationship:" he listens...and acts.

The most significant aspect of this entire case is that while changing their product was risky, there were two larger risks: 1) if RBA didn't address the demographic shift, then they would lose their market (i.e.: community schools) and 2) it would threaten the organization's sustainability if they didn't respond. While we can see that Read, Believe, Achieve excelled at choosing quality individuals to address the language and curricular issues of their product, choosing the right people to do the right work is a difficult and risky art—as we saw in Case 3C. In this Case, working with the consulting firm helped to not only adapt the curriculum, but gave crucial insight on the qualities and skills of the individuals they should hire to deliver the curriculum. This decision amplifies the reason why *The New Arts Entrepreneur* advocates the creation of a four-person venture startup team (accountant, lawyer, marketing professional and SCORE). Many times, we make early venture startup decisions based more on startup funds instead of having an understanding of what we need in both the present and the future. Yes, a cheaper accountant or marketing professional may save money in the short term, but we must also consider how these individuals can guide an emerging arts entrepreneur in the normal course of a venture's life; in this Case, RBA chose a consultant to guide them in making the best decision possible.

Factors Forcing the Decision

While it's fairly obvious that demographic changes in Read, Believe, Achieve's community are the primary drivers in this decision, we should not lose sight of the role K–3 school administrators/decision makers are playing in forcing this decision.

> Principals were pushing back when RBA offered them a program that was only in English, with RBA's standard explanation of "the students who speak English and Spanish will translate." Or, when RBA said, "We'll just work in your English classrooms," that plan was not okay with principals anymore, so more schools were saying no to RBA's program for their students.

RBA is confronting the same conundrum as Case 3B: something in their Steady State Model is changing (demographics) and their market (school administrators) is demanding they respond with a new product (i.e.: Spanish language curriculum). Again, they face the same broad trajectories as Case 3B: make an adjustment or slowly lose clients until it's no longer feasible to operate.

Though the paragraph above noted similarities with Case 3B, it would be a mistake to assume the cases are identical as there are some key differences. First, this is not a Policy shift in the Non-Profit Ecology or in the Supplemental Grid of RBA's Steady State Model. Instead, this is a shifting element in Read, Believe, Achieve's Geography Ecology (Figure 12.2 Case 3B). Second, since similar arts education and literacy organizations had not made the shift, RBA is making an *entrepreneurial* decision: if they risk adding a new product to their portfolio (a Spanish language version of their curriculum), the benefit is keeping and expanding their market versus *other* organizations meeting school administrator's needs. Throughout this Case, RBA recognized an opportunity to meet the needs of the market, which is a basic tenet of entrepreneurship. Without doubt, the organization is acting as an entrepreneurial non-profit. While it is true that both Case 3B and 3D involve risk, the risk in Case 3B is immediate as the financial impact was already occurring. However, the risk in this Case is more entrepreneurial as it concerns the time, money, logistics and the design of a curricular delivery method: teachers fluent in Spanish.

Decision Model

While it's comforting to believe the main thrust of a textbook solves all possible problems, we know this cannot be true. Case 3D demonstrates that despite the comfort of having tidy models to make decisions seem simple if we follow the steps, hybridization and innovation will eventually occur—which we see in A(a)rt almost constantly. In Case 3A and 3B we see the use of the Rational and Expertise models to make personal and organizational decisions. Though we present only a few cases for Read, Believe, Achieve, it might be tempting to suggest that if the two previous models were used in the past, future decisions would center around these two models. (Humans, after all, tend to find some level of comfort in behavioral patterns; hence our tendency to have "routines," which generate predictability and comfort). However, as Chapter 2 discussed, we make decisions every day using multiple models based on a myriad of circumstances. Again, one decision making model is *not* suitable for everything, all the time. Yet over time, we tend to gravitate towards a model grouping that may be informed (or influenced) by other models or groupings. This influence helps to create model hybridization. It also allows the process of decision making over time to be potentially creative, and demonstrates that decision making can be an evolutionary process—hence "learning from our mistakes" and "it worked well before, so it should this time."

Let's see if we can build an argument suggesting the decision-making model used in this Case is a hybrid of the Rational and Expertise models where the Expertise model is informing the Rational Model. Initially, we see a number of steps in the Expertise model. Step 1 (Observe the Problem in its Domain) is established in the first paragraph of the Case, where Patrick outlines both a broad context (read: Domain) for the main thrust of the Case and a localized context /Domain in paragraph two. Note that Step 1 in the Rational model (Identify the Problem) does not require identification in the context of a Domain. Step 2 of the Expertise model (Assess Aspects & Impact) occurs throughout the first part of the Case: discussion of studies, market decision makers (i.e.: school principals) demanding a new product, interviews, market/competitor behavior and the shift to grades K–3. This helped to establish Step 3 (Identify Patterns), when we read that other arts (and literacy) non-profits lacked a response to a changing Domain (i.e.: the K–3 Hispanic population was increasing).

It is here where we see a shift from the Expertise model to the Rational model. The shift occurs in part because Step 4 of both models concern the development of various courses of action. What we see then is the use of the same step in both models to shift from one model to another. Note that the RBA leadership analyzes potential options (i.e.: the risks of making the language shift or not) as Step 5 of the Rational model (Analyze each option) at the end of "Maybe forget about Spanish?" In the section "Risks: Adding Spanish," we see the rationale for the decision to establish a Spanish curriculum (Step 6 of the Rational Model—Decide Best Option). Note that most of that section outlines implementation (Step 7 of the Rational model). We see Step 8 (Evaluate the Decision) in the last three paragraphs of the case.

Now, while the two paragraphs above are a justification for the Expertise model informing the Rational model, one could also make the argument that there are aspects (or perhaps better put, a "philosophical feel") of the Analytical model as well. In part this is because both the Analytical and Rational model make up the Linear group.

We should note a pattern of decision making. Specifically, the *primary* model employed in Case Set 1 emerges from the Linear group. The only real exception we can see thus far is that aspects of the Expertise model are emerging from the Domain grouping. In many respects, this should not come as a surprise given the time difference between Case 3A and Case 3B—over a decade. Since the most difficult aspect of an arts business or organization is sustainability, leveraging one's experience making decisions over time is natural. Certainly, one never wants to make the same mistake twice and understanding an arts venture's ecologies is critical in making future decisions effectively.

Ecology Discussion

While the Ecologies are broad in nature, this case provides another solid example of how to refine ecologies specifically for a venture, as we saw in Case 3B. Typically this is done to provide a more articulate or contextualized view of the venture's ecological systems. Though one could make an argument that the Non-Profit Ecology could be modified, changing the Geography Ecology may better reflect Read, Believe, Achieve's situation in this Case.

For example, there are a few elements that 1) do not reflect the geographical concerns of RBA as a non-profit venture *as precisely as it could* and 2) there are likely some elements that could better reflect non-profit arts ventures generally. Cultural Tourism, Creative Economy Buy-In and the three venue elements do not fit well with the venture since 1) these five elements better reflect aspects of performance-based ventures and 2) there may be elements that could better articulate a non-profit venture more generally and RBA more explicitly (Table 14.1).

If we remove these five highlighted elements, we have a Geography Ecology that looks like the one in Table 14.2.

Since Read, Believe, Achieve's target community (or "market" in for-profit terms) is centered in Chicago, we should be able to better describe

Table 14.1 RBA Geographic Ecology Modification—Standard Geography Ecology

Economic conditions	Median household data	Real estate/retirees	Creative economy buy-in
Arts performance venues	Popular arts venues	Unique venues	Buzz
Cultural tourism	Foundations	Regional arts orgs beyond state or county arts orgs	Local arts philanthropy

Table 14.2 RBA Geographic Ecology Modification—In Process

Economic conditions	Median household data	Real estate/retirees	
			Buzz
	Foundations	Regional arts orgs beyond state or county arts orgs	Local arts philanthropy

the geographic ecological system RBA finds itself. Table 14.3 is the result of this modification.

Below is a brief explanation of the new elements in Table 14.3 and why they were added.

> **Local (Non-Arts) Educational Policy** – If these policies shift, RBA has options: they could ignore the Policy or they could act on the shift. Note that if a local educational board has the power to enact Policy, *but not law*, the organization may have options. However, if Policy becomes law, then an organization will need to follow those guidelines.
>
> **Demographic Shifts** – As we see in this Case, RBA is choosing to react to the Demographic Shift in their community. If there was another shift in the future, they would have the option of responding or not.
>
> **Board Member Assets** – RBA (as most arts non-profits) can choose Board Members to make the organization's mission a reality – especially if Policy, legal requirements or target communities change.
>
> **Qualified Instructor Pool** – If an educator pool does not have the qualifications to deliver a curriculum, any non-profit arts education organization effort will struggle.

A quick note about the one blank element in Table 14.3: Ecologies are not meant to be a specific size. Therefore, some will have more elements than others, which provides some freedom when fashioning an ecology for a specific venture.

Below is a very brief outline of why each of the following elements were retained in Table 14.3.

Table 14.3 RBA Geographic Ecology Modification—Result

Economic conditions	Median household data	Real estate/retirees	Local (non-arts) education policy
Demographic shifts	Board member assets	Qualified instructor pool	Buzz
	Foundations	Regional arts orgs beyond state or county arts orgs	Local arts philanthropy

Economic Conditions and Median Household Data – With these elements, RBA has a powerful argument to show funders that its mission is vital to the community – especially if Median Household Data begins to decline due to local Economic Conditions.

Buzz – This helps support both marketing and various client-based efforts within the community.

Foundations, Regional Arts Orgs and Local Arts Philanthropy – Most arts non-profits will have these three elements active since they articulate potential unearned revenue streams.

Real Estate/Retirees – The arguments for keeping this element active in the Ecology are strong on both sides. Certainly, one could consider retirees as potential Local Arts Philanthropy and eliminate the element due to redundancy. However, by keeping the element active, RBA can monitor real estate values, local zoning board changes, gentrification efforts, etc. Given the demographic shift in RBA's community already underway, Table 14.3 reflects potential real estate efforts (gentrification, for example) that might drive community members out of RBA's targeted school districts.

Ecologies can be dynamically modified to better reflect a venture's environments in order to generate a more accurate Steady State Model. As a venture matures during its sustainability phase, elements impacting the venture's decision making should be added to (or removed from) the venture's Ecologies as shown above.

Observations Part 1

Engage with professionals (accountants, lawyers, consultants, etc.) with the understanding that they are as much educators as they are professionals. Though you are in control of your venture and are making decisions daily, you have the opportunity every day to learn from them. Education, then, is a seldom discussed benefit of networking. In Read, Believe, Achieve's case, Patrick learned about the different qualities a Spanish-speaking educator would need to possess from working with the consulting firm. This, coupled with their arts education experience, enabled RBA to make a crucial decision about the one person who was going to deliver the product to the community face-to-face.

Though the effort was successful, the lack of Hispanic board members was a missed opportunity. Specifically, not having the cultural expertise at hand to help make the decision to embark on a Spanish language version of Read, Believe, Achieve's curriculum likely contributed to recognizing the demographic shift later than the school principals. Though we will never know, an Hispanic board member or two may have alerted RBA earlier on and instead of being in "reaction mode," they could have been in "scaling mode" and had more time to refine their curricular changes. Further, since non-profit board members can serve in many capacities, one role could have been as an intermediary between the schools, the Hispanic community and RBA. This may have given their efforts more legitimacy (and perhaps more collaboratively developed) if the community and the schools saw that board member as a trusted intermediary who could advocate for the new curriculum. However, to RBA's credit, the decision to have native Spanish speakers involved blunted this issue and fostered community buy-in.

Observations Part 2

Non-profit board members should always be selected for what they can bring to the organization in the future as well as the present. Though there is a belief that these individuals (as a group) are simply the financial source of last resort for an organization, this is a somewhat cynical view of their role. It may be better to construct a board based not simply on their belief in the organization, but for what they can do to sustain the organization so that it may continue to meet its mission. For example, the size and quality of the board member's network, their connection to the communities served, their potential for supporting positive PR efforts and yes—their connection to local foundations and private philanthropy.

Perhaps most interestingly, this Case identifies something seldom directly encountered in case studies like this: ethics driving an entrepreneurial decision; or more to the point, the mission of the organization driving the decision. Since all non-profits are legally obligated to pursue their stated mission(s), it may not come as a surprise that Read, Believe, Achieve chose this trajectory. However, again we see that entrepreneurial decisions are frequently made based on multiple factors. While it's true that some may strike out on their own with money or fame in mind, arts non-profits take a different tact. For these organizations, it's about the mission of the organization. Yes, they are legally obligated to pursue that mission and in RBA's case, the "moral" argument is as much about the mission as it is with the organization itself—morally, it appears as if Patrick had little choice. But there were additional aspects in play such as sustainability and market demographic shifts. Could Read, Believe, Achieve simply continue to pursue client schools, (i.e.: ignoring the shift) in an effort to address sustainability? Yes. But as the Case states, that was a market with little growth opportunity. Here, RBA was confronting a demographic shift growing exponentially and to not embrace the shift would be far less entrepreneurial, putting it at risk of not only losing sustainability but also abandoning its mission. So, in this case, one may see Read, Believe, Achieve's decision as not just about sustainability, but ethically—and entrepreneurially—meeting its mission.

Notes

1 National Center for Education Statistics, "Status and Trends in the Education of Racial and Ethnic Minorities," last modified July, 2010. Available at: https://nces.ed.gov/pubs2010/2010015/indicator1_1.asp#:~:text=In%20contrast%2C%20the%20Hispanic%20population's,to%2015.4%20percent%20in%202008.

2 Pew Research Center, "Hispanic Population Growth and Dispersion Across U.S. Counties, 1980–2020," last modified February 3, 2022. Available at: https://www.pewresearch.org/hispanic/interactives/hispanic-population-by-county/#:~:text=In%201980%2C%20the%20U.S.%20population,at%20least%2050%2C000%20Hispanic%20residents and Betsy Guzman, "Census 2000 Brief: The Hispanic Population," *United States Census Bureau*. Last modified May, 2001. Available at: https://www2.census.gov/library/publications/decennial/2000/briefs/c2kbr01-03.pdf.

3 The Editors of the Encyclopedia Britannica, "Hispanics in the United States: The U.S. Census of 2000," *Britannica*. Last modified April 4, 2006. Available at: https://www.britannica.com/topic/census-of-2000-1168856.

4 Claudio Sanchez, "English Language Learners: How Your State Is Doing," *National Public Radio*, (2017). Available at: https://www.npr.org/sections/ed/2017/02/23/512451228/5-million-english-language-learners-a-vast-pool-of-talent-at-risk.

5 Mark Mather and Patricia Foxen, "Toward A More Equitable Future: The Trends and Challenges Facing America's Latino Children," *National Council of La Raza*, (2016). Available at: https://unidosus.org/wp-content/uploads/2021/07/towardamoreequitablefuture_92916.pdf.

6 Diane August, Timothy Shanahan and Kathy Escamilla, "English Language Learners: Developing Literacy in Second-Language Learners—Report of the National Literacy Panel on Language-Minority Children and Youth," *Journal of Literacy Research* 41, no. 4 (2009):432–452.

Bibliography

August, Diane, Timothy Shanahan and Kathy Escamilla. "English Language Learners: Developing Literacy in Second-Language Learners—Report of the National Literacy Panel on Language-Minority Children and Youth." *Journal of Literacy Research* 41, no. 4 (2009):432–452.

Beckman, Gary D. *The New Arts Entrepreneur: Navigating the Arts Ecologies*. London: Routledge, 2022.

Guzman, Betsy. "Census 2000 Brief: The Hispanic Population" *United States Census Bureau*. Last modified May, 2001. Available at: https://www2.census.gov/library/publications/decennial/2000/briefs/c2kbr01-03.pdf.

Mather, Mark and Patricia Foxen. "Toward A More Equitable Future: The Trends and Challenges Facing America's Latino Children." *National Council of La Raza*, 2016, Available at: https://unidosus.org/wp-content/uploads/2021/07/towardamoreequitablefuture_92916.pdf.

National Center for Education Statistics. "Status and Trends in the Education of Racial and Ethnic Minorities." Last modified July, 2010. Available at: https://nces.ed.gov/pubs2010/2010015/indicator1_1.asp#:~:text=In%20contrast%2C%20the%20Hispanic%20population's,to%2015.4%20percent%20in%202008.

Pew Research Center. "Hispanic Population Growth and Dispersion Across U.S. Counties, 1980–2020." Last modified February 3, 2022. Available at: https://www.pewresearch.org/hispanic/interactives/hispanic-population-by-county/#:~:text=In%201980%2C%20the%20U.S.%20population,at%20least%2050%2C000%20Hispanic%20residents.

Sanchez, Claudio. "English Language Learners: How Your State Is Doing." *National Public Radio* 2017. Available at: https://www.npr.org/sections/ed/2017/02/23/512451228/5-million-english-language-learners-a-vast-pool-of-talent-at-risk.

The Editors of the Encyclopedia Britannica. "Hispanics in the United States: The U.S. Census of 2000." *Britannica*, 2006. Last modified April 4, 2006. Available at: https://www.britannica.com/topic/census-of-2000-1168856.

Case Set 4

A Fashion Industry Professional Responds

15

CASE 4A: QUIT YOUR DAY JOB?

Anderson Vincent has it all. His day job pays very well, and it requires almost no real work on his part. In one form or another, he has been doing this job for years, long enough to be able to do it "practically in my sleep," he says. Anderson has time to work on his own things on the side and his boss is fine with this arrangement. Only if there's a problem that solely Anderson can solve does his boss even want to see him.

There's just one problem: Anderson hates his day job. So, to make the situation tolerable, he asks his boss to give him a small office where he can do what he really cares about: create his own A(a)rt. Anderson's A(a)rt is not something that can be done by one person all alone, however. It needs a company of people to make it happen. His boss values Anderson's skills so much that—to keep him available—he agrees to provide the space. In that office, Anderson begins creating his own company.

Every day, Anderson goes to his office space, gets paid well for doing next to nothing and works on a new way to make his artwork happen in the world. He makes progress on his new venture, works on different logos and formulates an inspiring storyline about its importance. Anderson's focus is on the "aesthetics" of this new venture, how it will look and how markets will perceive his work.

Anderson feels he is making progress toward the day when he can quit his day job and spend all his time on his own thing. "Be patient, take

 DOI: 10.4324/9781003414483-20

the money, and get ready," he tells himself. Still, every morning he feels physically ill thinking about another day in his current job.

This is a familiar story for countless musicians, actors, visual artists, writers and other artists around the world—including Anderson Vincent, fashion designer. Even though this story can be told about experienced and successful artists, it is also often the case for artists in the early years of their career. How does an artist make the transition from day job to full-time artist? When does that artist quit their day job and go "all-in" on their art?

Reflection Question

1. Is having a day job and doing art on the side a good arrangement for an artist? Why or why not? When can it work?

"I've Done a Lot at a Young Age"

Anderson started designing clothes as a teenager, creating and selling swim trunks for fellow surfers on local LA beaches. His high school job was at Nordstrom's in the local mall. After high school, he pursued formal training in fashion design at Parsons School of Design in New York City.[1] He also attended the American College in Paris, where he worked as an assistant to young African-American designer Patrick Kelly.[2]

Not long after graduation from Parsons, Anderson worked for several design houses and was later hired by Italian designer Giorgio Armani as Senior Design Director. He got the job only after agreeing to start the next day. Anderson stayed at Armani for five years, followed by prestigious stints at various American clothing brands, including retail giants Gap and Target.

"I've done a lot at a young age," he said a few years later to Essence magazine. "I pushed myself hard, and I gave up a lot of my personal life for my work." For a while, he was creating art on the worldwide stage of retail clothing sales. Making things under well-known brands and for a worldwide audience of consumers was exciting.

Into the Woods

Eventually, Anderson grew disenchanted and uncomfortable with making things so many people purchased and so few needed. "I was making stuff just to spin off money, not stuff people actually need," he says now. "I was polluting the world with all the things I've made. It made me want to puke every morning on my way into work."

On a backpacking trip in the backwoods of Yellowstone National Park, a different idea began forming in Anderson's mind. Deep in the wild for 18 days, with a guide along "...just to keep me from getting lost or eaten by a bear," Anderson would sit alone at night around the campfire, thinking. He had brought along one pair of pants, one pair of shorts, two t-shirts, a pair of boots for hiking and a pair of light shoes for around the camp at night. "That was enough." What was enough back at home, for daily life? Could less stuff work in urban life? How could he stop being part of polluting the world? These thoughts haunted him for months after that backpacking trip.

Doing Bad, Wanting Good

Anderson was aware the fashion industry was polluting planet Earth. That's exactly what made him sick on his way to work each day. Clothing is second only to agriculture in the amount of pollution it creates.[3] Making clothing accounts for 8% of global greenhouse gas emissions, greater than airline flights and maritime shipping combined.[4] Thousands of chemicals, many known to be carcinogens, are used to finish fabrics.[5] Fashion ranks third—behind oil and paper—in using 10% of the water used by all industries, which is enough water to hydrate 110 million people for an entire year.[6] Just 15% of clothing and footwear are reused or recycled in the United States; the remainder are dumped into landfills or incinerated.[7] Diverting these textiles from landfills and into recycling programs would be equivalent to eliminating the carbon emissions from more than seven million cars.[8]

The more he thought about it, the more Anderson wanted to be part of something very different. Starting with his expertise as a fashion designer, Anderson wanted to design clothes you could wear to dinner at a fancy New York restaurant, then wear the next day to go hiking in the mountains. He wanted to use reclaimed fabric to keep it out of landfills. Fabrics manufactured using toxic chemicals would be avoided. As a former surfer, Anderson wanted to use less water in making the fabrics as well. He knew he wanted a lot...and was undaunted.

Wanna be Starting Something

In 2012, Anderson decided to take the next year off to decompress. During that year, former employers kept pestering him to come back and help them on a project basis, solving problems they felt only he could solve. They made it hard to say no, dangling big money for minimum effort.

Finally, after a year of "floating," as he calls it, he let one of his former employers lure him back, to do projects. Part of the deal was a small office, where he could work on whatever he wanted, whether it had anything to do with his employer or not. This was his chance to bring his campfire ideas about sustainable fashion to life.

Creating a clothing company, then running it, was not something Anderson had ever done before. However, he had run parts of some very large companies—including major fashion design houses—and even made broken business units successful again. At this point, he had been around the fashion industry for years. Could starting a whole new company be that different?

How the Fashion Industry Works: An Overly Simplistic View

Some define the fashion industry as consisting of four parts. First are raw material producers: fabric and textiles producers, as well as leather and fur. Second are apparel manufacturers, which includes designers. A few companies use their own production facilities for some or all of the manufacturing process, but most rely on separately owned manufacturing firms or contractors to produce garments to the fashion company's specifications. The third part is distribution: department stores, specialty stores, factory outlet stores, boutiques, online e-shops and TV home shopping. Last are those who assist fashion businesses in marketing to other levels of the industry and consumers, including fashion media, professional and trade organizations, promotion agencies and public relations specialists.

In the field of women's apparel, manufacturers typically produce several product lines (collections) per year, which they deliver to retailers at predetermined times of the year. Some "fast fashion" manufacturers produce new merchandise even more frequently. An entire product development team is involved in planning a line and developing the designs. Materials (fabric, linings, buttons, etc.) must be sourced, ordered, and samples made for presentation to retail buyers.

The fashion industry across the entire world was on an upswing in 2013 when Anderson took his year off. Global sales in 2012 increased 3.5%, as a baseline, then increased 4.5% more in 2013, 5.1% in 2014, and 5.5% in 2017, which was Anderson's new company's first full year in business. In 2019, just prior to the COVID pandemic, sales growth was 5.9%.[9] Looking back now, it was a good time to start a clothing company. But what kind of company should it be? How much of the four-part process should Anderson's new company attempt?

"You're Afraid to do It"

For several years, Anderson spent his spare time working on the "aesthetics" of his possible new company. "I played with different logos, the storyline for this new brand." He knew the core idea would be "clothes for walking more-lightly on this Earth." This means having fewer clothes in your closet but each piece is more functional, doing multiple things for you. He wanted everything to reflect that core idea. Anderson's new venture would be all his, the whole world would know this was his creation. This was appealing.

Yet whenever he did work for his part-time employer/benefactor in this period, he remained unhappy. His work was still helping people buy "stuff" they didn't need—and this "stuff" was still polluting the world.

To try out the designs he had in mind, on real customers, Anderson launched a *Kickstarter* campaign in May, 2013, with a goal of selling $50,000 of his new designs. He reasoned this would be a sure way to show progress. Was he getting close to launching? It was a huge success, selling $68,770 of his new designs in a matter of days, far exceeding his goal.

Was he moving fast enough? How could he move any faster, in the amount of time he was able to devote to this venture versus projects from past employers? The money they were paying him was too good to ignore and side benefits were compelling—especially the former employer supporting his new venture by giving him an office. Maybe he just needed to be patient and happy that he could see his future enterprise taking shape.

Three years went by. One day Anderson was unloading on his best friend about how long it was taking to feel ready to launch. He had always received blunt feedback from this person, which made him the one Anderson went to almost without even knowing he needed feedback.

"You're afraid to do it," his friend responded.

Anderson sat in stunned silence. He thought his friend would recognize his progress. Instead, this trusted advisor told him he was fooling himself. "It was almost like he punched me," Anderson says. Then he realized this friend was 100% right. "I'd been hiding from it. I was dipping my one foot into the water, like with the *Kickstarter*, not jumping in with both feet." Anderson thought he was making progress by getting things done.

"No you're not," came his friend's response.

Reflection Questions

1. Is Anderson ready to commit 100% to his A(a)rt?
2. What additional data should Anderson uncover in order to make this decision?
3. Is his continued data search just another excuse not to jump?

Committing 100% to Art

In the summer of 2016, just one week after his best friend said "You're afraid to do it," Anderson stopped everything he was doing and devoted 100% of his energy to launching his venture. "I should have gone all-in three years earlier, right after doing that *Kickstarter*," Anderson now says. Only once he was "all-in" did he start looking at all the details: finances, pricing, etc…"I made the decision to jump all-in, then looked for data."

Though Anderson was primarily a fashion designer, he also knew many aspects of the industry and how to put his art out in the world. "I've got a weird brain," Anderson says. "That's why people hired me to do things for their companies—I can make designs and I can make things happen, business-wise. Most designers can't do both."

However, he quickly learned there were holes in his knowledge. Starting and running an entire fashion *company* became an education. Raising money from investors, for starters, was new to Anderson. "I was totally naive about that, about the process you have to play with different investors," he admits. He also didn't know the total cost and supporting structure it would take to make this big leap. "It was kind of bliss, to not know a lot of it. But it was also sort of frustrating when I met someone who *did* know. All these unfamiliar words were coming out of their mouths." He read books at night on everything he didn't know, "… from cap tables to what a convertible note was and how did that work?"[10]

Anderson also learned there would be no way to actually launch Seordna—the name he gave his company—unless he jumped in with both feet and was totally committed. "Money people can smell if you're not 100% in," he says. "They don't invest unless you're all-in."

Running at Full Speed

When Anderson Vincent finally made the decision to launch Seordna, he was anxious, but also excited. He used his *Kickstarter* designs and within six months, the website and online ordering platform were live:

> Once we said "Go," we moved really fast. We had a manufacturer lined up, too. The best manufacturer in the world. Now the manufacturer was asking questions, buying things, putting things in the works. You've got people building out the website. This means you're burning money.

Anderson had been taking his time, but now, he was running at full speed. For the next three years, Seordna's revenues doubled annually, reaching $6.7 million in 2019. Going into 2020, he projected revenue to double again. Seordna was buying fabrics and stockpiling inventory at their manufacturing partners in China to meet projected demand. This would, finally, get the company to profitability.

Then came the pandemic.

Discussion: Case 4A — Quit your Day Job?

Summary

This is a hybrid Case. On the A(a)rt side, it describes a situation some emerging arts entrepreneurs encounter before venture startup. Yet on the business side, it describes a remarkably talented artist apparently surrounded by success at every turn. In this discussion, we examine Anderson's experiences more broadly and then focus on a number of key issues in the last two subsections.

From a "life lesson" perspective, the first section of the Case describes what most emerging arts entrepreneurs (and many college students) experience: the dreaded "day job." (Let's acknowledge the fact that Anderson was fortunate to secure some enviable positions during his "day job" days, however). For some, "day jobs" are simply an exchange of labor for money, where neither party is emotionally invested in the other. On the other hand, some experience these positions as (at worst) a low point in their lives where they feel as if they've abandoned their values for something else: money, maintaining a lifestyle, etc. The common denominator is that these jobs *tend not to be* what people *really* want to do. (If you are in this position now, know you are treading a well-worn path). However, it should be said that some "day jobs" have both extrinsic and intrinsic benefits.

Anderson, however, is in an interesting position. On the surface, it looks as if his multitude of "day jobs" would be something any emerging fashion designer would regard as the pinnacle of a meaningful career. He is having early success beyond imagination, clearly making a name for himself in the fashion industry and most importantly, learning how to negotiate a complex Fashion Ecology. Yet, as the Case describes, a sense of disenchantment emerges based on Anderson's values and experiences. Success, it appears, has consequences.

Seordna is Anderson's response to his values. His concern about textile design inefficiency and the fashion industry's environmental impact are values he feels strongly about, but for some reason, we see Anderson (as his friend opined and Anderson agreed) appearing fearful of launching. Leveraging a successful Kickstarter into a launch would be the most logical next step. Why should someone with his design resume slow roll the launching of a venture where he has 1) demonstrated a marketable design and 2) secured proof-of-concept?

If fear was truly the problem, there is one aspect that *may* play a part in this slow-roll: the fear of success. To be clear, this discussion is not about psychoanalyzing, it's about trying to understand decisions, which is a process. Anderson's "fear" as he described it was revealed by a friend as a truth Anderson immediately understood. In a short time, he apparently overcame that fear. However, "fear" typically has a source. In parts of this book, we've broadly described one's *habitus* as the collection of experiences in different *fields* of life. We could say, then, that if Anderson was feeling fearful about Seordna's success, his *habitus* generated that decision based on the previous *fields* he experienced.

Most entrepreneurs (including Anderson) will say they were at least somewhat apprehensive when launching their businesses; this is a reasonable, human response to risk. But we should also note that artists have opinions about their creative capacities—valid or not. Creation demands many tangible and intangible negotiations and we suggest that belief in—and validation of—one's goals helps to *temper* fear, as we see in Anderson's Kickstarter success. However, an honest assessment of fear residing in self (which Anderson clearly engaged in after his friend's comment) generates an informed understanding and *choice* about that fear.

Factors Forcing the Decision

Anderson is negotiating two significant issues. First is his dissatisfaction with the environmental impact of clothing manufacture and inefficient clothing design. Many textile students are well aware of these issues, and for Anderson, his "day jobs" are increasingly in conflict with his values. For Anderson, the environmental arguments are compelling, and his role in sustaining these impacts are becoming unbearable.

Some readers would point out that without a change in how Seordna clothing is manufactured, the company would still create a negative environmental impact. This is true. But one of Seordna's design innovations is in a garment's potential multiple uses—an aspect embedded into the designs. This is an important part of the venture's "environmental response" and feeds deeply into the value proposition for environmentally conscious markets; it also addresses Anderson's dissatisfaction with the industry and his role in its production. Additionally, using recycled materials (another design parameter) and design efficiency was another response—strong value points for certain markets.

Weighing the issue of Seordna still contributing to the industry's problems (granted, on a smaller scale) versus its design innovations is difficult for those not enmeshed in the textile industry. Broadly speaking, there is an important entrepreneurial lesson here: it is rare that a single innovation solves every problem. Many times, small innovations and efficiencies bring about larger *sustainable* change over time. For example, an original iPhone would be almost useless in the third decade of the 21st century; it's taken time to develop innovations in the product and for software developers to leverage those innovations.

The second issue Anderson negotiates is his experience with the Fashion and Textile Ecology. One would rightly surmise that his "day jobs" provided an education about the industry and without being extremely familiar with it, Seordna could not have been as successful as it was in such a short time. This helps us understand that when launching a venture, an idea, a deeply held value or an innovation is only one part of the equation. Knowing in which ecology the venture will reside is the next critical step. As any fashion entrepreneur will attest, breaking into the fashion industry is extraordinarily difficult—more difficult than most arts industries given its complexity, potential supply chain issues and skilled labor requirements. His experience in the industry, knowledge of the Fashion Ecology and leveraging his network make Seordna a success.

What we have then, is a fashion venture launched due to a deeply held personal value (environmentalism) and an accompanying design to manifest that value. We note again that Anderson's knowledge of the Fashion Ecology (i.e.: fashion industry) served as a catalyst to make Seordna a reality. This helps us re-frame the potential purpose of a "day job." Specifically, if one accepts a "day job" to serve one's future goals, that job is leveraged. If the "day job" does not serve one's goals and nothing is gained by this service, then it really *is* a "day job." There's nothing wrong with this, but in many cases, one's A(a)rt goals suffer as a result of time allocated for purposes not serving those goals. Again, we have to eat and unless you produce your own food, it takes money to eat;

the choice to take a less-desirable "day job" to eat is an understandable decision. But if one has a choice, getting a "day job" serving your entrepreneurial goals is likely a far better decision as Anderson demonstrates.

Decision Model

One of the benefits of the *Entrepreneurial Ecology of the Arts* is that one can not only see and analyze the individual elements of the ecology in which a venture resides, but also identify patterns and relationships occurring with the elements. For example, if one element is experiencing stress, other elements can adjust to that stress and keep the ecology stable. In this case, Anderson is at the center of a Fashion and Textile Ecology and is perfectly positioned through his "day jobs" to engage with—and observe—many of the elements in this Ecology daily. This suggests that Anderson knows not only the elements in the Ecology but how they react when stressed. Another example: the fashion industry supply chain is both complex and tenuous. If there is a cotton shortage due to weather conditions in one part of the world, this will stress cotton producers in other parts. Given that cotton is a critical component in textile manufacturing, Anderson would adjust his product delivery dates, which stresses inventory projections and could result in a revenue loss unless there was enough inventory to overcome the shortage.

Most readers would suggest that given Anderson's experience in the industry and his knowledge of the Fashion and Textile Ecology, his decision-making model should be a part of the Domain group: Expertise or Intuitive. This is a strong argument, especially if one considers his experience in recognizing patterns within the Ecology. What supports the argument is that *patterns* appear in both models. However, this Case demonstrates that identifying a single model based on the narrative may not always be easy.

If we agree that a Domain model is likely the model Anderson is using and that *recognizing patterns* is (at least) partially the basis for our decision model identification, then examining the model's parameters will likely tell us the model he is using. (Table 15.1 outlines the steps in each model and also appears in chapter 2). Since understanding *patterns* is the core of our analysis, we see a difference between the two models: Expertise, Step 3 (Based on one's understanding and experience within a domain,

Table 15.1 Expertise and Intuitive Decision Model Steps

Step	Expertise	Intuitive
1	Observe the problem at hand and make *sense* of it in its domain	Identify the problem
2	*Assess* as many aspects of the problem as possible and determine how it may impact the situation.	Scan the environment for cues to *recognize patterns*
3	Based on one's understanding and experience within a domain, *identify patterns*	Select *one* potential course of action, based on experience, knowledge, and training
4	Based on the domain, goals, issue at hand, etc., determine potential courses of action	Consider potential course of action through to outcome
5	Determine *a single* course of action appropriate to both the issue and the domain	If chosen course of action will not produce desired outcome, alter it and retest
6		If altered course of action still not deemed workable, discard and look for alternative
7		Test alternate course of action until viable option found
8		Implement the chosen course of action

identify patterns) and Intuitive, Step 2 (Scan the environment for cues to *recognize patterns*). The Expertise model is explicit in *identifying patterns*, while the Intuitive model is explicit in *recognizing patterns*—there is a critical difference between the two. Being able to *recognize* something is different than being able to *identify* something. In this case, when we "recognize" something, we are explicit in allowing our recognition to be fine-tuned. (i.e.: we recognize a generality). When we "identify" something, we are sure that our identification is a *more accurate* or more fine-tuned understanding of a pattern's essence. (i.e.: we identify a specificity). For example, we can *recognize* a bird from far away but can *identify* the exact species when we are closer. The question now is whether Anderson was *recognizing* the environmental impact of his "day jobs" or he *identified* the impact of his daily actions. This is hard to determine given the case narrative, so if we analyze each step more closely, that may help.

Let's examine Step 3 of the Expertise Model (Based on one's understanding and experience within a domain, *identify patterns*). Anderson's work within the fashion industry *could have* given him the opportunity to see and better understand how both his "day jobs" and discrete actions allowed him to identify patterns. He was at the creative center of design houses and had some managerial experience in these organizations. It makes sense, then, that his decision *could be based* on his experience and proximity to the industry. Looking at Intuitive Model's Step 2 (Scan the environment for cues to *recognize patterns*), we must make the determination if Anderson's experience in the fashion industry (seeing both the good and the bad) and his desire to become an entrepreneur as a response, was based on *scanning the environment*, or in this context, *scanning the fashion industry*. The verb is key: scanning. Since we only know Anderson was experiencing dissatisfaction with his role in the industry and we do not have an example in the Case narrative of a personal experience causing this angst, one *could make an argument* that Anderson was using the Intuitive model.

Since we cannot 100% determine the decision-making model Anderson was using by examining the *pattern*, we could look at the model's total steps and try to decide that way. The Case ends with Anderson starting Seordna and experiencing some significant success. What we don't see is Anderson launching Seordna, having it fail for some reason and starting another company—Step 5 of the Intuitive model. This means that Anderson is using the Expertise model and not the Intuitive model, as that model allows for action failures and further attempts at solving problems.

COVID becomes an issue at the end of this Case. An astute reader will wonder if Anderson's values or goals will change—based on *patterns* of some kind—that will force him to move away from the Expertise model. This type of thinking is helpful for all arts entrepreneurs as each decision one makes has consequences. Before COVID enters at the end of the Case, Anderson's decision to launch Seordna seems like a good decision using the Expertise model; after all, his industry experience clearly helped him succeed. Looking forward, however, an unprecedented pandemic may make this decision far more impactful than it initially appeared.

Ecology Discussion

While we have been speaking about Anderson's knowledge of the Fashion and Textile Ecology, we also encounter these sentences in the Case narrative: "However, he quickly learned there were holes in his knowledge. Starting and running an entire fashion *company* became an education." This likely came as a surprise to a few readers and indeed, is a bit of a shock. We would rightly expect someone with this level of experience—and early success—to *know* Seordna's ecological system, making a launch relatively easy. The facts, however, paint a different picture.

Before we get into why Anderson finds launching an "**entire** fashion company" challenging, let's examine Figure 15.1 (This part of the discussion is to help readers unfamiliar with the industry get a taste of this complex ecological system). Figure 15.1 is a very broad view of this ecology and many elements are not listed, such as color scientists, marketing, weaving machine engineers, investors, etc., due simply to space.

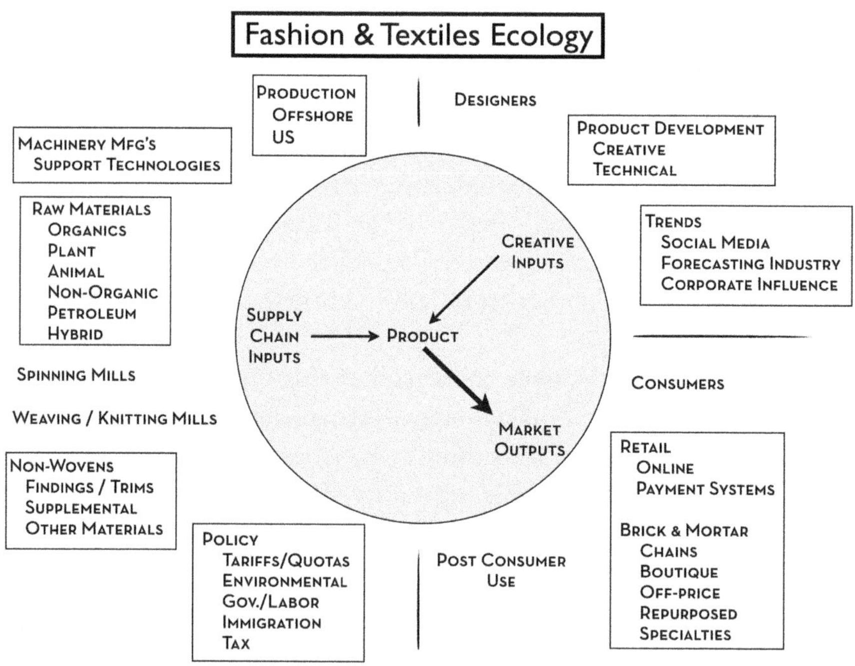

Figure 15.1 Fashion and Textile Ecology.

What makes it even more challenging is its dynamism. For example, if a certain color or material is trending, designers, marketers, fabric manufacturers and many others will respond to the trend. Additionally, trends can occur multiple times per year. To say that the fashion industry is dynamic and complex is an understatement.

Hopefully, it is clear that Anderson was going to have *both* an easier *and* more difficult time launching Seordna. Grasping the sheer size and complex inter-relationships between the elements is not only daunting, trying to launch a company of Seordna's size and potential impact so quickly is not a one-person job. Engaging these elements in the order they need to occur requires a "big picture" or "ecological" view, much like an orchestra conductor. Yet his "day job" experience certainly helped, as he could leverage both his knowledge and his network.

What we have in this Case, then, is something quite common—a *partial* understanding of the venture's ecology. Anderson obviously knew far more than just the primary aspects of the Fashion and Textile Ecology and given Seordna's quick success, it seems as if he leveraged the Ecology successfully. But once he started engaging with *some* of the elements more discreetly (as seen in the description of capitalization tables in the narrative), he was in education mode (like many new entrepreneurs) and had to learn these new aspects in the moment. The fact that he leveraged his understanding of the Fashion and Textile Ecology in the way he did, says much about his values, experience and, importantly, his "day jobs."

Notes

1 Parsons School of Design, "About Parsons." Accessed November 16, 2023. Available at: https://www.newschool.edu/parsons/about.

2 Fashion Institute of Technology, State University of New York, "1954-1990 – Patrick Kelly," *Fashion History Timeline*. Accessed November 16, 2023. Available at: https://fashionhistory.fitnyc.edu/1954-1990-patrick-kelly.

3 Climate Trade, "The World's Most Polluting Industries," last modified May 11, 2023. Available at: https://climatetrade.com/the-worlds-most-polluting-industries.

4 Quantis, "Measuring Fashion." Accessed July 3, 2023. Available at: https://quantis.com/wp-content/uploads/2018/03/measuringfashion_globalimpactstudy_full-report_quantis_cwf_2018a.pdf.

5 K. Stevens, "Chemicals In Textile Production," *European Outdoor Group*. Last modified January, 2018. Available at: https://assets-global.website-files.com/5ed628f951e6c112227290bb/5f3812b771c81db7f5a24c1a_EOG%20Chemicals%20in%20Textile%20Production%20low%20res.pdf.

6 See Nathalie Remy, Eveline Spellman and Steven Swartz, "Style That's Sustainable: A New Fast-Fashion Formula," *McKinsey & Company*. Last modified October 20, 2016. Available at: https://www.mckinsey.com/capabilities/sustainability/our-insights/style-thats-sustainable-a-new-fast-fashion-formula and Seaside Sustainability, "Fast Fashion Series, Part 2: Fast Fashion and Water Pollution," last modified pril 4, 2023. Available at: https://www.seasidesustainability.org/post/fast-fashion-series-part-2-fast-fashion-and-water-pollution#:~:text=It%20is%20estimated%20that%20the,million%20people%20for%20a%20year.

7 United States Environmental Protection Agency, "Facts and Figures About Materials, Waste and Recycling: Nondurable Goods: Product-Specific Data." Last modified December 3, 2022. Available at: https://www.epa.gov/facts-and-figures-about-materials-waste-and-recycling/nondurable-goods-product-specific-data#ClothingandFootwear.

8 Alden Wicker, "Fast Fashion Is Creating An Environmental Crisis," *Newsweek Magazine*, September 1, 2016. Available at: https://www.newsweek.com/2016/09/09/old-clothes-fashion-waste-crisis-494824.html.

9 P. Smith, "Market Growth of the Apparel Industry Worldwide From 2012 to 2020," *Statista*. Last modified July 27, 2023. Available at: https://www.statista.com/statistics/727541/apparel-market-growth-global.

10 A capitalization table details who has ownership in a company, including all company shares. A convertible note is a form of short-term debt. In effect, an investor is loaning money to a start-up and instead of getting principal plus interest in return, they can convert it to equity in the company at a later date.

Bibliography

Beckman, Gary D. *Navigating The New Arts Entrepreneur: the Arts Ecologies*. London: Routledge, 2022.

Bikart, Joseph. *The Art of Decision Making: How we Move from Indecision to Smart Choices*. London: Watkins Publishing, 2019.

Climate Trade. "The World's Most Polluting Industries." Last modified May 11, 2023. Available at: https://climatetrade.com/the-worlds-most-polluting-industries.

Fashion Institute of Technology State University of New York. "1954-1990 – Patrick Kelly." *Fashion History Timeline*. Accessed November 16, 2023. Available at: https://fashionhistory.fitnyc.edu/1954-1990-patrick-kelly.

Ferrell, O.C., John Fraedrich and Linda Ferrell. *Business Ethics: Ethical Decision-Making and Cases*. Boston: Cengage, 2019.

Knouse, Steven B. and Robert A. Giacalone. "Ethical Decision-Making in Business: Behavioral Issues and Concerns." *Journal of Business Ethics* 11, no. 5/6 (1992): 369–377.

Parsons School of Design. "About Parsons." Accessed November 16, 2023. Available at: https://www.newschool.edu/parsons/about.

Quantis. "Measuring Fashion: Environmental Impact of the Global Apparel and Footwear Industries Study." Accessed July 3, 2023. Available at: https://quantis.com/wp-content/uploads/2018/03/measuringfashion_globalimpactstudy_full-report_quantis_cwf_2018a.pdf.

Remy, Nathalie, Eveline Spellman and Steven Swartz. "Style That's Sustainable: A New Fast-Fashion Formula." *McKinsey & Company*. Last modified October 20, 2016. Available at: https://www.mckinsey.com/capabilities/sustainability/our-insights/style-thats-sustainable-a-new-fast-fashion-formula.

Seaside Sustainability. "Fast Fashion Series, Part 2: Fast Fashion and Water Pollution." Last modified April 4, 2023. Available at: https://www.seasidesustainability.org/post/fast-fashion-series-part-2-fast-fashion-and-water-pollution#:~:text=It%20is%20estimated%20that%20the,million%20people%20for%20a%20year.

Smith, P. "Market Growth of the Apparel Industry Worldwide From 2012 to 2020." *Statista*. Last modified July 27, 2023. Available at: https://www.statista.com/statistics/727541/apparel-market-growth-global.

Stevens, K. "Chemicals in Textile Production." *European Outdoor Group*. Last modified January, 2018. Available at: https://assets-global.website-files.com/5ed628f951e6c112227290bb/5f3812b771c81db7f5a24c1a_EOG%20Chemicals%20in%20Textile%20Production%20low%20res.pdf.

Trenton, Nick. *Think in Models: A Structured Approach to Clear Thinking and the Art of Decision-Making*. Self-published, Nick Trenton, 2019.

United States Environmental Protection Agency. "Facts and Figures About Materials, Waste and Recycling: Nondurable Goods: Product-Specific Data." Last modified December 3, 2022. Available at: https://www.epa.gov/facts-and-figures-about-materials-waste-and-recycling/nondurable-goods-product-specific-data#ClothingandFootwear.

Wicker, Alden. "Fast Fashion Is Creating an Environmental Crisis." *Newsweek Magazine*, September 1, 2016. Available at: https://www.newsweek.com/2016/09/09/old-clothes-fashion-waste-crisis-494824.html.

16

Case 4B: Do the Right Thing?

Global pandemics are dire. Before the COVID era, Anderson Vincent worked hard to position his company, Seordna, as comfortable clothing for travel. Now there was no travel. The company's revenues dropped two thirds in the pandemic's first year. Most clothing brands were slashing staff, which is something Anderson told his staff he did not want to do. "That's not me," he declared. He had a commitment to his employees, as well as his profits.

Then, on May 25, 2020, a black man in Minnesota was murdered by a white police officer. George Floyd's last minutes of life were caught on video by a 17-year-old bystander and soon watched by millions across the United States. Within days, protests began in cities across the US. Some protests turned violent. On the day George Floyd was memorialized in the town of his birth, June 6, 2020, massive, peaceful protests were held nationwide demanding police reform.

Anderson says:

> George Floyd's death really affected me. As a black man, I've always felt the pressure to do more, be exceptional, be well-spoken. I have to do all these things so I can fit in the world the way I want. I'm going through this George Floyd thing and I'm watching people be really upset. I'm upset. I'm just fed up with

DOI: 10.4324/9781003414483-21

> the idea that I don't belong in this culture, that there are people who think I don't belong.

A worldwide pandemic and a national racial incident were both making the large inequities in America more visible. Anderson says:

> I'm watching it all on TV, like all of us. All the people falling through the social safety net. I'm watching the people driving through food banks, the long lines of cars. I'm thinking, "Those aren't poor people's cars. They look just like my car. That could be my car." Then we're hearing about all the kids that go hungry in this country. It's like the Band-Aid keeps getting ripped off all these things I was sort of hiding from.

Soon, Anderson's thoughts turned inward:

> I was using Seordna to have this conversation about consumerism, but I was part of helping the financial world by making my clothes overseas. I wasn't creating jobs in America. I was *taking away* jobs in America. I was just having this one-sided idea that you could wear less and we could make it sustainable. But who gives a damn if your clothes are sustainable if you can't feed your kids? Or if your neighbor doesn't have a job?

And then came the supply chain problems. The company was soon living a supply chain nightmare, like most companies around the world. Almost as soon as the pandemic started, it was difficult to get fabric to the factory in China where much of Seordna's manufacturing occurred. To make matters worse, it became difficult to move finished products from China to the United States.

United States clothing manufacturing typically occurs in Asia because of cost. Workers in Asia—particularly China—are paid far less than workers in America. The average garment worker in China is paid between $161 to $357 per month in US dollars.[1] Many, however, are paid on a piece-rate basis, so their pay can fluctuate greatly.

Anderson realized a supply chain nightmare was not the only thing wrong with having Seordna's clothing manufactured in Asia. One reason he quit working for big fashion brands was because he no longer wanted to pollute the Earth with clothing people didn't need. How could he feel comfortable shipping his designs halfway around the globe just so Americans would have what they wanted—even if he was telling people it was fine, just buy less? Should he continue providing jobs to Asian workers when people in America (especially in poor communities where inequities were so clearly exposed by the pandemic and the George Floyd incident) needed jobs?

What to do?

Like many, Anderson read press stories everyday about how other brands were dealing with the pandemic. His competitors were cutting staff to the bare minimum, wondering when the pandemic would end and if their companies would exist when it was over. Cutting staff bothered Anderson at an emotional level. He already declared to his entire team that he had no intention of cutting jobs. With revenue declining by two thirds, he still needed to cut costs. He also needed some way to revive revenues, to encourage consumers to return and buy travel clothes when there was no current travel.

One way to fix the revenue issue, Anderson thought, was new messaging emphasizing the comfort of his designs. "Transitioning your customers' thinking from travel to comfort isn't that easy," he says. If he was going to go that route to get more revenue, he needed to invest more money in advertising. He did not believe that would work, however. "We can't advertise our way to success," he declared.

In order to offset the environmental effects of manufacturing in—and shipping from—China, Seordna joined the One Percent for the Planet initiative, promising to donate one percent of revenues to organizations working on making the planet a cleaner place.[2] These organizations included Surfrider, American Rivers, and the Environmental Voter Project.

Weighing heavily on Anderson's mind and heart, still, were all the inequities in American society exposed by the pandemic and the death of George Floyd. Anderson was born in Memphis and raised in Los Angeles. Now, in New York City or anywhere else he went, he looked like

George Floyd, his car looked like those in long food pantry lines, and his neighbors and their neighbors looked just like families all over America who were hurting. What would help? What action could he and Seordna take to make a real difference?

Anderson decided to do something radical. "I decided we were going to bring all of our manufacturing back to the US. We were going to make Seordna clothing in communities that needed jobs," he says. At this point in his fashion career, Anderson was sure he could make it work. So, he jumped, telling his team one day on a Zoom call, "We are going to change the way we manufacture all our clothing. We are bringing those jobs home." He decided to call this Seordna initiative American Made.

Reflection Questions

1. Should Anderson have made this decision? Was it the "right" thing to do? Why or why not?
2. What were his other options? Consider both his business's needs and concern about social inequities in America.
3. What role did Anderson's emotions play in making the decision to move Seordna's production back to America? List the positive role of emotions in his decision, then the negative aspects, if you think there are any.

Creating Jobs for People in America

Anderson says:

> I had no business making this decision versus some other one. We were struggling just to stay afloat. I was just pissed off. I actually foolishly believed I could find enough people in the country that had the skills that we could just go into these communities and put them back to work.

There was much to learn.

He first tested his idea in New York City. All Broadway shows stopped in March, 2020, and costume professionals were, like many, out of work. Now it was July, four months into the pandemic. Anderson secured as many as 40 of these skilled professionals and set them to work making Seordna products from their homes.

This pilot effort taught Anderson a few important things about bringing production back to America. For one, you could produce high-quality clothing in a skilled workforce location. It also showed Anderson how high the costs were in America—New York City, in particular—for that skilled labor. Now he was calculating what he saved on transporting products from Asia and comparing those costs to the higher labor cost in NYC. The numbers didn't balance. Seordna could manipulate other inputs, however, to help get the financials to work. "We got very, very smart with our fabric purchasing," Anderson says.

Ultimately, those Broadway tailors and seamstresses went back to Broadway when shows started opening again. Thus, Anderson was forced to pause and look at what else he learned from the New York City pilot: 1) skilled labor in New York City would rather be sewing for hit shows on Broadway and will go back as soon as possible and 2) New York City was not the target community Anderson hoped to serve. Broadway seamstresses already had good paying jobs, as did a good percentage of their neighbors in surrounding communities. If Seordna was going to completely disrupt its business model to create jobs for people in under-resourced American communities, Anderson needed to find one of those communities.

Gee's Bend, Alabama

Isolated at a bend in the Alabama River just southwest of Selma, Alabama, Gee's Bend looked like one of those communities. The median income of its 700 residents is $12,000 per year and jobs have been scarce since 1962, if not before.[3] In that year, the ferry disappeared one day without notice from local officials. That ferry was the lifeline for Gee's Bend. It was the quickest way to connect to Camden to shop, work, go to school or receive medical care, as there wasn't a hospital or doctor on the Bend. People in Camden who held power said the ferry just wasn't up to it anymore. People in Gee's Bend suspected it was a response to demonstrations for racial justice and voting rights. The ferry did not return for nearly four decades.[4]

Gee's Bend has a long tradition of textile A(a)rt production—especially sewing and quilts. Their unique and beautiful quilts are exhibited worldwide and appear in American museums such as the Museum of Fine Arts, Houston, and the Milwaukee Art Museum. Gee's Bend quilts were assembled from scraps of fabric (well-worn blue jeans, shirts and skirts), then sewn together in striking, artful designs by residents, many of whom trace their ancestry to enslaved people from Pettway Plantation.[5] This is a town without many jobs, and a long tradition of sewing.

When Anderson went looking for a community for his second sewing pod, Gee's Bend was not hard to find.[6] A good friend had a strong connection to Gee's Bend quilters through the Souls Grown Deep Foundation and was happy to make an introduction.[7] They secured a meeting with the Foundation and Gee's Bend representatives so Anderson could pitch his idea of establishing a pod in Gee's Bend, which could create ten or more good-paying jobs. What Gee's Bend brought to the table was low-wage workers, some of whom might already possess sewing skills from their quilt making. This could be a win-win.

Gee's Bend said yes. The Souls Grown Deep Foundation, operationalized to give back to the Gee's Bend community, provided financial support totaling $600,000. The Foundation was able to provide funding to Seordna—a for-profit entity—as an "impact investment," rather than as a philanthropic grant.[8]

Start-up costs burned through this initial funding. There are a few buildings in Gee's Bend, though none of them suitable for dozens of commercial sewing machines with proper lighting and air conditioning. Anderson decided on converting a house for the effort. Sewing machines were purchased and, finally, training the first group of seamstresses to manufacture Seordna designs began.[9]

He quickly understood his new model for American production works best as follows: train those with no skills at $15 per hour at first. As skills and efficiency increase, boost the hourly rate to $25. Finding people willing to start at $15/hr and eager to sew was not a problem. The problem was the amount of training required to raise a worker's skill up to the level of quality and productivity that made Seordna's designs marketable.

It turns out that sewing quilts and sewing a pair of Seordna pants are not the same kind of sewing at all. Thus, most of the company's new hires in Gee's Bend required much more training than Anderson anticipated. Once they were trained to make one Seordna product, making others required even more training. When someone was being trained, they were not producing clothes. Anderson was burning through cash with little revenue to show for his effort, again.

Eagle Butte, South Dakota

Before Gee's Bend was fully operational, Anderson was already working on a site for another pod, this time in Eagle Butte, South Dakota on the Cheyenne River Reservation. A staff member of a local business development non-profit was at a conference and met someone who knew Anderson. This launched a conversation about bringing Seordna to Cheyenne River.[10]

In square miles, Cheyenne River Reservation is the fourth largest of over 300 tribal reservations in the United States.[11] Like many reservations, particularly those like Cheyenne River that do not run casinos to generate jobs and revenue for their members, this location suffers from some serious social problems. Eagle Butte has a population of 1,260 as of the 2020 census.[12] The teen suicide rate is 3.5 times the rate in the US as a whole.[13] Unemployment on the reservation, according to the U.S. Census Bureau's American Community Survey for 2013–2017 was 26.4%, more than four times the average of 6% in the US during the same period.[14] Like many smaller communities in America, the largest employer is the hospital.[15] There are not many other jobs on the reservation's 4,266 square miles. Nearest cities to Eagle Butte are Pierre, South Dakota's capital 90 miles away, with a population of 14,091, and Bismarck, 163 miles away, with 74,138 residents.[16]

Anderson had a strong sense that anyone he hired for this new pod would require training to become a skilled maker of even the simplest Seordna designs. That said, he knew the Cheyenne Reservation was the right place to establish the company's next sewing pod because he could feel the community's creativity. As he drove around Eagle Butte during his first few visits, he also saw the critical need for jobs and economic opportunity.

South Dakota was announced as the site for the next pod in December, 2021. At the time, Anderson said it would take several months to establish the pod for online sales. Ultimately, the pod hired its first employees at the end of August, 2022, and as of May, 2023, products are not shipping from this pod because Seordna is still in the training process.

Anderson was learning that the main cost pushing manufacturing jobs to Asia—skilled labor—was very hard to manipulate in America. A starting wage of $15 per hour for unskilled garment makers was many times more than the cost of skilled labor in China. Further, it took many hours to train unskilled makers to the level Seordna needed.

Other than labor, there were few other costs Anderson could manipulate. The cost of fabric was the same whether Seordna purchased it in Asia or America or anywhere else in the world. Costs for transportation went down when Seordna didn't have to ship finished product from Asia to America for American customers, however. Marketing costs were the same, regardless of where the clothes were being manufactured.

Anderson also realized the cost of labor was a problem. That cost was eating up all his start-up funds. Adding that cost into the price he would have to charge for a shirt or pair of pants would make it harder and harder to sell any Seordna clothing.

He set out to do what he thought was the right thing: bring jobs back to poor communities in America. That was still the vision and the goal. But how to make it work financially, given what Anderson learned from the first two pods in NYC and Gee's Bend? Some kind of adjustment was clearly necessary, or Seordna would go out of business.

Reflection Questions

1. How can Seordna make its American Made initiative work, bringing jobs back to America's under-resourced communities, at a cost that is still attractive to consumers?
2. How can Seordna "do the right thing" and also make their business work financially?

Training People in America

A possible answer to Anderson's training costs problem was found in his own recent experience in Gee's Bend. That community had a foundation (the Souls Grown Deep Foundation, mentioned above) that cared about the community, and more jobs for Gee's Bend residents was a start. Souls Grown Deep invested $600,000 to pay start-up costs to bring Seordna there. This began with creating the physical space for production: painting, wiring for the sewing machines, air conditioning, the sewing machines themselves, etc. After months of getting this ready, however, Anderson had no more startup funds for training the residents. So, he looked for other donors who would help. He found several, such as the corporate foundation of the statewide electrical company serving Gee's Bend. They were willing to invest in job creation.

"Why are you paying for it?" asked a friend when Anderson brought this up with him. "Raise grants to train the makers. There's tons of money out there for training people in America."

For Anderson, this made sense. "The moment I put that out there, we had people who were like 'I'm a foundation. I have tons of money, and that's exactly where I want to put it.'"

Seordna has, to date, received commitments to support its pods from the Bush Foundation, Marguerite Casey Foundation, and Walton Foundation. Most are doing this as "impact investing," since Seordna is *not* a non-profit that can receive traditional grants. "We just have to deliver the outcomes they (the Foundations) are required to show the Federal government."

Five other tribes contacted Anderson asking how they can get a pod in their community. One, having casinos, is different from his current tribe in South Dakota meaning the tribe has plenty of money for funding the startup and training costs.

Has this been good for sales? Anderson says:

> It is another reason for our customers to buy our clothes. We've added a younger demographic as our customer. That demographic, 21 to 35 year olds, was elusive to us before we launched American Made. We were 35–55 year olds (demographic) before

> that. We also have a better sell-through when we talk about the American Made product.[17]

"We just can't make our product fast enough today," he says. Happily, lack of serious production from the American pods, so far, has not yet been a disaster. Seordna expected to double in sales again in 2020 before the pandemic hit. Planning included stockpiling inventory of finished product from the China factory. That inventory surplus would be used to fill orders, while the pods get up to speed.

To date, customers can get most of the Seordna products they order. Of course, this situation cannot continue forever. Right now, American Made pods are responsible for 19% of Seordna's inventory. Sooner than later, pods must become the prime manufacturers of Seordna's product.

Reflection Questions

1. Should Anderson expand the pods to other native American locations?
2. Has Anderson determined how to balance the "right thing" for under-resourced communities in America, and also for his business?

Discussion: Case 4B — Do the Right Thing?

Summary

Inspiration comes in many forms. For many, its impact is a fork in the road where one either chooses to act or not. Case 4B describes Anderson as deeply affected by the George Floyd tragedy, which served as his inspiration to launch Seordna's new manufacturing effort. Interestingly, he acted *through* the company, primarily, instead of by other means. According to the narrative, his decision to move the company's manufacturing back to the US was an ethical act, which had business consequences. The Case shows us the consequences—both meaningful and challenging—of these inspired actions. His decision demonstrates that holding true to one's ethical foundations *typically* takes effort. Nothing good, it seems, comes easy.

Anderson's decision to begin this transition by initially moving production to New York City was, arguably, genius. With a skilled workforce available due to the pandemic, he demonstrated "proof of concept;" a clothing brand *could* make a profit manufacturing on the American shore. This was crucial not only in a business sense, but also as proof that acting according to one's ethics was—for Anderson—the right thing to do. When he began losing his NYC-based labor force, an opportunity emerged in Gee's Bend, then in Eagle Butte—both economically depressed areas.

Interestingly, Seordna (a for-profit business) began receiving impact investments from non-profit foundations for training new employees. When this occurs, Seordna (as an entity) changes dramatically. Anderson's decision to bring manufacturing back to the US is not necessarily an entrepreneurial or innovative decision as there has been a movement to on-shore manufacturing for decades; it is more an ethical decision. Yet this decision puts the company at some risk and with Anderson's firm commitment to not lay off employees during the pandemic, the risk becomes increasingly grave; spending money on training skilled workers is depleting Seordna's finances. However, once the company receives these impact investments for training workers in economically disadvantaged areas, the business enters the realm of *social* entrepreneurship. Yes, this is still a for-profit fashion brand, but in this new realm, *Seordna* becomes something more.

Social entrepreneurship is best described by Gregory Dees, one of the movement's most significant scholars. He defines social entrepreneurs as those who:

> ...play the role of change agents in the social sector, by:
>
> - Adopting a mission to create and sustain social value (not just private value)
> - Recognizing and relentlessly pursuing new opportunities to serve that mission
> - Engaging in a process of continuous innovation, adaptation, and learning
> - Acting boldly without being limited by resources currently in hand, and
> - Exhibiting heightened accountability to the constituencies served and for the outcomes created.[18]

Let's see if Seordna meets Dees's definition.

1. *Adopting a mission to create and sustain social value (not just private value).* As a for-profit, Seordna (in addition to its environmental and design concerns) is about making a profit. When Anderson moves manufacturing to the US and trains economically and socially disadvantaged communities to create these products at a fair and equitable wage, the company has a **mission**—just like a non-profit organization. It **creates and sustains social value** by going into these communities, investing foundation dollars in training and—importantly—not abandoning its commitment simply because it may be challenging in the short term.
2. *Recognizing and relentlessly pursuing new opportunities to serve that mission.* Despite the increased time investment in training workers at Gee's Bend, Seordna identifies the Eagle Butte community and sets up another manufacturing pod. Despite the fact that Gee's Bend wasn't yet *fully* trained to produce products, the company **recognized and relentlessly pursued a new opportunity** to fulfill its new **mission**.

3. *Engaging in a process of continuous innovation, adaptation, and learning.* Anderson had to design a new training program for the Gee's Bend community, which was an **adaptation** required when shifting from trained workers to untrained. Setting up the Gee's Bend facility was a **learning experience** for Anderson, as was Eagle Butte. Seordna **innovated** by exploring a relationship with five other tribal communities with resources to support the effort, thus creating a second funding stream to support more pods' initial training.
4. *Acting boldly without being limited by resources currently in hand.* Anderson did not abandon Gee's Bend when it was becoming a financial strain. In fact, despite being **limited by resources currently in hand,** he was creative and pursued new funding to support Seordna's **mission.**
5. *Exhibiting heightened accountability to the constituencies served and for the outcomes created.* Seordna has not abandoned its new mission or the new pods. Despite not being able to "…make our product fast enough today" due to the training challenges, the company is being **accountable to the constituencies served and the outcomes created.**

According to Dees's definition, we could make a strong case that Seordna is engaging in the five pillars of social entrepreneurship. This means it is not only an entrepreneurial venture founded on sustainable principles but, in this new realm, the company is a change agent in the communities it serves. It exists then, in two parallel environments, serving two different constituencies (a for-profit market and challenged communities), with two different, intersecting value propositions (profit and community impact). This meets Anderson's goals and likely appeals to his market's values.

It seems, then, that Anderson has a win-win on his hands. There's 1) plenty of interest and support in moving manufacturing to US shores, 2) Seordna has parallel value streams, 3) there were no layoffs during the pandemic, 4) Anderson's very risky business decision during a pandemic appears to be a success, 5) Seordna is still profitable and 6) is positively impacting communities in need. Yet there are consequences of this success. A short list would include: 1) temporarily negotiate two supply chains as he transitions to US manufacturing, 2) manage and make decisions for both a for-profit arts business and a social enterprise, 3) continue his design creation, 4) manage a training system for new workers and 5) remain ethically responsible in his business decisions. This is not an easy job in the best of circumstances. While it is true that people can be hired to manage some of these responsibilities, *someone* needs to guide and make final decisions concerning these efforts.

Factors Forcing the Decision

George Floyd's murder was the primary factor in Anderson's decision to transition Seordna's manufacturing to the US. Yet he was not the only entrepreneur to respond to this tragedy. In fact, entrepreneurs, corporations and foundations (among others) felt a need to respond in a manner that served the social good. Racial equity, environmental and funding efforts emerged almost overnight across the country. Large corporations like Nike, Ben & Jerrys, Facebook and Amazon (among many others) either released strong statements against the Floyd incident or pledged money to support disadvantaged communities of color.[19] Due to Black Lives Matter protests bringing attention to the inequities of African-American business loan and credit line decisions, business ownership in these communities immediately increased across the country.[20] Seordna was on its way to sustainability by this time and, therefore, wasn't a part of this increase directly, but as an African American-owned business, it was positioned to take advantage of an easier loan and credit landscape.

This new funding landscape extended to both non-profit organizations and social entrepreneurs. Foundations were looking to impact communities during this time and for them, the more effective the better. Viewed from a non-profit perspective, Seordna's new effort was positioned perfectly to leverage this shift as well. For example, Gee's Bend is an African-American majority (98% according to 2021 census data) community with an unemployment rate of 21.7% at the beginning of the pandemic and a median household income $20,000 below the state average in 2019.[21] When combined with the corporate and lender response to George Floyd's death, Gee's Bend's high unemployment rate, its demographic makeup and being in the14th poorest county in the US, it's no wonder Seordna secured foundation-based monies.

What we have then, is what one might call the "George Floyd Effect." In essence, the dramatic murder of an African-American man on a street in Minnesota impacted not only US culture, it changed the lending and granting priorities of US banks, corporations and foundations. On a national scale, this is a significant social shift. Anderson (like so many others) internally wrestled with George Floyd's death and its implications for the African-American community; his response was to change Seordna's business model. He began this Case as an arts entrepreneur, and because of a decision to better disadvantaged communities *through* his fashion brand; he ended this Case as an arts-based social entrepreneur.

Decision Model

As Anderson deliberated about launching Seordna in Case 4A, he used a Domain-based decision-making model, in part because he was embedded in the domain of the fashion industry. In this Case, he is deciding how to respond to the death of George Floyd and the social impacts of COVID simultaneously. Since these are social issues, one would expect him to stay in this model grouping as he found himself in two domains concurrently: the African-American community and a world community reeling from COVID. Of course, with Seordna he was still in the fashion industry, which is another domain; indeed, he was negotiating *three* domains in the midst of two serious, national crises simultaneously.

It seems logical to continue using the same decision model in this grouping since he is *recognizing patterns* in these domains and trying to respond. For some readers, his negotiations around these patterns may seem emotionally-based, leading one to think an Instinctive-based model (Creative or Heuristic) would be used. Though Anderson is negotiating these crises on many levels—including emotionally—just because an arts entrepreneur might be emotionally impacted around a situation does not mean they will react in that way; nor does it mean they are using a model from the Instinctive model group.[22]

As with Case 4A, the keys to determining the decision-making model Anderson used in this Case are the *patterns* steps of the Models: Step 3 of the Expertise model (Based on one's understanding and experience within a domain, *identify* patterns) and Step 2 of the Intuitive model (Scan the environment for cues to *recognize* patterns). We can look to the Decision Model section of the Case 4A Discussion and apply the same comparative logic: if Anderson ran into problems at Gee's Bend and abandoned the effort there, then secured Eagle Butte and used a different approach (Step 5 of the Intuitive model—If chosen course of action will not produce desired outcome, alter it and retest), then an Intuitive model identification is appropriate. However, since Anderson did not abandon Gee's Bend, an Expertise model identification is likely best in this Case.

While Anderson is using the same decision model in both Cases 4A and 4B, we should *not* conclude the following: if a venture is tightly integrated within a domain of some kind (industry, trade, craft, etc.) a model in the Domain group is appropriate. As we have made clear, there is not *one* best model arts entrepreneurs should use when making decisions about their ventures. Anderson could have easily used a Linear group model if the decision was data-driven. (i.e.: based on Seordna's training and startup costs, projected revenue, fabric shipping costs, etc.). Likewise, he could have made a snap decision to move manufacturing to the US using the Heuristic model. In this Case, he did neither. This suggests Anderson's decision making thus far in the Case Set *tends to be* developing solutions lying *within* domains.

Ecology Discussion

The last paragraph immediately above sets us up well for an ecology discussion of this Case. Before we do, however, we remind the reader that Anderson is negotiating three distinct domains simultaneously: the fashion industry, the African-American experience in the US and a global pandemic. From an ecology perspective, Anderson is squarely in the Fashion Ecology during his negotiations. However, now that Seordna's business model is more social entrepreneurship-based, is there a Social Entrepreneurship Ecology we should consider? This is somewhat debatable. In broad strokes, a Social Entrepreneurship Ecology would have four quadrants: dedicated policy and financial inputs, community output and perhaps marketing. While one could insert this as a part of a Steady State Model, it could become somewhat unwieldy and cause confusion.

Perhaps a better solution would be to integrate these aspects into a single ecology.[23] If we envision the right side of the ecology as representing the entire Fashion Ecology (see Figure 15.1 from Case 4A, with the "Consumer" element pulled out and highlighted) and the left side as the main pillars of a Social Entrepreneurship Ecology, we have a (somewhat) better view of Anderson's decision-making environment.[24] (See Figure 16.1). As discussed in Case 4A, the fashion industry is both complex and dynamic. When including the additional challenges of the social entrepreneurship component—which is now part of Seordna's manufacturing effort—it is not far off to say that Anderson is *almost* operating a non-profit organization *inside* of Seordna. Before we have that discussion, let's talk very briefly about social entrepreneurship ventures.

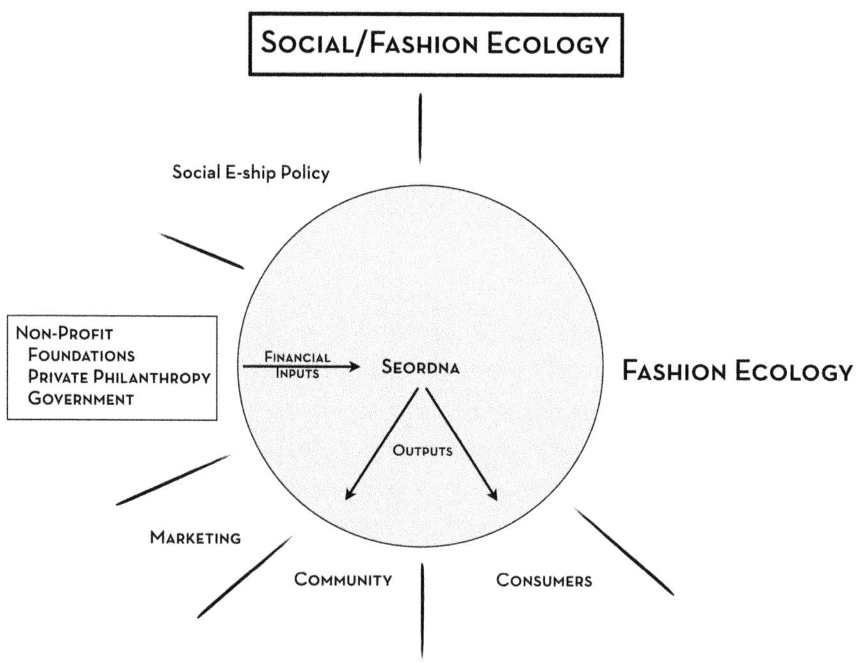

Figure 16.1 Seordna's Social/Fashion Ecology.

First, a social entrepreneurship venture can be incorporated as either a for-profit, a non-profit organization or some variation such as a B-corp or a low-profit company (L3C). These ventures look similar to a non-profit because of their social-based mission. Seordna is clearly a for-profit entity but it now has a social entrepreneurship component. We can tell it has this component because 1) there is a community served and 2) there is a revenue stream from foundations, private philanthropy or government to fund the effort.

The elements on the left side of Figure 16.1 (as a group) can be called the "Social Entrepreneurship" group and comprise the four elements listed in the first paragraph of this section. A brief explanation of each appears below.

Social Entrepreneurship Policy: This element functions similarly to the Arts Policy element in the Non-Profit Ecology. In essence, much of this group's elements are impacted by policy efforts focusing on social entrepreneurship.

Marketing: This element is critical for social entrepreneurship ventures. If there is no marketing about the venture's mission, for-profit businesses, their markets, funders or potential communities, it can be difficult to engage with these organizations.

Communities: This element acts exactly the same as in the Non-Profit Ecology where 501(c)3 organizations focus their mission on these groups.

Financial Inputs: This group of elements should be familiar for those familiar with *The New Arts Entrepreneur* because they are the same ones in the Non-Profit Ecology: foundations, private philanthropy, earned income (in Seordna's case) and government (of all kinds).

What we have in this group are two of the three primary inputs of the Non-Profit Ecology, including one major output, communities. For most, it would seem that a social entrepreneurship venture is actually a non-profit organization as far as its ecological construction. It is not. Since there is no *critically-weighted* consensus on a definition of social entrepreneurship—sans Dees' model—it almost exists as a concept in search of proof that such a thing exists.[25] Yet we know it *does exist* when 1) for-profit entities engage in non-profit-similar missions, 2) these

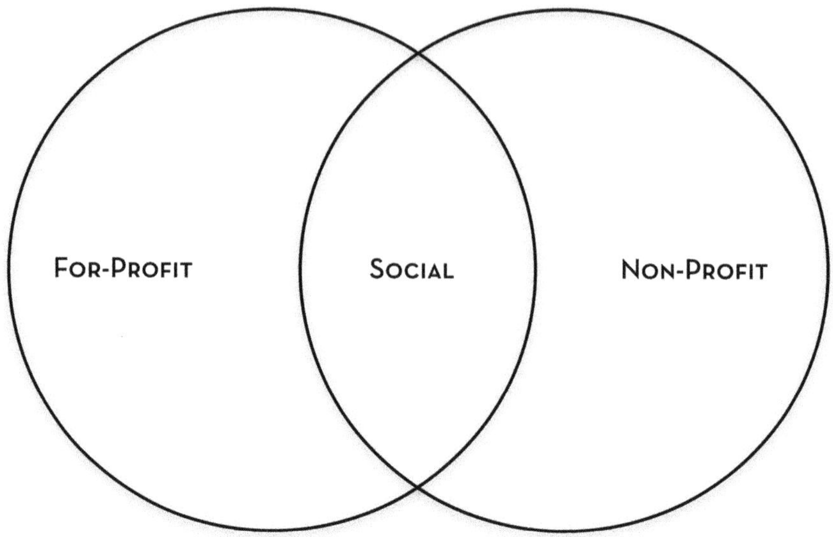

Figure 16.2 Seordna's For- and Non-profit Venn Diagram.

ventures earn a profit and 3) we already proved Seordna is engaging in social entrepreneurship from the Summary discussion above. Without going into an overly academic explanation, it might be best to consider Social Entrepreneurship not as an ecological system, but a *concept* allowing an intermingling of the For- and Non-Profit ecologies where the pillars of each fuse ways that creates something new, yet recognizable. Figure 16.2 illustrates this idea.

Notes

1 Business and Human Rights Resource Centre, "Impacts of COVID-19 on China's Garment Sector," accessed November 16, 2023. Available at: https://www.business-humanrights.org/en/from-us/covid-19-action-tracker/china/#:~:text=Background%20information%20on%20garment%20sector&text=The%20minimum%20wage%20varies%20by,for%20food%2C%20attendance%20and%20seniority.

2 One Percent for the Planet, "Our Story." Accessed November 16, 2023. Available at: https://www.onepercentfortheplanet.org/about/story.

3 NEST, "Gee's Bend." Accessed November 16, 2023. Available at: https://www.buildanest.org/geesbend.

4 Clyde Haberman, "Martin Luther King's Call for Voting Rights Inspired Isolated Hamlet," *New York Times*, March 8, 2015. Available at: https://www.nytimes.com/2015/03/09/us/gees-bend-alabama-martin-luther-king-voting-rights-1965.html.

5 Kyes Stephens, "The History of Gee's Bend, Alabama," *The Quilts of Gee's Bend in Context*. Accessed November 16, 2023. Available at: https://www.auburn.edu/academic/other/geesbend/explore/history.htm.

6 For the remainder of this Case Set, we will be using the term "pods" to describe the communities Anderson engages to manufacture Seordna clothing. One could consider Anderson's pilot effort in NYC a "pod."

7 Souls Grown Deep Foundation, "About: Souls Grown Deep Foundation." Accessed November 16, 2023. Available at: https://www.soulsgrowndeep.org/foundation/about.

8 According to the Foundation's annual report, this was done through a convertible note. As we learned in Case 4A, this means the foundation is loaning money to a relatively new entity, which can be converted into equity in the entity (i.e.: Seordna) at a later date.

9 Good quality, commercial-grade sewing machines can cost upwards of $5,000–$8,000 each.

10 Kristi Eaton, "Nimble Maker Pods Give Fashion Jobs a Light Footprint," *Reasons to Be Cheerful*. Last modified May 11, 2023. Available at: https://reasonstobecheerful.world/nimble-maker-pods-give-fashion-jobs-a-light-footprint.

11 Wikipedia, "List of Indian Reservations In The United States." Accessed November 16, 2023. Available at: https://en.wikipedia.org/wiki/List_of_Indian_reservations_in_the_United_States.

12 Place Explorer, "Eagle Butte," *Data Commons*, accessed November 16, 2023. Available at: https://datacommons.org/place/geoId/4617620/?utm_medium=explore&mprop=count&popt=Person&hl=en.

13 Tatanka Luta, "The Research: Cheyenne River Statistics." Accessed November 16, 2023. Available at: https://tatankaluta.org/research-page-2.

14 See Center For Native American Youth at The Aspen Institute, "Fast Facts About Native American Youth and Indian Country." Accessed November 16, 2023. Available at: https://www.aspeninstitute.org/wp-content/uploads/files/content/images/Fast%20Facts.pdf, Federal Reserve Bank of Minneapolis, "Cheyenne River Reservation." Accessed November 16, 2023. Available at: https://www.minneapolisfed.org/indiancountry/resources/native-community-data-profiles and U.S. Bureau of Labor Statistics, "Civilian Unemployment Rate." Accessed November 17, 2023. Available at: https://www.bls.gov/charts/employment-situation/civilian-unemployment-rate.htm.

15 Thomas C. Ricketts, III and Paige E. Heaphy, "Hospitals In Rural America," *Western Journal of Medicine* 173, no. 6, (Dec. 2000): 418–422.

16 Travel Math, "Cities Near North Eagle Butte, South Dakota." Accessed November 16, 2023. Available at: https://www.travelmath.com/cities-near/North+Eagle+Butte,+SD.

17 "Sell-through" is a key performance indicator in retail, which measures the ratio of units in inventory versus units sold to customers. In other words, if you make a lot of product, and don't sell much of it, that's a bad sell-through rate. A good sell through rate is when you sell everything you make, having nothing left sitting on inventory shelves.

18 Gregory Dees, "The Meaning of Social Entrepreneurship," reformatted and revised, 2001. Available at: https://centers.fuqua.duke.edu/case/wp-content/uploads/sites/7/2015/03/Article_Dees_MeaningofSocialEntrepreneurship_2001.pdf.

19 There has been a number of studies suggesting these financial pledges are disproportioned and difficult to enforce. See Tracy Jan, Jenna McGregor and Megahn Hoyer, "Corporate America's $50 billion Promise," *The Washington Post*. Last updated Aug. 24, 2021. Available at: https://www.washingtonpost.com/business/interactive/2021/george-floyd-corporate-america-racial-justice.

20 Raffi E. García and Alberto Ortega, "Racial Protests and Credit Access" (working paper, last revised Oct. 19, 2023). Available at: https://doi.org/10.2139/ssrn.4304551.
21 For population demographics, see CensusReporter.org, "Census Tract 347," accessed July 12, 2023. Available at: https://censusreporter.org/profiles/14000US01131034700-census-tract-347-wilcox-al. For household income data, see City-data.com, "Boykin, AL." Accessed July 12, 2023. Available at: https://www.city-data.com/city/Boykin-Alabama.html. For unemployment rates, see Federal Reserve Bank of St. Louis (FRED), "Unemployment Rate for Wilcox County, AL." Accessed July 12, 2023. Available at: https://fred.stlouisfed.org/series/ALWILC1URN.
22 As a reminder, the models in the Instinctive group are somewhat timed-based: the Heuristic model is better used when a quick or critical decision is required and the Creative model is more effective when the decision is not time-critical.
23 Portions of the ecology below are inspired by Rone Roux, "Merging Social and Arts Entrepreneurship to Empower Music Students," working paper, Stellenbosch University, April 24, 2023.
24 Ibid.
25 Dees, Gregory. "The Meaning of Social Entrepreneurship."

Bibliography

Business & Human Rights Resource Centre. "Impacts of COVID-19 on China's Garment Sector." Accessed November 16, 2023. Available at: https://www.business-humanrights.org/en/from-us/covid-19-action-tracker/china/#:~:text=Background%20information%20on%20garment%20sector&text=The%20minimum%20wage%20varies%20by,for%20food%2C%20attendance%20and%20seniority.

Beckman, Gary D. *The New Arts Entrepreneur: Navigating the Arts Ecologies*. London: Routledge, 2022.

CensusReporter.org, "Census Tract 347." Accessed July 12, 2023. Available at: https://censusreporter.org/profiles/14000US01131034700-census-tract-347-wilcox-al.

Center For Native American Youth at The Aspen Institute. "Fast Facts About Native American Youth and Indian Country." Accessed November 16, 2023. Available at: https://www.aspeninstitute.org/wp-content/uploads/files/content/images/Fast%20Facts.pdf.

City-data.com, "Boykin, AL," Accessed July 12, 2023. Available at: https://www.city-data.com/city/Boykin-Alabama.html.

Dees, Gregory. "The Meaning of Social Entrepreneurship." Reformatted and revised, 2001. Available at: https://centers.fuqua.duke.edu/case/wp-content/uploads/sites/7/2015/03/Article_Dees_MeaningofSocialEntrepreneurship_2001.pdf.

Eaton, Kristi. "Nimble Maker Pods Give Fashion Jobs a Light Footprint." *Reasons To Be Cheerful*. Last modified May 11, 2023. Available at: https://reasonstobecheerful.world/nimble-maker-pods-give-fashion-jobs-a-light-footprint.

Federal Reserve Bank of Minneapolis. "Cheyenne River Reservation." Accessed November 16, 2023. Available at: https://www.minneapolisfed.org/indiancountry/resources/native-community-data-profile.

Federal Reserve Bank of St. Louis (FRED). "Unemployment Rate for Wilcox County, AL" Accessed July 12, 2023. Available at: https://fred.stlouisfed.org/series/ALWILC1URN.

García, Raffi E. and Alberto Ortega. "Racial Protests and Credit Access." Working paper, last revised Oct. 19, 2023. Available at: https://doi.org/10.2139/ssrn.4304551.

Haberman, Clyde. "Martin Luther King's Call for Voting Rights Inspired Isolated Hamlet." *New York Times*, March 8, 2015. Available at: https://www.nytimes.com/2015/03/09/us/gees-bend-alabama-martin-luther-king-voting-rights-1965.html.

Jan, Tracy, Jenna McGregor and Megahn Hoyer. "Corporate America's $50 billion Promise." *The Washington Post*, updated Aug. 24, 2021. Available at: https://www.washingtonpost.com/business/interactive/2021/george-floyd-corporate-america-racial-justice.

NEST. "Gee's Bend." Accessed November 16, 2023. Available at: https://www.buildanest.org/geesbend.

One Percent for the Planet. "Our Story." Accessed November 16, 2023. Available at: https://www.onepercentfortheplanet.org/about/story.

Place Explorer. "Eagle Butte." *Data Commons*. Accessed November 16, 2023. Available at: https://datacommons.org/place/geoId/4617620/?utm_medium=explore&mprop=count&popt=Person&hl=en.

Ricketts, Thomas C. III and Paige E. Heaphy. "Hospitals In Rural America." *Western Journal of Medicine* 173, no. 6 (Dec. 2000): 418–422.

Roux, Rone. "Merging Social and Arts Entrepreneurship to Empower Music Students." Working Paper. Stellenbosch University, April 24, 2023.

Souls Grown Deep Foundation. "About: Souls Grown Deep Foundation." Available at: https://www.soulsgrowndeep.org/foundation/about.

Stephens, Kyes. "The History of Gee's Bend, Alabama." *The Quilts of Gee's Bend in Context*. Available at: https://www.auburn.edu/academic/other/geesbend/explore/history.htm.

Tatanka Luta. "The Research: Cheyenne River Statistics." Accessed November 16, 2023. Available at: https://tatankaluta.org/research-page-2.

Travel Math. "Cities Near North Eagle Butte, South Dakota." Accessed November 16, 2023. Available at: https://www.travelmath.com/cities-near/North+Eagle+Butte,+SD.

U.S. Bureau of Labor Statistics. "Civilian Unemployment Rate." Accessed November 17, 2023. Available at: https://www.bls.gov/charts/employment-situation/civilian-unemployment-rate.htm.

Wikipedia. "List of Indian Reservations in The United States." Accessed November 16, 2023. Available at: https://en.wikipedia.org/wiki/List_of_Indian_reservations_in_the_United_States.

17
Case 4C: How to Retain Employees?

Anderson Vincent had a problem: he was hiring people for his big idea but they weren't staying. His company, Seordna, hired 21 people for clothing manufacturing training in early September, 2022, at the Cheyenne River Reservation in South Dakota. This was Seordna's newest maker pod. By February 1, 2023, training was in its fifth month and only six trainees remained. Though they were paid during this time, 15 had left.

Employee retention was not only a problem, it threatened Anderson's goals for Seordna. He confided:

> Our most important thing, the thing that makes us win, is retention. If we're going to spend six to eight months training someone, and then they leave, we've just burned eight months, and we've burned a boatload of money and resources and time. That sets us back. So, how do you get people to stay? How do you create an environment where they love what they're doing?

Not long ago, Anderson found a funding source that shared his vision for US manufacturing jobs: charitable foundations. These foundations mainly care about creating jobs in under-resourced communities and training unskilled people for these jobs. Seordna could do that, so foundations funded the company's efforts. They assumed sales revenue would

DOI: 10.4324/9781003414483-22

keep the organization growing and jobs secure. However, to make this work, Seordna needed to retain these workers.

"You Need to Flip your Model"

Anderson was frustrated. In response to the George Floyd murder in summer 2020, he staked the future of the company on doing the right thing for under-resourced communities. This was not just a business decision he made, but also a deeply felt personal mission. In July of 2020, he told his team he was moving all of Seordna's clothing manufacturing back to America. Now it was 2022 and it seemed like nothing was working quite well enough. He had been unable, so far, to ignite sales and grow revenue back to pre-pandemic levels.

"Why is my business not working?" he asked. He knew one of the reasons: "We're spending all our resources—money, people—on American Made, not on Seordna, the brand," he said. With less work on the brand (advertising and other ways of communicating with customers, for example) sales and revenue suffered.

Discussing this with one of his investors, Anderson heard this insight: "You need to flip your model. You are thinking you have a really interesting product model that you are now manufacturing in a new location. You need to start thinking of it as a really interesting manufacturing model that can make high-quality products for anyone." What would it mean, though, to truly put manufacturing at the core of Seordna? What would need to change?

As he struggled to increase revenue and retain skilled makers for his new pods, Anderson asked himself another question: "Am I committed to building a world-class American Made initiative?" American Made was now his manufacturing method. If he was committed to it, then the pods he was creating needed to be world-class. World-class started with high quality. Specifically, straight hems, flat seams and durability. It also meant high productivity, with each employee making enough pants or shirts per paycheck to keep the cost of labor per piece low enough that prices were within reach of consumers.

He had never been in the manufacturing business before launching American Made. Anderson had always been a fashion designer who partnered with manufacturers to produce his designs. Was he really committed now to doing all that was necessary to be a world-class clothing manufacturer?

"I actually love all that stuff," Anderson said. "Like the Toyota Production System, where people teach themselves to get more and more efficient." To be truly ready to make that commitment, he knew the next problem he had to fix was retaining trained sewers. Where to start and what to do?

Reflection Questions

1. What options does Anderson have to help Seordna retain more of the people it hires and trains as makers?
2. How should he go about deciding which options to choose?

Creating a World-Class Manufacturer

The first thing Anderson did was bring in someone who could help Seordna create a better hiring process. "We had people we hired who would come for two weeks of training, get paid, then disappear for two weeks," Anderson says. "Then they'd show back up and think they still had a job. They've never had a position where they're expected to show up like that."

For starters, the consultant helped Seordna create better interview questions, to get underneath the surface-level answers they were getting from candidates. To do this, they looked at those Anderson hired who were doing everything well. What were their qualities and characteristics that made them good employees for Seordna? Then they asked themselves, "What questions can we ask to elicit answers that tell us whether a candidate does or does not have those same characteristics?"

Working with the consultant, Anderson realized he couldn't "… save everyone on the reservation. I have to find those who really see the opportunity." He came to understand that some people had issues beyond those that Seordna could solve: substance and domestic abuse, no history of employment, lack of motivation to seize this opportunity.

"I went from a place of 'I'm saving the world' to 'I'm building a business' and allowing people who want this opportunity to come into it."

Anderson's team also looked at how to do firing, in case they hired anyone who emerged as a bad fit. "We wanted to get those people out as soon as possible. It's cancerous to have people who don't want to do the work."

The team was also learning about the size of pods:

> It doesn't really work to have teams that are bigger than six or eight people each. Navy SEAL teams are between five and eight people. There's research on this. We've learned it by watching our pods work. If you get bigger than eight, two leaders emerge. It splinters the team. Now we have what we call a 'pioneer' team of six. The next team gets to learn from them, but they work separately from the first team, on something else (i.e. pants vs. shirts). Training the next pod, in addition to their garment making, gives the first pod members a chance to earn more. It also fills them with a sense of pride.

Once some of these changes were made, they were formalized into an operating model. Seordna could use that for launching new sites. This included how to train the next trainers, and incentive pay for outstanding work.

Anderson could now step back and assess what other things needed to change to truly create a world-class manufacturing company and retain its employees. He had the experience of starting and running pods in three locations: New York City, Gee's Bend, and the Cheyenne River Reservation. What had he learned in each?

He soon realized he was running two businesses. A friend in China had pointed him toward this idea and now Anderson understood what he meant. Obviously, the first business, which he had been running since launching Seordna, was a clothing brand business—designing great clothes, sourcing fabrics, and marketing to consumers. The second business, which became part of Seordna with the launch of American Made, was the manufacturing business—hiring, training and managing people to sew at a world-class level.

Anderson knew he did not have enough people or resources to continue running both businesses. If he continued trying to do that, both would continue to struggle. The lack of attention to employees at the pods would result in unacceptable attrition. Sales would suffer from insufficient time and money spent on marketing. Anderson knew many aspects of the whole business. He also knew he could not do it all. Even a multi-talented, experienced and dedicated artist like Anderson was constrained by limits. There was only so much time in the day.

He decided to focus 100% of his own and the company's energy on American Made, the manufacturing business. This was a leap of will. Anderson was not sure this would be enough. If he could guarantee hiring the right people and they stayed, his pods would start producing more of his designs, and costs for each piece would decrease. What more could he do to make sure this happened?

Reflection Questions

1. Seordna is obviously struggling after moving its manufacturing to the United States. Did Anderson miss something?
2. What else could Anderson do to increase employee retention?
3. How could Seordna test alternative courses of action, to determine which are most viable?

Giving Employees a Stake

In early 2023, Anderson took what some would call a radical and risky step. He decided the solution to his employee retention problem was to restructure the ownership of his company. This started with Anderson putting manufacturing at the core of what Seordna now does.

Anderson says:

> Once I embraced that thought, it was like, well, I really should be sharing our revenue with all stakeholders, including makers.

> So, we're looking at ways to give employees a share in company profits. Other companies do this. We are considering different types of trusts and things so we can split some of the equity, then give it to the makers. It takes away some of my equity, and some of my investors' equity, too.

How might this work? "We'll pay people to train our makers. Then we'll pay for wrap-around services. All of this is with foundations' money." Wrap-around services may include childcare, financial literacy classes, wealth-building ideas, diet and obesity coaching, and domestic violence help. "Foundations will also pay for facilities and machinery and things to train people. When they graduate, they're paid by Seordna buying the products they made," Anderson adds. Seordna then sells these finished products at a profit.

In this model, Seordna will be only one of several customers for whom the pods at Gee's Bend and Cheyenne River fabricate designs. The pods would be the world-class manufacturing model Anderson's friend in China outlined. Each user of the manufacturing platform, including the Seordna brand, can focus on fashion design and marketing. If this increases revenues as expected, there's more business for the pods.

How does this structural change improve worker retention? Giving employees an ownership stake incentivizes them to perform. It gives them pride and dignity that few manufacturing jobs offer. Will it work? It is too soon to tell. Anderson explained:

> We're still making this transition. It's hard, really hard. I make it sound easy. It's really, really hard. It doesn't happen overnight. However, when it works, it's really going to work. Once the model is done, people will look back and go, "Well, that was really smart. You had a brilliant plan." But it wasn't the plan when I started. It has evolved in a way I would never have guessed. My plan was really to solve a different problem. Now I truly believe we're going to invite others onto this platform, because we can solve a lot more problems for them, such as speed to market. This model of manufacturing could begin a trend that would revolutionize blue collar jobs in America.

Reflection Questions

1. What do you think of Anderson restructuring the entire company and giving equity to the pods themselves? Will it work? Can it improve staff retention?
2. What other issues does Seordna have at this point? How will restructuring affect those issues, positively or negatively?
3. If you were an employee at one of Seordna's pods, how would you respond to this change in business model? How could Seordna approach you in a way that makes you feel comfortable and empowered?

Discussion: Case 4C — How to Retain Employees?

Summary

In this last Case in the Set, we see some partial outcomes of Anderson's decision to move into the social entrepreneurship space: 1) his workload increased significantly and 2) solving manufacturing issues with the pods is becoming a challenge. In the midst of these issues, he realizes Seordna must change its employee relations and modify its business model. Adding a social mission and changing the company's business model to reflect that mission was not easy, but has the potential to address Anderson's goals outlined in the previous two Cases.

Anderson described the financial impact of his decision in Case 4C:

> "We're spending all our resources—money, people—on American Made, not on Seordna, the brand," he said. With less work on the brand (advertising and other ways of communicating with customers, for example) sales and revenue suffered.

These two sentences are critical as it sets the stage for the rest of the Case. Note the simple if-then statement: *if* Seordna uses its resources to support a social mission, *then* there are no resources for marketing the brand. (As we saw in the Case 4B Discussion, marketing is one of the pillars of a social entrepreneurship effort). From a business perspective, this is not just problematic, it's a warning sign the company and its new mission are potentially at risk.

A critical point emerges in the Case when Anderson realizes he's running two businesses: not a fashion business with a social mission but a fashion business *and* a manufacturing business *with* social missions. He then considers potential decision *outcomes* around this realization:

> Anderson knew he did not have enough people or resources to continue running both businesses. If he continued trying to do that, both would continue to struggle. The lack of attention to employees at the pods would result in unacceptable attrition. Sales would suffer from insufficient time and money spent on marketing. Anderson knew many aspects of the whole business. He also knew he could not do it all.

This is a precise (albeit simplified) way of considering possible outcomes. Again, we see the if-thens: *if* this occurs, *then* that will occur. Note Anderson's concern about the success of both *Seordna* and the manufacturing pods broadly, not just one part of this entire effort. Clearly, he is dedicated to his goals and the company's new social mission as a unified entity. Seordna used to be a platform for Anderson's clothing designs but now it's a platform for social change. This was his goal from the initial Case of this Set.

Given the realization from the Case narrative above, Anderson makes the risky and bold decision to shift to the manufacturing business. Some readers might argue he should reduce funding for Gee's Bend and Eagle Butte and direct those resources to marketing and brand building—if not abandoning the effort altogether. Yet this strategy compromises Seordna's social mission and the ethical foundations Anderson established in Case 4A. Transforming the company into a manufacturing business not only meant his design work *might* need to take a back seat initially, Seordna's business model would need to change. With this new focus, the company not only retains its social mission (if not amplifies it), it creates a new revenue stream. For this to occur, the pods must operate efficiently, profitably and produce quality products. The pods were not meeting these parameters.

As a solution, Anderson focuses on the employees. Instead of revamping the training program or replacing local community labor with skilled garment workers, he takes a more holistic approach and centers his effort on providing as much equity to employees as possible. He does this primarily by revenue sharing, which depletes both his and investors' profits slightly, but provides employees with a sense of ownership in the company. Perhaps the most mission-based aspect of this effort is Anderson's planned "wrap around" services.[1] This, combined with the revenue sharing, demonstrates an authentic, mission-based investment in the pods and their communities.

Factors Forcing the Decision

Anderson is negotiating the growing pains of an established entrepreneurial venture and its new social mission. While it is common for businesses to experience *many* challenges around these transitions, we can identify two in the Case narrative. The first is best said by Anderson himself, as quoted above: "We're spending all our resources—money, people—on American Made, not on Seordna, the brand." Second is his clear dedication to Seordna's new social mission. However, we also see the reality of this integration: social missions need funding and if the funding evaporates, so does the venture and its mission.

In Case 4B, we saw that directing Seordna's resources into American Made was the impetus for seeking foundation grants. While many issues can arise when resources are strained in this way, a common response for most businesses and corporations is to decrease the marketing budget. For arts businesses, this is a self-inflicted wound, especially in highly competitive market environments like the fashion industry. If this pillar of any arts startup is not developed, markets that would likely support a social mission simply can't find the venture. Likewise, Seordna is a for-profit entity and needs financial resources to not only exist, but to fund the social mission as well. Anderson is correct in observing that the company's resource allocation strategy to fund its social mission is unsustainable; if Seordna is not making money, it fails.

Having established that Anderson is fully committed to American Made, we note another resource needing consideration. The time required for any business to establish a social mission is significant and Anderson's time investment (as a CEO) is likely incredible. Yet it is *his* role to envision and manage the execution of this new vision. While we may think sending a text or email requires little time, when one is communicating dozens of times a day (likely with decisions attached to many), time becomes a limited resource.

Considering only these two factors, a merger of resources forced this decision. When it comes to resource allocation, Anderson's commitment to Seordna's new social mission is also a resource. His *passion* for the mission (as demonstrated by the time and effort required to make American Made sustainable) is as much a resource as the bottom line of a balance sheet. This *intangible* resource is hard to financially quantify other than saying he's getting paid to do it, but this critique may be short-sighted. For example, if we say that someone has a "vision" for an arts venture, can we *absolutely* quantify its potential impact, project its yearly income and costs, etc? And what is the value of "vision" itself? Is the *capacity* for creating a "vision" or possessing "passion" quantifiable? The point is that we can see the *outcome* of passion in quantifiable terms (yearly income, units shipped, etc.), yet the *capacity* to possess, generate and act on one's passion—as an intangible asset—is seldom discussed, yet critical and limited.

Decision Model

Here we see a change in how Anderson approaches his decision to revise Seordna's business model. In the first two Cases in this Set, he used the Expertise Model because he was making decisions squarely within the domain of the fashion industry. With Seordna's social mission established, the additional decision to change its business model is not something Anderson approached casually. With a decision of this magnitude, we should consider a few issues before identifying his decision-making model.

First, let's determine the broad outline. Manufacturing clothing is a part of the Fashion and Textile Ecology and Anderson is not considering shifting from this ecology. Seordna is, however, also in a hybrid Ecology with a significant Social Entrepreneurship component (see Figure 17.3).[2] This means the possible decision outcome is within the Social/Fashion Ecology, but with a shift in weighting (from design) to the manufacturing aspect of the Ecology. Given his history of Domain-based decision models through this Case Set, we would expect Anderson to stay in this decision model group. Identifying the "correct" model for this decision, however, may be a matter of perspective.

From a *Case Set* perspective one could argue that Anderson is still in the Domain group given Seordna's new business model. When looking at it from this perspective, Case 4B is the beginning of an Intuitive model (Step 3—Select *one* potential course of action, based on experience, knowledge and training) and Case 4C describes Step 5 (If chosen course of action will not produce desired outcome, alter it and retest). This is a compelling argument if we (again) consider the entire Set.

However, if we examine the discrete decision-making perspective of shifting to a manufacturing-centric business, we again come to this section of the narrative:

> Anderson knew he did not have enough people or resources to continue running both businesses. If he continued trying to do that, both would continue to struggle. The lack of attention to

> employees at the pods would result in unacceptable attrition. Sales would suffer from insufficient time and money spent on marketing. Anderson knew many aspects of the whole business. He also knew he could not do it all.

This is a perfect example of Step 4 (Consider potential course of action through to outcome) of the Intuitive Model. Here, we see exactly what the Step articulates. In fact, we could create two decision trees for the quote above (Figures 17.1 and 17.2).

Here, Anderson is considering potential courses of action through to outcome. However, if we agree that models in the Domain group are being used throughout the Case Set, then we also get a glimpse into Anderson's decision *style*. Clearly, he is always thinking about solving

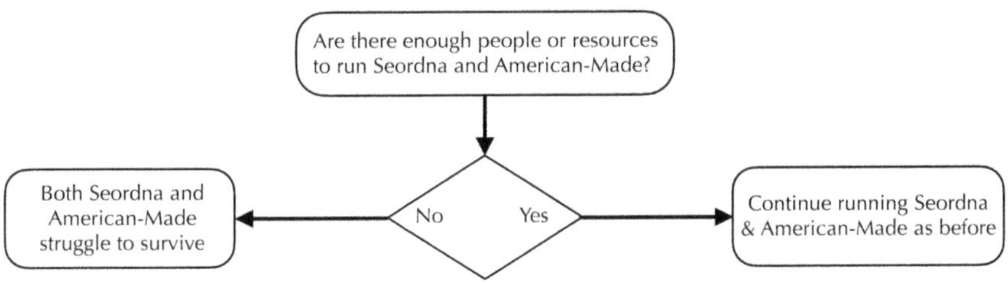

Figure 17.1 Seordna Decision Tree 1.

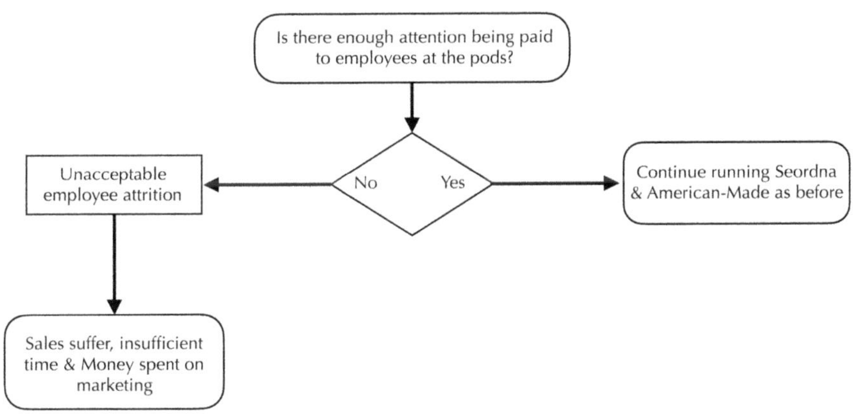

Figure 17.2 Seordna Decision Tree 2.

problems within ecologies (i.e.: domains). This should not be a surprise given his past work in—and knowledge of—the fashion industry. Additionally, Anderson should continue using the Domain group (from a Case Set perspective) since there are so many elements in the Social/ Fashion Ecology; more elements means more interactions and potential opportunities.

Ecology Discussion

Given the decision under discussion in this Case (and the previous paragraph), we would expect no change to Anderson's use of the Social/ Fashion Ecology. With the exception of one additional element, this is a valid assumption. Accounting for this change simply means adding Seordna's new revenue stream: American Made's future, non-Seordna clients. While we could add this element to the supplemental box in a Steady State Model, this element is a critical revenue stream and adding it to the Ecology itself is more appropriate and accurate. As Figure 17.3

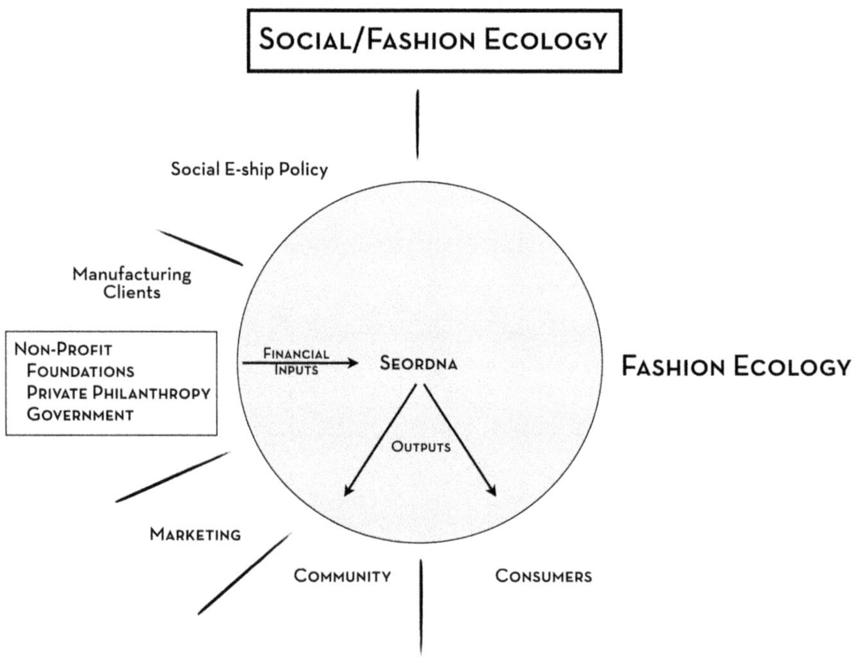

Figure 17.3 Seordna Social/Fashion Ecology with Addition.

indicates, the element "Manufacturing Clients" appears in the left side of the ecology (i.e.: the social entrepreneurship pillars) as a separate element in the Financial Inputs group.

Ultimately, Anderson is not only using, but *leveraging* the Social/Fashion Ecology. Since he knows the Ecology's elements and is quickly learning how the Ecology operates, it makes sense to leverage the system to its fullest potential as an arts entrepreneur: innovative solutions *typically* can be found within an Ecological system without *necessarily* seeking solutions from unrelated Ecologies.[3]

Notes

1 The class activity for this Case specifically addresses this effort in the corresponding teaching note.
2 There is a slight change in this Ecology from the previous case, discussed in the Ecology section below.
3 It should be said when one introduces elements or innovations from unrelated ecologies, markets can become somewhat disoriented. Though this does not occur consistently, effective and targeted communication can eliminate this issue if it arises.

Bibliography

Beckman, Gary D. *The New Arts Entrepreneur: Navigating the Arts Ecologies*. London: Routledge, 2022.

Bikart, Joseph. *The Art of Decision Making: How we Move from Indecision to Smart Choices*. London: Watkins Publishing, 2019.

Guo, Chao and Wolfgand Bieleield. *Social Entrepreneurship: An Evidence-Based Approach to Creating Social Value*. San Francisco: Jossey-Bass, 2014.

Kickul, Jill and Thomas S. Lyons. *Understanding Social Entrepreneurship: The Relentless Pursuit of Mission in an Ever Changing World*. 3rd edition. London: Routledge, 2020.

Trenton, Nick. *Think in Models: A Structured Approach to Clear Thinking and the Art of Decision-Making*. Self-published, Nick Trenton, 2019.

INDEX

For Product Safety Concerns and Information please contact our EU representative GPSR@taylorandfrancis.com
Taylor & Francis Verlag GmbH, Kaufingerstraße 24, 80331 München, Germany

www.ingramcontent.com/pod-product-compliance
Ingram Content Group UK Ltd.
Pitfield, Milton Keynes, MK11 3LW, UK
UKHW020359160925
462952UK00021B/1004
* 9 7 8 1 0 3 2 5 3 9 5 7 7 *